The 50 Greatest Cartoons
As Selected by 1,000 Animation Professionals

Turner Publishing, Inc.
ATLANTA

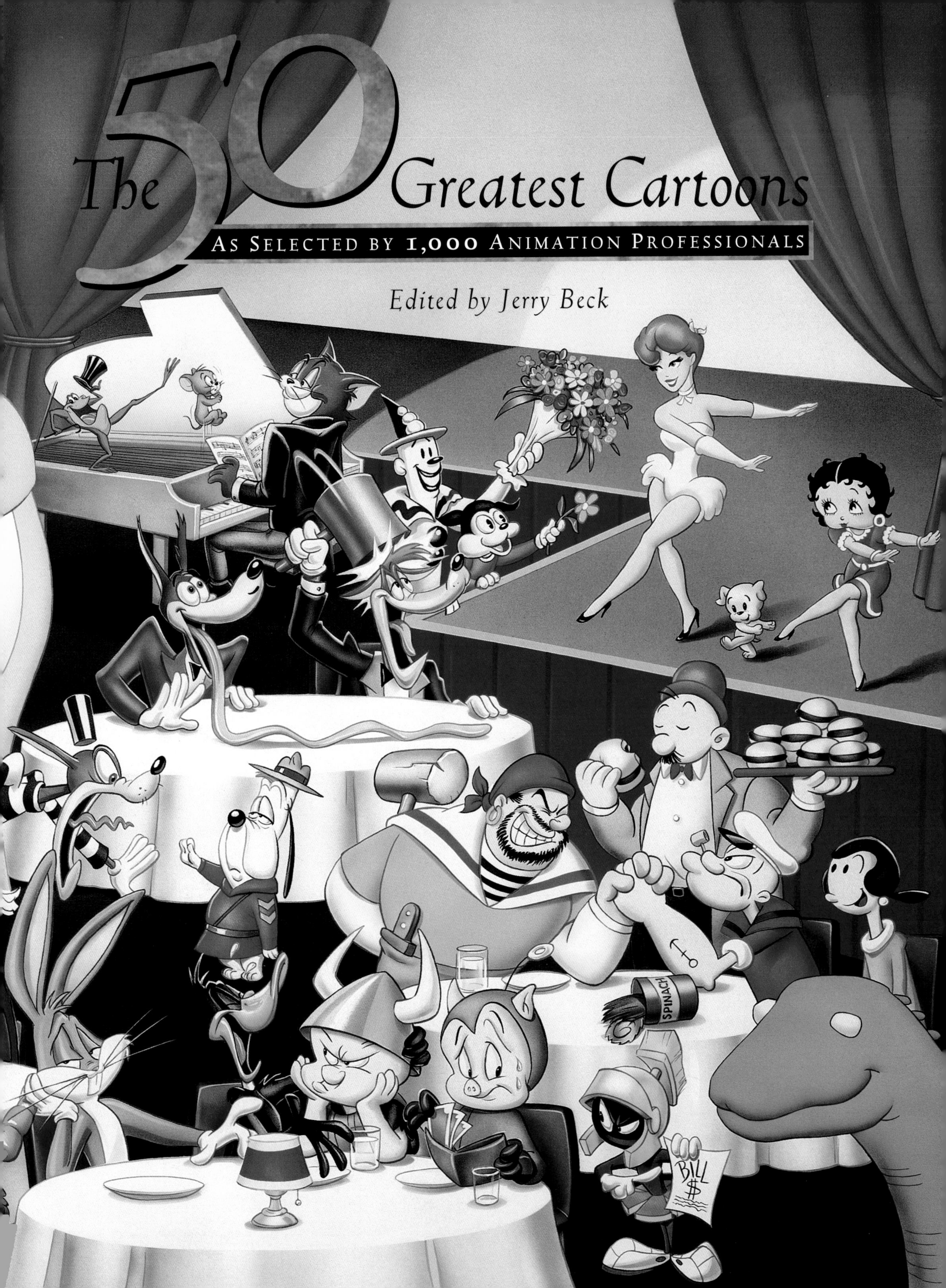
The 50 Greatest Cartoons
As Selected by 1,000 Animation Professionals
Edited by Jerry Beck
SPINACH
BILL $

Published by Turner Publishing, Inc.
A Subsidiary of Turner Broadcasting System, Inc.
1050 Techwood Drive, N.W.
Atlanta, Georgia 30318

First Edition 10 9 8 7 6 5 4 3 2 1

Library of Congress Cataloging-in-Publication Data
The Fifty Greatest Cartoons : As Selected by 1,000 Animation Professionals / edited by Jerry Beck.
p. cm.
Includes index.
ISBN 1-878685-49-X
1. Animated films—United States—Catalogs. I. Beck, Jerry.
NC1766.U5F54 1994
791.43'3—dc20 94-20780
CIP

Distributed by Andrews and McMeel
A Universal Press Syndicate Company
4900 Main Street
Kansas City, Missouri 64112

Produced by Layla Productions, Inc. and Sammis Publishing Corp.
Art direction by Michael Walsh and Karen Smith
Art coordination by Bee Espy

Printed in the U.S.A.

COVER ARTWORK CHARACTER KEY

1 *A Unicorn in the Garden*
2 *Bambi Meets Godzilla*
3 *Superman*
4 *The Man Who Planted Trees*
5 Man *(The Tell-Tale Heart)*
6 Squirrels *(Peace on Earth)*
7 *Quasi at the Quackadero*
8 Dora and The Dover Boys
9 Red *(Red Hot Riding Hood)*
10 Red *(Little Rural Riding Hood)*
11 Coal Black *(and de Sebben Dwarfs)*
12 Red *(Little Red Riding Rabbit)*
13 Mouse and Canary *(King Size Canary)*
14 Michigan J. Frog *(One Froggy Evening)*
15 Tom and Jerry *(The Cat Concerto)*
16 Koko the Clown and Bimbo *(Snow White)*
17 Red *(Red Hot Riding Hood)*
18 Betty Boop *(Minnie the Moocher)*
19 Pudgy (Betty Boop's dog)
20 Red, Grandma and Wolf *(Red Hot Riding Hood)*
21 Woody Woodpecker *(The Barber of Seville)*
22 *The Cat Came Back*
23 *Bad Luck Blackie* and White Kitty
24 Sylvester *(The Scarlet Pumpernickel)*
25 Wolf Cousins *(Little Rural Riding Hood)*
26 Goofy *(Clock Cleaners)*
27 Mickey Mouse *(Brave Little Tailor)*
28 Minnie Mouse *(Brave Little Tailor)*
29 Donald Duck *(The Band Concert)*
30 Pluto
31 Felix the Cat *(Felix in Hollywood)*
32 Wolf *(Northwest Hounded Police)*
33 Droopy *(Northwest Hounded Police)*
34 Bluto *(Popeye the Sailor Meets Sindbad the Sailor)*
35 Wimpy *(Popeye the Sailor Meets Sindbad the Sailor)*
36 Popeye *(Popeye the Sailor Meets Sindbad the Sailor)*
37 Olive Oyl *(Popeye the Sailor Meets Sindbad the Sailor)*
38 Mark Anthony and Pussyfoot *(Feed the Kitty)*
39 *The Big Snit*
40 *Gerald McBoing Boing*
41 *Rooty Toot Toot*
42 Bugs Bunny *(Rabbit of Seville)*
43 Daffy Duck *(Duck Amuck)*
44 Elmer Fudd *(What's Opera, Doc?)*
45 Porky Pig *(Duck Dodgers in the 24 1/2th Century)*
46 Marvin the Martian *(Duck Dodgers in the 24 1/2th Century)*
47 *Gertie the Dinosaur*

Contents

Editor's note 6
A Brief History of Animation 9
An Animation Time Line 12
Animation Hall of Fame 22
A Gallery of Cartoon Stars 23
What Makes a Cartoon Great? 26

The Fifty Greatest Cartoons 29

1. *What's Opera, Doc?* 30
2. *Duck Amuck* 36
3. *The Band Concert* 40
4. *Duck Dodgers in the 24½th Century* 44
5. *One Froggy Evening* 48
6. *Gertie the Dinosaur* 52
7. *Red Hot Riding Hood* 56
8. *Porky in Wackyland* 60
9. *Gerald McBoing Boing* 64
10. *King-Size Canary* 68
11. *Three Little Pigs* 72
12. *Rabbit of Seville* 74
13. *Steamboat Willie* 78
14. *The Old Mill* 80
15. *Bad Luck Blackie* 82
16. *The Great Piggy Bank Robbery* 84
17. *Popeye the Sailor Meets Sindbad the Sailor* 88
18. *The Skeleton Dance* 92
19. *Snow White* 94
20. *Minnie the Moocher* 98
21. *Coal Black and de Sebben Dwarfs* 102
22. *Der Fuehrer's Face* 106
23. *Little Rural Riding Hood* 108
24. *The Tell-Tale Heart* 112
25. *The Big Snit* 116
26. *Brave Little Tailor* 120
27. *Clock Cleaners* 124
28. *Northwest Hounded Police* 126
29. *Toot, Whistle, Plunk and Boom* 130
30. *Rabbit Seasoning* 132
31. *The Scarlet Pumpernickel* 136
32. *The Cat Came Back* 138
33. *Superman* 140
34. *You Ought to Be in Pictures* 144
35. *Ali Baba Bunny* 148
36. *Feed the Kitty* 150
37. *Bimbo's Initiation* 152
38. *Bambi Meets Godzilla* 154
39. *Little Red Riding Rabbit* 156
40. *Peace on Earth* 158
41. *Rooty Toot Toot* 160
42. *Cat Concerto* 162
43. *The Barber of Seville* 166
44. *The Man Who Planted Trees* 168
45. *Book Revue* 170
46. *Quasi at the Quackadero* 174
47. *Corny Concerto* 178
48. *A Unicorn in the Garden* 180
49. *The Dover Boys* 182
50. *Felix in Hollywood* 184

Other Great Cartoons 186
Illustrations 187
How to Find the Fifty Greatest Cartoons 188
Animation Art Sources and ASIFA 189
Index 190
Acknowledgments 192
Illustration and Contributor credits 192

Editor's Note

This volume is an elaborate program book for the cartoon festival of my dreams. The fifty cartoons showcased here were chosen in a survey of more than one thousand animators, cartoon historians, and animation professionals. Their decisions turned into my pleasure—I got to rescreen all the films to confirm their consensus.

No single person picked these fifty films. All of us, myself included, have many favorites which did not make the final cut. But to my delight, this is an extraordinarily well-rounded collection of classic animation. While it is full of popular Disney, MGM, and Warner Bros. films, it also includes cartoons by Walter Lantz, the Fleischer Studios, UPA, and the National Film Board of Canada, as well as pioneering efforts like *Gertie the Dinosaur* and the work of contemporary artists.

Many of those polled are members of the New York, Hollywood, Portland, and San Francisco chapters of ASIFA (Association Internationale du Film D'Animation—see page 189 for more information), a film society made up of animators, film students, and cartoon buffs. Ballots were also sent to members of the Society for Animation Studies, one hundred animation studios, and film critics at more than one hundred periodicals. All were asked to rank their favorite cartoons from numbers 1–50; any film, foreign or domestic, classic or contemporary, was eligible, so long as it was short (less than thirty minutes) and cel animated (a special exception was made for *Gertie the Dinosaur*, which was animated with paper). The ballot was tallied by weighing each choice with its ranking.

Of the thousands of cartoons produced since 1908, there are probably a few hundred more that could have made the grade; we have listed the runners-up at the end of the list of fifty, but even that does not cover every worthy cartoon. I think everyone reading this book will find at least one or two absences that they consider inexplicable, and might even wonder why one or two of those present merit inclusion. Many of those polled remarked that they had trouble comparing cartoons of vastly different styles and artistry, qualifying their lists with voluminous notes. Every voter used his or her own criteria, but the decision came down to a simple question: Is this a classic cartoon? The answer for every cartoon included is, of course, yes!

The Fifty Greatest Cartoons celebrates these cartoons with prime examples of original animation art, chosen from the greatest private collections and galleries located all over the world. We've also used frame enlargements from rare 35mm prints, pencil sketches, and seldom-seen advertising material to illustrate selected cartoons. Artist and Fleischer historian Leslie Cabarga provided us with two original paintings (*Snow White* and *Bimbo's Initiation*); animation director Daryll Van Citters helped us illustrate *King-Size Canary*, *Duck Amuck*, and *The Scarlet Pumpernickel*.

In addition to a concise plot synopsis, full credits, and production information, each cartoon is given a critical appraisal from a distinguished animation pundit. I'd like to especially thank these critics for sharing comments, insights, and wisdom with us. (See page 192 for their credits.)

This book is a tribute to fifty very special cartoons. But the only true way to appreciate these films is to see them–at animation festivals, on television (you can catch many of them if you glue yourself to The Cartoon Network, The Disney Channel, and Nickelodeon), or by purchasing videotapes and laser discs. I encourage you to seek out the fifty greatest cartoons and see what all the fuss is about. You'll have a marvellous time doing it. I did!

—*Jerry Beck*
Hollywood, California
1994

My first impression on reading this list of the fifty greatest cartoons is what a superb gathering it is. I do believe that you could blindly shuffle the entire pack of cartoons several times and put them down in random order and it would in every case—no matter how often the shuffle—represent a great and amazing overview of the eighty-odd years of this wonderful, youthful craft of ours. If you put them down alphabetically, *What's Opera, Doc?* would probably be last and I would still be delighted and honored to be there. A special hosanna to Jerry Beck for providing this star-spangled tribute to animation—a worthy craft indeed.

CHUCK JONES

A Brief History of Animation

The history of animation encompasses several stories. Like all histories, it begins with individuals, in this case creative and inventive people whose talent, ingenuity, and vision allowed them to go beyond an art form as they'd found it. Because animation combines artistry and technology, its history also involves the development of techniques and procedures which varied from simple paper cutouts to elaborate computer setups. Many of these innovations were created against the backdrop of the complex studio system of Hollywood; the stories of these studios are another element of animation history, as is the development of unique artistic styles associated with these studios. And finally, the characters created by mere mortals often took on immortal and fantastic lives of their own, and their biographies are another integral part of animation history. Throughout this book, you will find these components highlighted in sidebars. In this chapter, we will attempt to unite them in a cohesive chronology.

The earliest attempts at animation can be found in cave drawings of animals drawn with legs in several positions to imitate motion. The effort to analyze motion on film culminated in an experiment by photographer Edward Muybridge. To settle a bet made with Leland Stanford (then governor of California) as to whether all four feet of a racehorse were off the ground at the same time, Muybridge set up twelve cameras with tripwires; as a horse passed each one, a photograph was snapped. By looking at all twelve pictures, Stanford was able to see that at one point none of the horse's hooves were touching the ground. Muybridge found a way to project these animated images and showed them to Thomas Edison, who was inspired to invent the kinetescope. By looking through this machine, viewers could see a flickering, minute-long motion picture. The movie industry had been born.

Animated films began as an offshoot of trick photography movies, or "trick films," popular in the early 1900s. In the beginning, just the novelty of an animated drawing was enough to captivate audiences who were getting used to seeing live-action moving pictures. As audiences gained sophistication, cartoon makers kept the public's attention with broader humor, appealing characters, and better drawings. Two early experimenters were J. Stuart Blackton, with his *Humorous Phases of Funny Faces* (1906), in which an unseen hand draws words and pictures, and French

Below: Muybridge's experiment. Above, right: In a filmed introduction to his vaudeville act, Winsor McCay drew Gertie for a group of friends in a New York restaurant.

HOW A CARTOON IS MADE

Many people are amazed when they learn how much skill, effort, and labor are involved in the making of a cartoon. Thousands of drawings and cels, and dozens of finished background paintings—plus a script, musical score, special effects, and voices—are required for each seven-minute short. Every animation studio followed its own production procedures, but most followed the same general plan.

In most studios, ideas were fleshed out on storyboards, where gags were plotted and refined. Usually, dialogue was recorded before the drawing commenced, so that animators could time their sequences to the words being spoken. Once the story was finalized, the work was divided up; in most cases, several animators worked on every cartoon. For every second of film time, between twelve and twenty-four drawings were created, each only slightly different than the preceding one. The master animators drew the main poses for each character, expertly capturing motion and expression; "in-betweeners" drew the rest. These drawings were then traced onto celluloid by inkers; the back of the cels were painted to exact specifications. For the average short film, about four thousand animation drawings and cels were required.

At the same time, background paintings were prepared by layout and background artists. Cameramen combined the cels and backgrounds, shooting each cel against the proper background in continuity, frame by frame. Musical scores and special effects were then added to the finished film.

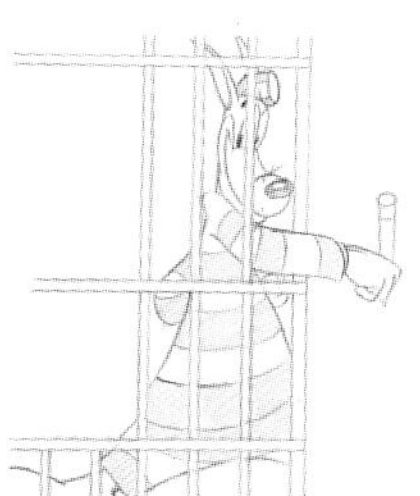

Two important stages in the creation of animation: Above: Animation drawings from *Northwest Hounded Police*. Thousands of animation drawings are produced, each slightly advancing the motion. Below: Cel and cel with background from *Duck Dodgers in the 24½th Century*. Animation drawings were traced onto celluloid; backgrounds were painted separately. Cameramen combined the cels with the proper backgrounds and shot them in sequence.

artist Emil Cohl, who made *Fantasmagorie* (1908), in which stick figures metamorphosize against a black background.

But the creation of animation as an art is often credited to newspaper cartoonist Winsor McCay, who produced more than four thousand meticulously drawn pictures for his first animated cartoon, *Little Nemo* (1911). His second film, *The Story of a Mosquito,* portrays an encounter between a drunken man and a mosquito. In his third cartoon, he made another giant leap forward by imbuing his character, Gertie the Dinosaur, with a personality. The mischievous Gertie eats, breathes, laughs, and cries—and even today *Gertie the Dinosaur* is considered one of the greatest animated films ever produced (it is number six in this book). As Leonard Maltin wrote in *Of Mice and Magic*, "Winsor McCay breathed life into an inanimate character, and this was his greatest achievement. It did not go unnoticed. Gertie was so successful that it made people forget the animated films that preceded it, even McCay's. For years, Gertie has been named in film histories as the first animated cartoon. With all its impact, it might as well have been."

TECHNOLOGY

Throughout the years, animators have embraced technical innovations to make their laborious job easier, the finished films look better, and the images more spectacular. The first major innovation was the use of celluloid overlays. In the earliest animated cartoons, such as those of Winsor McCay, the artist had to draw everything in the picture, over and over on paper, with only slight changes in each drawing to create the illusion of movement. Pioneer cartoonist producer J. R. Bray first patented the use of celluloid sheets in 1914 to paint the static background. The moving characters, still drawn and animated on paper, were shot through the clear portion of the cel overlay. Artist Earl Hurd patented the use of cels later the same year, transferring the animated characters from paper to cels and photographing them over the static background art—the basic method of cel animation still practiced today. The use of cels shortened production schedules and made possible the mass-production of animation.

Max Fleischer invented the rotoscope in 1918 as another method of speeding up cartoon production. This device enables an animator to trace live action photography one frame at a time for animation purposes; actors were filmed simulating the desired action, so that animators could see and capture the movement of actual

The following time line does not purport to be an all-inclusive history of animation. Listed in the time line are notable highlights in chronological order, including important films, famous creators, and technical achievements.

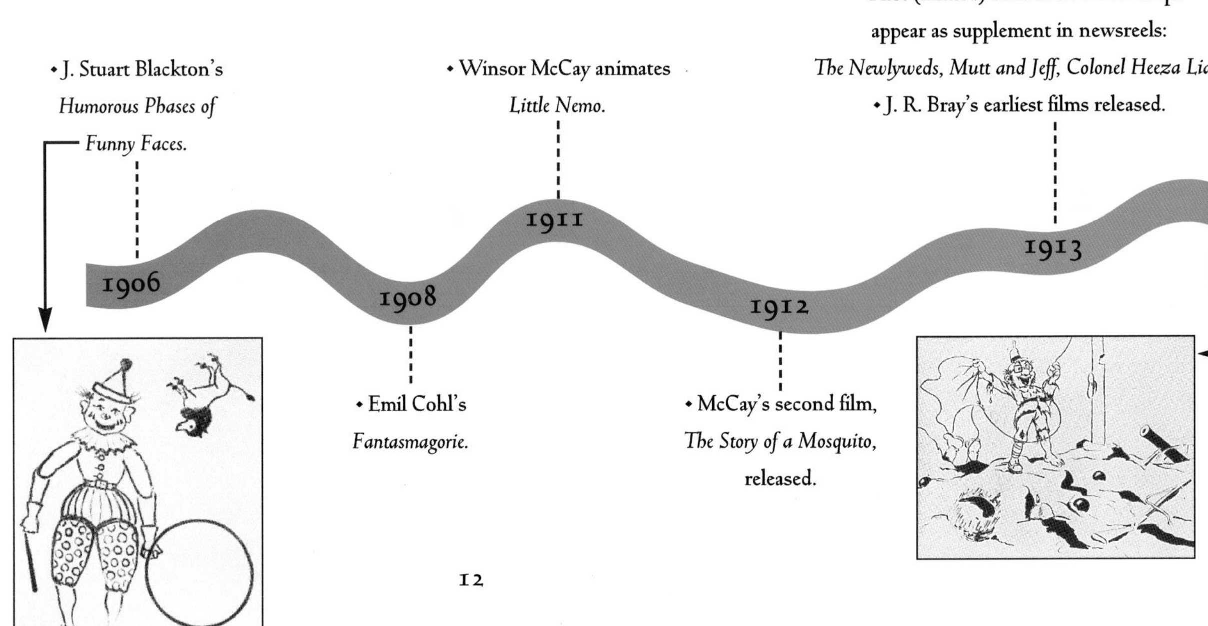

• J. Stuart Blackton's *Humorous Phases of Funny Faces.*
1906
1908
• Emil Cohl's *Fantasmagorie.*
• Winsor McCay animates *Little Nemo.*
1911
1912
• McCay's second film, *The Story of a Mosquito,* released.
• First (limited) animation comic strips appear as supplement in newsreels: *The Newlyweds, Mutt and Jeff, Colonel Heeza Lia*
• J. R. Bray's earliest films released.
1913

This illustration accompanied Fleischer's patent application for the rotoscope.

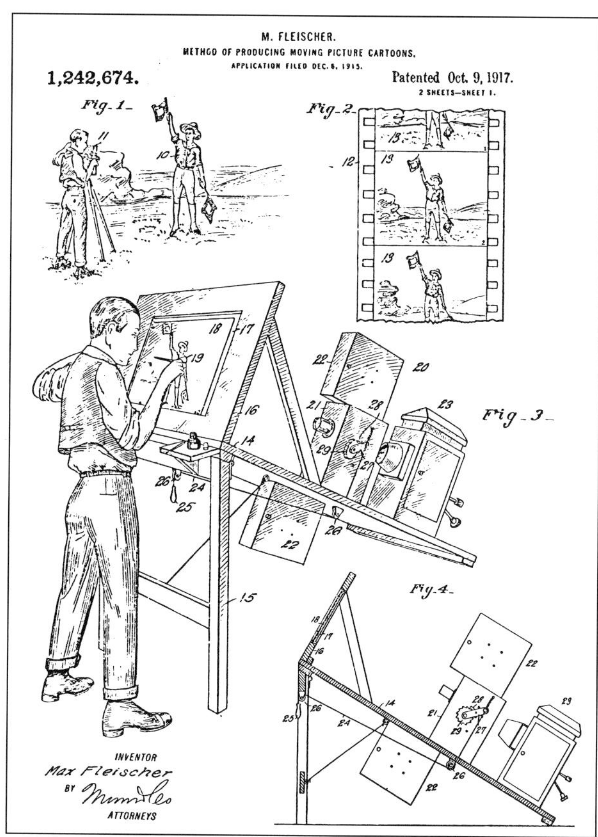

bodies. Though not as practical as Max envisioned, the rotoscope has become a valuable tool in the special-effects field and has enhanced many animated features, including *Gulliver's Travels* and *Lord of the Rings*.

Color and sound, 3-D and CinemaScope, all came to animation at the same time that Hollywood adopted these advancements for live-action subjects. Prints still survive of hand-tinted color cartoons made during the silent-film days, including McCay's *Little Nemo*. Max Fleischer experimented with sound cartoons in 1924 with a series of sing-along DeForrest Phonofilms, but it was Walt Disney who popularized sound cartoons when he introduced Mickey Mouse in *Steamboat Willie* (1928) and put full spectrum 3-strip Technicolor on the map with *Flowers and Trees* (1932).

Bringing visual depth to animation had been an ambition since the 1930s when Ub Iwerks and Walt Disney each developed separate multiplane systems, and Max Fleischer's studio built three-dimensional sets for their cartoons. The early 1950s brought on a 3-D craze in which several studios brought popular characters (including *Bugs Bunny, Popeye, Woody Woodpecker,*

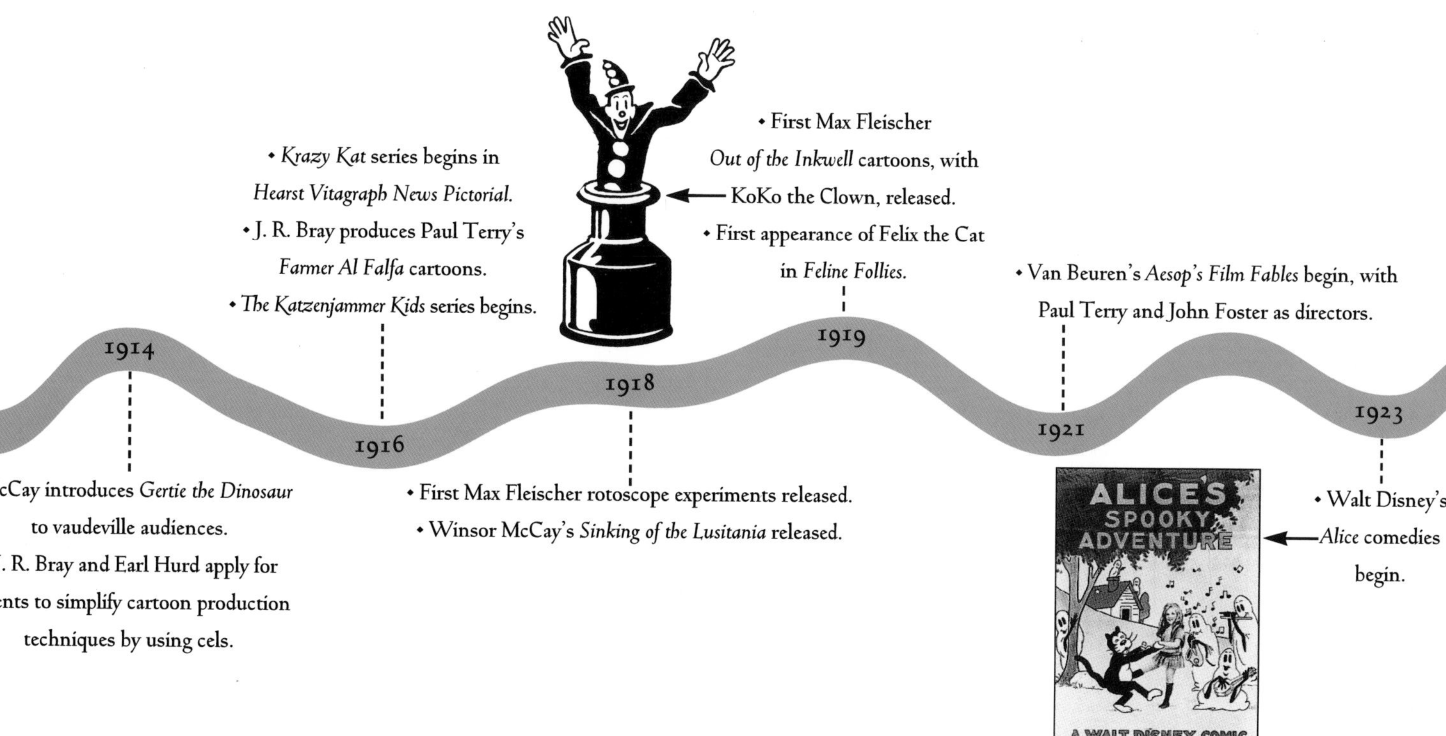

1914
McCay introduces *Gertie the Dinosaur* to vaudeville audiences.
• J. R. Bray and Earl Hurd apply for atents to simplify cartoon production techniques by using cels.
1916
• *Krazy Kat* series begins in *Hearst Vitagraph News Pictorial.*
• J. R. Bray produces Paul Terry's *Farmer Al Falfa* cartoons.
• *The Katzenjammer Kids* series begins.
1918
• First Max Fleischer rotoscope experiments released.
• Winsor McCay's *Sinking of the Lusitania* released.
1919
• First Max Fleischer *Out of the Inkwell* cartoons, with KoKo the Clown, released.
• First appearance of Felix the Cat in *Feline Follies.*
1921
• Van Beuren's *Aesop's Film Fables* begin, with Paul Terry and John Foster as directors.
1923
• Walt Disney's *Alice* comedies begin.
ALICE'S SPOOKY ADVENTURE
A WALT DISNEY COMIC
M.J. WINKLER
DISTRIBUTOR.N.Y.
WINKLER PICTURES

Donald Duck, and *Casper)* to the fore, with the help of irritating glasses.

Wide-screen CinemaScope has been used for many shorts (especially ones featuring UPA's *Mr. Magoo* and MGM's *Tom and Jerry)* and feature-length films *(Lady and the Tramp* and *Raggedy Ann and Andy*, among others). CinemaScope backgrounds are wider, and layouts are designed for horizontal staging in an effort to fill our peripheral vision; the technique was used to great effect, particularly in the Disney shorts *Toot, Whistle, Plunk and Boom* (1953) and *Grand Canyonscope* (1954). CinemaScope cartoons look best in big theaters on large screens—rare in these days of tiny multiplex cinemas and home-video screens—making them hard to appreciate today.

The next major technological advance was the development of xerography in the late 1950s. Xerox duplication of pencil art onto cels—eliminating the inking process—became the industry norm during the 1960s. This speeded production and was championed by TV animation producers, though surprisingly it was the Disney Studio that first made use of the procedure. The scratchy line of xerography has many fans mourning the lost art of hand inking. In recent years, colored inks have softened the harsh look of xerographed animation cels.

Today, computer generated ink-and-paint has completely eliminated the use of cels in many films and television shows. Tightly cleaned-up animation drawings can be scanned directly into the computer and colored, with the final finished frames output directly to 35mm nega-

• Leon Schlesinger produces first Looney Tune, Hugh Harman and Rudolph Ising's *Sinkin' in the Bathtub*, starring Bosko.

• Fleischer's Betty Boop appears in *Dizzy Dishes* and *Barnacle Bill*.

• First Technicolor cartoon sequence by Walter Lantz in *King of Jazz*.

• *Adventures of Prince Achmed* is first animated feature, by Lotte Reiniger, produced in Germany.

• Disney and Ub Iwerks create first three Mickey Mouse cartoons: *Plane Crazy, The Gallopin' Gaucho*, and *Steamboat Willie*.

1924 1926 1927 1928 1929 1930 1931

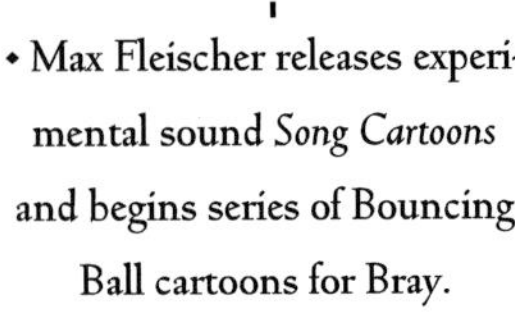

• Max Fleischer releases experimental sound *Song Cartoons* and begins series of Bouncing Ball cartoons for Bray.

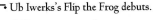

• Disney's Oswald the Lucky Rabbit series debuts.

• First Silly Symphonies cartoon, *The Skeleton Dance*, released.

• Ub Iwerks's Flip the Frog debuts.

• Dick Huemor creates *Scrappy* cartoon for Columbia Pictures.

• Van Beuren's Tom and Jerry cartoons begin.

• First Merrie Melodies cartoon release *Lady Play Your Mandolin*, starring Foxy tives. In addition, complex computer-generated dimensional background settings, surpassing the multiplane sequences created by Disney and Fleischer in the 1930s, can easily be composited into the scene.

But just as in the day of Winsor McCay and J. R. Bray, it still takes a human artist to draw each character movement by hand. That hasn't changed and probably never will. The technical innovations of the past century have helped filmmakers improve their craft and significantly contributed to the continuing popularity of the art form.

THE STUDIO SYSTEM

Winsor McCay worked more than one year, personally drawing twenty-four frames for each second of screen time, to make just one animated film like *Gertie the Dinosaur.* Other cartoonists like J. R. Bray and Raoul Barre realized that mass producing a quantity of animation could be a profitable business. Thus the first studios to create animated cartoons were founded in 1913, making possible the creation of a volume of animation.

The studio system eventually produced a "Golden Age," the period from 1930 to the late 1950s, during which every major Hollywood studio released new cartoons to theaters, animation studios—like Disney, Warner Bros., MGM, and UPA—thrived and innovated, and the quality of the films was at a peak.

In the beginning, the studios, the cartoonists, and the movie industry itself were located in New York City. The first cartoon series were adapted from major newspaper comic strips—*Mutt and Jeff*, *Krazy Kat*, *The Katzenjammer Kids*, etc.—or arose from the pens of New York-based print cartoonists like Gregory LaCava, Pat Sullivan, and Paul Terry.

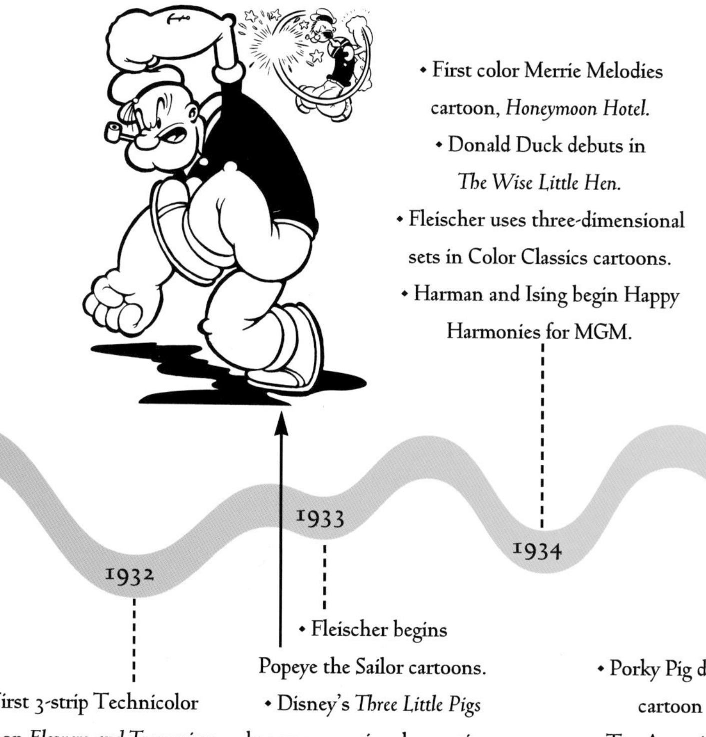

1932

• First 3-strip Technicolor cartoon *Flowers and Trees* wins first Oscar for animation.

1933

• Fleischer begins Popeye the Sailor cartoons.
• Disney's *Three Little Pigs* becomes a national sensation.

1934

• First color Merrie Melodies cartoon, *Honeymoon Hotel.*
• Donald Duck debuts in *The Wise Little Hen.*
• Fleischer uses three-dimensional sets in Color Classics cartoons.
• Harman and Ising begin Happy Harmonies for MGM.

1935

• Porky Pig debuts in Merrie Melodies cartoon *I Haven't Got a Hat.*
• Tex Avery joins Warner Bros. studio and starts Termite Terrace unit.

1936

• Carl Stalling begins music supervision at Warner Bros.
• Van Beuren studio closes.
• *Popeye the Sailor Meets Sindbad the Sailor* is first extra-length short cartoon released by Fleischer.

1937

• *Snow White and the Seven Dwarfs* premieres.
• *Porky's Duck Hunt* introduces Daffy Duck.
• Bob Clampett directs first cartoon, *Porky's Badtime Story.*
• Mel Blanc begins cartoon voice career.
• Multiplane camera first used in *The Old Mill.*

One of the earliest known photographs of Walt Disney.

Though still prized as the forerunners of modern cartoons, these cartoons displayed little of the skill and artistry of modern cartoons or of Winsor McCay. McCay berated his colleagues at a testimonial dinner, "Animation should be an art . . . but what you fellows have done is [make] it into a trade." Quality returned when Otto Messmer breathed life and personality into Felix the Cat, whose adventures in the 1920s were remarkably well crafted as well as funny. The Fleischer studio was responsible for further advances in both animation technique and plot development. But the cartoon as we know it today was developed by one man, and that man was Walt Disney.

A relative youngster to the field when he entered it in 1923, Disney was determined to match his rival animation studios in quality. By 1927, his Hollywood studio was producing the most sophisticated cartoons on the screen. His desire to compete with and better his rivals led to his popularizing synchronized-sound cartoons in 1928. Throughout the 1930s, the Disney studio dominated the field in innovation and direction; it was Walt Disney who brought fine artistry to the "trade" of animation, providing training for his artists and appreciation and support for their work. As Chuck Jones said, "Because of Disney, people sat up and took notice of the cartoon. . . . He prepared, fought, and bled for a ground where the artist could flourish and

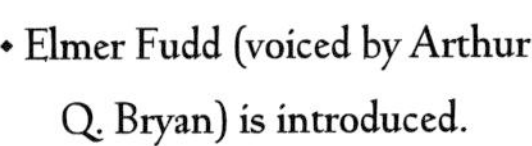

1938

- *Porky's Hare Hunt* introduces early Bugs Bunny.
- First Chuck Jones cartoon, *The Night Watchman*.

1939

- Elmer Fudd (voiced by Arthur Q. Bryan) is introduced.
- Feature films by Fleischer *(Gulliver's Travels)* and Disney *(Pinocchio)* are released.

1940

- Bugs Bunny in Tex Avery's *A Wild Hare* asks "What's up, Doc?" for the first time.
- Lantz's Woody Woodpecker and Hanna-Barbera's Tom and Jerry debut.

1941

- Fleischer begins Superman cartoons.
- Disney releases *Dumbo*.
- Frank Tashlin creates *The Fox and the Crow* for Columbia's Screen Gems studio.

1942

- Terrytoons debuts the *Mouse of Tomorrow* (Mighty Mouse).
- Tweety and Beaky Buzzard are introduced by Bob Clampett.
- Disney releases *Bambi*.
- Paramount Pictures ousts the Fleischer brothers, and establishes Famous Studios.

1943

- Leon Schlesinger produces *Pvt. Snafu* cartoons for the U.S. Army.
- Tex Avery directs the first Droopy cartoon and *Red Hot Riding Hood* for MGM.

1944

- Schlesinger sells his cartoon studio to Warner Bros; Looney Tunes and Merrie Melodies produced in color from this point on.
- At MGM, Jerry Mouse dances with Gene Kelly in *Anchors Aweigh* and Tex Avery introduces *Screwy Squirrel*.

where a new art form could grow—not only at his studio, but throughout the world."

Every other studio began imitation series based on Disney's lead: Where Disney had Silly Symphonies, Warner Bros. released Looney Tunes and Merrie Melodies; MGM began Happy Harmonies; Columbia had Color Rhapsodies; Paramount presented Color Classics; and RKO weighed in with Rainbow Parade cartoons. Fairy tales and fables were adapted in color cartoons, and happy-go-lucky Mickey Mouse imitations danced in the black-and-white releases. By the time Disney premiered *Snow White* in late 1937, the other studios had granted the crown to Uncle Walt.

The Fleischer studio was Disney's biggest rival during the 1930s, with Betty Boop and Popeye eventually surpassing the Disney characters in popularity. The rough but highly cartoony artwork was characteristic of the New York studio and provided the cartoons with an individual identity that other studios lacked. Despite the crudeness of the artwork, the early Fleischer cartoons contain a surreal atmosphere that gives them a depth and sophistication; because they can be enjoyed on many levels, they have become cult classics. But they too succumbed to the pressure of keeping up with the Disneys, and as the thirties wore on, the Fleischer cartoons became cuter and more standard.

The Warner Bros. cartoons were the most influential animated shorts of the 1940s. Tex Avery and the zany Termite Terrace crew decided to ignore the beauty and polish of the emerging Disney style and concentrate on something Walt and his followers were leaving

Opening credits for a Color Rhapsody cartoon.

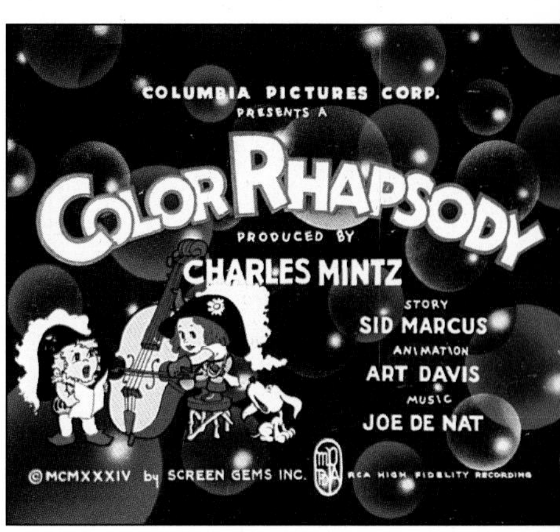
COLUMBIA PICTURES CORP.
PRESENTS A
COLOR RHAPSODY
PRODUCED BY
CHARLES MINTZ
STORY
SID MARCUS
ANIMATION
ART DAVIS
MUSIC
JOE DE NAT
©MCMXXXIV by SCREEN GEMS INC.
RCA HIGH FIDELITY RECORDING

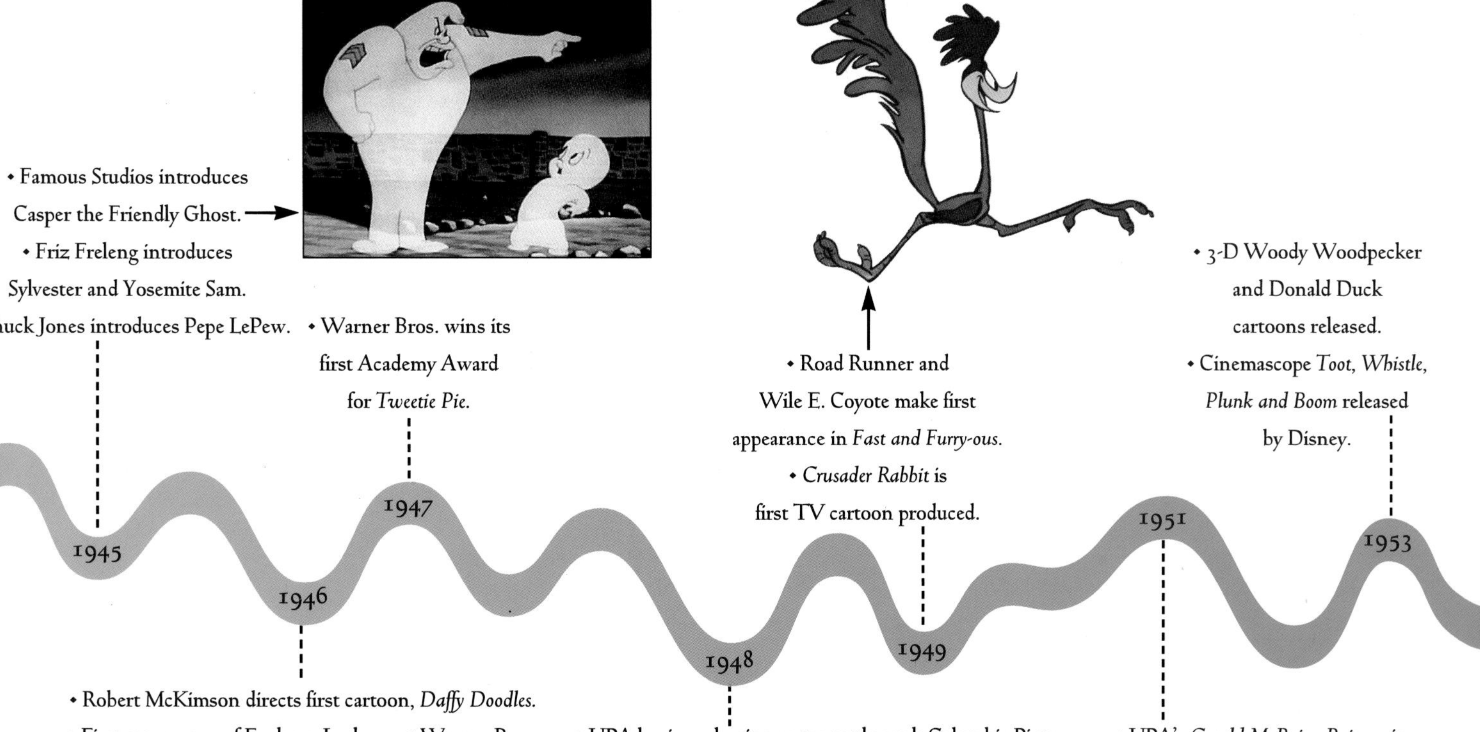
1945
• Famous Studios introduces Casper the Friendly Ghost.
• Friz Freleng introduces Sylvester and Yosemite Sam.
huck Jones introduces Pepe LePew.
1946
• Robert McKimson directs first cartoon, *Daffy Doodles*.
• First appearance of Foghorn Leghorn at Warner Bros. and Heckle and Jeckle at Terrytoons.
1947
• Warner Bros. wins its first Academy Award for *Tweetie Pie*.
1948
• UPA begins releasing cartoons through Columbia Pictures.
1949
• Road Runner and Wile E. Coyote make first appearance in *Fast and Furry-ous*.
• *Crusader Rabbit* is first TV cartoon produced.
1951
• UPA's *Gerald McBoing Boing* wins Academy Award, inaugurating UPA's new graphic style.
1953
• 3-D Woody Woodpecker and Donald Duck cartoons released.
• Cinemascope *Toot, Whistle, Plunk and Boom* released by Disney.

behind: comedy. Avery and his comrades in arms Frank Tashlin, Bob Clampett, Chuck Jones, and Friz Freleng dished out funnier drawings, outrageous gags, and bigger laughs—and introduced us to a menagerie of cartoon superstars more popular today than ever before: Bugs Bunny, Daffy Duck, Porky Pig, the Road Runner, Tweety, Pepe LePew, and many more. More than one-third of the fifty cartoons in this volume were produced by this studio—evidence of the talent involved and the popularity of their work. Musician Carl Stalling, voice actor Mel Blanc, and dozens of great animators (including Rod Scribner, Virgil Ross, Ben Washam, Abe Levitow, and Ken Champin) and storymen (including Michael Maltese, Tedd Pierce, and Warren Foster) were among the crew working for the legendary Warner directors. Their work is known for its comedy, but it never lacked in quality.

MGM also went for the laughs after disappointing results with Hugh Harman and Rudolf Ising's Disney-style shorts in the 1930s. The directing duo of Joseph Barbera and William Hanna gave the studio a starring cat-and-mouse team, Tom and Jerry, and earned seven Academy Awards. MGM also gave Tex Avery (who moved to MGM from Warner Bros. in 1942) a chance to perfect the gag cartoon with a series of films that begat Droopy, Screwy Squirrel, and the eye-popping *Red Hot Riding Hood.*

United Productions of America began a series of stylish short subjects, released by Columbia Pictures, that influenced every studio from Hollywood to Zagreb, Yugoslavia, during the 1950s. Based on limited animation and modern graphic art, UPA's cartoons were popular with the critics and the public, with characters such as the near-sighted Mister Magoo and Gerald McBoing Boing leading the way.

The Hollywood cartoon studios of the golden age turned cartoons into an art form. The pioneer animators were a creative community who inspired each other toward greatness, and in turn their best work continue to influence the best work in animation today.

The personal styles of cartoon directors first became prevalent in the 1940s. Clampett, Jones, and Avery emerged and influenced the way gag cartoons were constructed. But UPA in the fifties was the true turning point. It proved that individual animation design, far from the lush Disney styles, could be popular. Chuck Jones and John Hubley began using stylized characters and abstract back-

BUGS BUNNY in his FIRST LAUGH RIOT IN 3 DIMENSION

LUMBER JACK-RABBIT

A WARNER BROS. LOONEY TUNE CARTOON

TECHNICOLOR

1954

• 3-D Bugs Bunny and Casper cartoon released.
• First appearance of Tasmanian Devil.
• Disney closes cartoon shorts unit.

1955

• Paul Terry sells his studio, Terrytoons, to CBS.

1956

• MGM closes cartoon unit.

1957

• Hanna-Barbera begins TV animation with "Ruff and Reddy."

1958

• *Knighty Knight Bugs* wins Academy Award, Bugs Bunny's only Oscar.

1959

• "Rocky and His Friends" debuts.
• UPA feature, *1001 Arabian Nights*, released.

1960

• "The Bugs Bunny TV Show" and "The Flintstones" debut on prime-time television (both ABC).
• First use of Xerox process in animation, in Disney's short, *Goliath II*.

grounds in the early 1940s. World War II forced animators to work faster on training films and learn how to communicate information quicker with limited animation and modern graphics. When UPA began making theatrical shorts after the war, Stephen Busustow, John Hubley, Bob Cannon, and their crew used these economic methods to create stylish films that influenced animation around the world.

The UPA studio opened the door to different techniques and ideas. From the simple line art of *Gerald McBoing Boing* and Thurber's *A Unicorn in the Garden* to the abstract renderings of *The Tell-Tale Heart*, a new message went out to animation filmmakers. A backlash formed against Disney realism as artists learned the medium could be used for personal artistic inventions.

Since then, the diverse styles of animation have proved to be unlimited. And independent animation has provided a cornucopia of different styles from artists everywhere. Personal visions have been realized in short films and full-length features, from the Pannonia Studio in Hungary to the famed Zagreb Studio of Yugoslavia, with works sponsored by such institutions as the National Film Board of Canada and London's Channel 4.

ANIMATION FOR TELEVISION

In 1956, a new era in animation began with the creation of "The Boing Boing Show," the first network animated series. Aimed at adults, it featured classic UPA cartoons, clever bridging animation, and offbeat new shorts. (Actually, the first made-for-television animation appeared in commercials, done by such master animators as Otto Messmer in 1941 and Shamus Culhane in 1947. Another early effort was Jay Ward and Alex Anderson's *Crusader Rabbit* cartoon series in 1949.) But starting in 1956, a steady stream of animation—both new and classic—was introduced to a new generation of cartoon fans through this powerful new medium.

The pioneers of television animation were competing with their theatrical counterparts—just as other early television programming competed with movies

"The Flintstones" (top) and "The Jetsons" (above), created by Hanna-Barbera during the boom years of television animation, utilized limited animation techniques.

1961
- *Ersatz*, from Zagreb Studio, is first foreign animation to win Academy Award.

1962
- Bob Clampett's "Beany and Cecil" cartoons debut on TV.

1963
- Warner Bros. animation studio closes.
- "Astro Boy," first Japanese animated TV series, debuts.

1964
- DePatie Freleng begins Pink Panther theatrical cartoon series; first cartoon, *The Pink Phink* wins Oscar.
- "Jonny Quest" premieres.

1965
- "A Charlie Brown Christmas," prime-time special debuts.

1966
- Filmation's first series "Superman" debuts on Sunday morning.
- Walt Disney dies, December 15.
- Chuck Jones creates "How the Grinch Stole Christmas."

1967
- Terrytoons and Paramount close animation studios.

and radio programs—and needed to maintain artistic quality. The early TV toonists relied on dialogue and narration, so their products were closer to contemporary radio shows than to theatrical cartoons. The artists had to demonstrate great visual skill, since, for budgetary reasons, each of their drawings was seen for much longer than the one-twelfth of a second that is standard for theatrical animation. Much of the art in the early years was highly stylized, a result of UPA influence and the ingenuity of cartoonists who needed to compensate for lack of movement with creative artwork.

Like "The Boing Boing Show," many early TV shows were aimed at adults. Jay Ward's "Rocky and Bullwinkle" (1959), Hanna–Barbera's "The Flintstones" (1960), and Bob Clampett's "Beany and Cecil" (1962) rank with the funniest television, live or animated, ever produced. Other shows were geared for youngsters, including "Colonel Bleep," Jack Schleh's highly stylized space adventures, animated segments on "Bozo the Clown" (1959), and "Tom Terrific" (1957), created by Gene Dietch for "The Captain Kangaroo Show."

In 1957, William Hanna and Joseph Barbera, fresh from seventeen years of Tom and Jerry theatricals for MGM, began amazingly successful (and still-vibrant) careers in television animation with the Ruff and Reddy series. Using strong character designers like Ed Benedict and veteran storymen like Michael Maltese and Warren Foster, Hanna-Barbera's television cartoons became a national sensation with a succession of stars like Huckleberry Hound (1958), Quick Draw McGraw (1959), and Yogi Bear (1961). "The Flintstones" 1960 premiere in an 8:30 P.M. time slot spawned a slew of prime-time cartoons—"The Alvin Show," "Top Cat," "Calvin and The Colonel" (all 1960); "The Jetsons" (1962), and "Jonny Quest" (1964) were joined by evening showings of "The Bugs Bunny Show," "The Bullwinkle Show," "Beany and Cecil," and "The Famous Adventures of Mr. Magoo" in an escalating cartoon boom. Soon, ultra-low-budget producers offered quirky and sometimes hilarious productions, such as Sam Singer's "The Adventures of Pow-Wow" (1957), "Bucky and Pepito" (1958), and "Courageous Cat and Minute Mouse" (1960); Ken Snyder and Fred Crippen's "Roger Ramjet" (1965); and Cambria Studio's "Clutch Cargo" (1959) and "Space Angel" (1962), which used the Syncro-Vox technique of matching live-action mouths to static drawings. Even theatrical producers took the plunge, with UPA producing "Dick Tracy" (1961) and "Mr. Magoo" (1960), Terrytoons creating "Deputy Dawg" (1960), Paramount beginning "The New Casper Cartoon Show" (1963), and Walter Lantz hosting "The Woody Woodpecker Show." Imports from Japan ("Astroboy,"

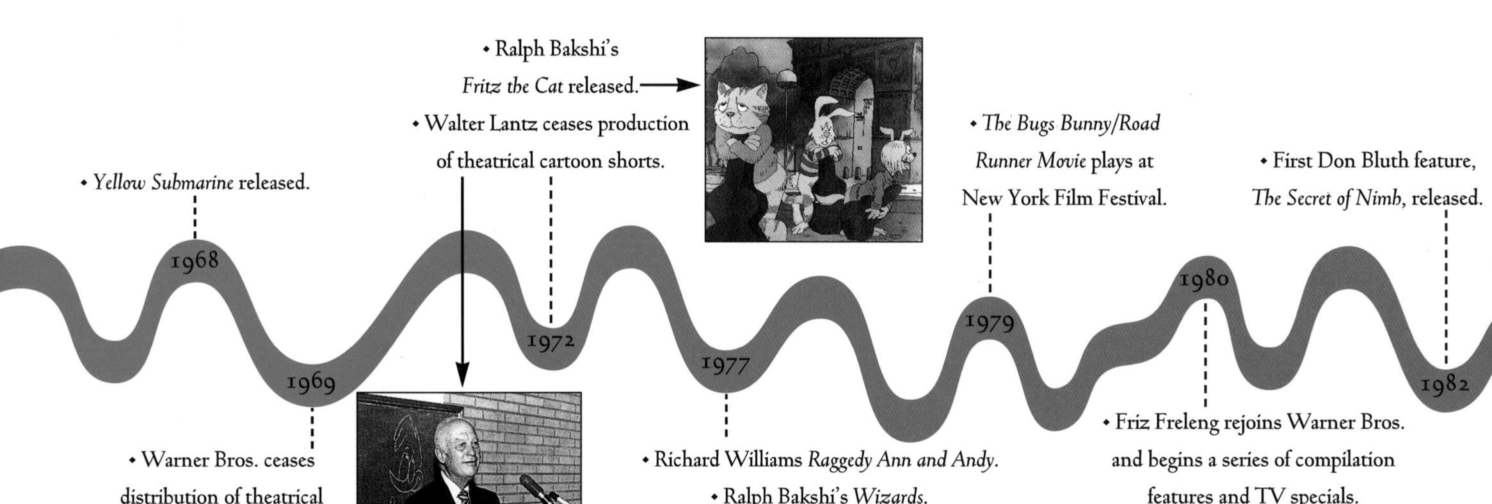
• *Yellow Submarine* released.
1968
1969
• Warner Bros. ceases distribution of theatrical cartoon shorts.
• Ralph Bakshi's *Fritz the Cat* released.
• Walter Lantz ceases production of theatrical cartoon shorts.
1972
1977
• Richard Williams *Raggedy Ann and Andy*.
• Ralph Bakshi's *Wizards*.
• John Hubley's final film, *A Doonesbury Special*.
• *The Bugs Bunny/Road Runner Movie* plays at New York Film Festival.
1979
1980
• Friz Freleng rejoins Warner Bros. and begins a series of compilation features and TV specials.
• First Don Bluth feature, *The Secret of Nimh*, released.
1982

1963; "Gigantor," 1966), England (Halas and Batchelor's "Do-Do the Kid from Outer Space") and France ("Tin-Tin") rounded out the Golden Age of television animation of the late fifties and sixties.

The next years saw a decline in evening series, replaced by highly acclaimed and popular specials, encouraged by the success of "A Charlie Brown Christmas" (1965) and Dr. Suess's "How the Grinch Stole Christmas" (1966). Among the best of these were Chuck Jones's "Horton Hears a Who" (1970), Richard Williams's "A Christmas Carol," and Bill Melendez's "The Lion, the Witch, and the Wardrobe" (1979). The later 1960s also brought forth a barrage of comic-strip characters on Saturday morning, including Superman, the Lone Ranger, Archie, and Spiderman. By the mid-eighties, these were replaced by merchandise-driven action cartoon characters such as G.I. Joe and the Smurfs.

In 1987, Ralph Bakshi's Saturday-morning CBS series "Mighty Mouse: The New Adventures" surprised everyone with humor, something animation had forgotten. Disney continued this change for the better with "Duck Tales," (1987), a fully animated series starring their famous characters. Warner Bros. and Amblin Entertainment's "Tiny Toon Adventures" (1989) revived "wacky" cartoons for afternoon viewing, and "The Simpsons" (1990) brought animated satire back to prime time and to a primarily adult audience.

The future of made-for-television animation—and for the animation industry as a whole—has never looked brighter. In addition to popular feature-length films, new and diverse high-quality programming is being produced for network television ("Batman: The Animated Series," Fox, 1992; "Family Dog," CBS, 1993); for cable networks ("The Ren and Stimpy Show," Nickelodeon, 1991) and directly for the home video market ("Tiny Toons Adventures: How I Spent My Vacation," 1992). Ted Turner launched an international Cartoon Network in October 1992, and the Public Broadcasting System produced its first made-for-television animated feature in 1993. Cable networks such as The Disney Channel, USA, MTV, and The Family Channel are actively producing new cartoon series. Television is now the primary market for animation. It is on television that the next generation of great animators will ply their craft, make us laugh, and dazzle our senses.

1983
- TV animation producer DIC enters the U.S. market with Inspector Gadget.

1985
- Bugs Bunny gets star on Hollywood Walk of Fame.

1987
- Steven Spielberg presents *An American Tale.*
- Ralph Bakshi's "Mighty Mouse: The New Adventures."

1988
- *Who Framed Roger Rabbit?* opens.

1990
- "The Simpsons" begins weekly airings.
- *The Rescuers Down Under*, the first Disney film completed with computerized ink and paint.

1991
- "The Ren and Stimpy Show" premieres on Nickelodeon.
- *Beauty and the Beast* nominated for an Oscar in the Best Picture category.

1992
- The Turner Cartoon Network starts.
- "Batman: The Animated Series" debuts.

1993
- Steven Spielberg presents *Animaniacs.*

Animation Hall of Fame

Winsor McCay
(1867–1934)
Popular American cartoonist and illustrator who introduced the possibilities of animation with his milestone films *Little Nemo, Gertie the Dinosaur,* and *The Sinking of the Lusitania.*

Max Fleischer
(1884–1972)
Inventor of the rotoscope and the head of the most innovative animation studio of the 1920s and 1930s. Fleischer pioneered sound cartoons, the combination of live action with animation, three-dimensional sets, and extra-length cartoons. His studio also brought KoKo the Clown, Betty Boop, and Popeye to the screen.

Otto Messmer
(1892–1983)
Creator and animator of Felix the Cat, the first animated cartoon personality to become a star. Messmer also made the first animated television commercial in 1941 and pioneered the animated billboard for the Douglas Leigh Corporation.

Walter Lantz
(1900–1994)
Creator of Woody Woodpecker and Chilly Willy and veteran cartoon maker whose studio launched the careers of Tex Avery, Virgil Ross, Clyde Geromini, Shamus Culhane, and many others. Lantz produced theatrical cartoon shorts longer than any other studio, more than fifty years, and he won an Oscar for Special Achievement in 1979.

Walt Disney
(1900–1966)
Perhaps the most important figure in twentieth-century animation. Creator of Oswald Rabbit and Mickey Mouse in the 1920s, he later made significant contributions to the development of sound cartoons, personality animation, color, the multiplane camera, and feature-length animation.

Friz Freleng
(1906–)
Animator and director of classic Warner Bros. cartoons. Freleng created many characters, including Porky Pig, Sylvester, Yosemite Sam, and the Pink Panther, and was instrumental in developing Bugs Bunny, Tweety, Speedy Gonzales, and the Goofy Gophers. He won many Oscars, including ones for *Tweetie Pie* (1947), *Knighty Knight Bugs* (1958), and *The Pink Phink* (1964).

Tex Avery
(1908–1980)
Animator and director responsible for the wacky Hollywood cartoon style of the 1940s. Directed the first cartoons of Daffy Duck and Bugs Bunny for Warner Bros. and created Droopy, Screwy Squirrel, and Red Hot Riding Hood for MGM.

William Hanna (1911–) and **Joseph Barbera** (1905–)
Codirecting duo for seventeen years at MGM, where they produced the multi-Academy Award-winning Tom and Jerry series. Beginning in 1957, they revolutionized animation for television, forming their own company and creating Huckleberry Hound, Yogi Bear, the Flintstones, the Jetsons, Jonny Quest, Scooby Doo, and many, many others.

Chuck Jones
(1912–)
Director and creator responsible for many classic cartoons and characters: The Road Runner, Wile E. Coyote, Pepe LePew, Michigan J. Frog, Marvin Martian, and Charlie Dog are but a few of his creations. Jones contributed significantly to the personality development of Daffy Duck, Elmer Fudd, and Bugs Bunny, and won Oscars for *For Scentimental Reasons* (1949), *So Much for So Little* (1949), and *The Dot and the Line* (1965).

Bob Clampett
(1913–1984)
Inspired director of classic Warner Bros. Looney Tunes. Instrumental in the development of Porky Pig, Daffy Duck, and Bugs Bunny. Created Tweety, Beaky Buzzard, and Beany and Cecil.

A Gallery of Cartoon Stars

KEY: (Principal creator/studio/year of debut)

Felix the Cat
(Otto Messmer/Pat Sullivan/1919)
Unlike his comic strip contemporaries, Felix was the first star of animated cartoons who was created and developed for the screen. Otto Messmer's personality animation gave the character a charm that endeared him to silent film audiences, and he was the first cartoon star to be mass-merchandised.

Mickey Mouse
(Walt Disney, Ub Iwerks/Disney Studio/1928)
The always upbeat Mickey Mouse, the first talking cartoon star, became a national symbol of happy days ahead during the darkest moments of the Depression. Mickey established the Disney studio as a leader in animation, and he is best known today as the Sorcerer's Apprentice in *Fantasia* (1940) and as the original host of TV's "Mickey Mouse Club" (1955–59).

Betty Boop
(Grim Natwick/Fleischer Studios/1930)
The sexy star of Max Fleischer's 1930s cartoons was a take-off of "Boop-oop-a-doop" singer Helen Kane. Many of Betty's cartoons are cult classics today due to their outrageous humor, sexual innuendoes, and jazzy scores by talents such as Cab Calloway and Louis Armstrong. The Motion Picture Production Code of 1934 forced the animators to lengthen her skirt and end her risqué adventures with KoKo the Clown and Bimbo in favor of much safer antics with Grampy and Pudgy. Her voice was provided by Mae Questel.

Popeye
(E. C. Segar/Fleischer Studios/1933)
Created as a supporting player for the comic strip "Thimble Theater" in 1929, the gruff-talking sailor became a star in the comics and gained even more fame in the Paramount cartoon shorts. Fleischer's cartoons were outrageous and inventive to begin with, and their take on Popeye made him the most popular cartoon character of the 1930s.

Donald Duck
(Clarence Nash (voice)/Disney Studio/1934)
Clarence Nash's unique voice was the basis of Donald Duck, first animated by Art Babbit and Dick Huemor in *The Wise Little Hen*, directed by Wilfred Jackson. His hot-tempered personality was developed in subsequent cartoons and his popularity soon eclipsed Mickey Mouse as the biggest star of Disney's short cartoons.

Porky Pig
(Friz Freleng/Warner Bros./1935)
Created as part of a cast of animal characters—in the mode of "Our Gang," which included Porky and Beans, Ham and Ex, Ollie Owl, etc.—for the Merrie Melodies cartoon *I Haven't Got a Hat*, Porky became the unlikely star of a series of black-and-white Looney Tunes and was developed by Tex Avery, Bob Clampett, and Frank Tashlin. He ultimately became the symbol of Warner Bros. cartoons with his closing signature line, "That's all, folks."

Daffy Duck
(Tex Avery/Warner Bros./ 1937)
Daffy started out as a complete screwball in his earliest cartoons with costar Porky Pig. He mellowed out by the 1950s into a selfish egotistical foil for Bugs Bunny and Elmer Fudd. According to Chuck Jones, Mel Blanc based the voice characterization on producer Leon Schlesinger's unique speech pattern.

Tom and Jerry
(William Hanna, Joseph Barbera/MGM/1940)
This cat and mouse duo rarely spoke, but we always knew what was on their minds. Hanna and Barbera spent seventeen years coming up with the funniest ways to make mayhem with the pair, and won seven Oscars doing it.

Bugs Bunny
(Tex Avery/Warner Bros./ 1940)
Avery directed *A Wild Hare*, the first cartoon in which Mel Blanc asks "What's up, Doc?" in his now-famous Brooklyn/ Bronx accent, but the bunny was a collaboration among Avery, Chuck Jones, Bob Clampett, Ben Hardaway, Cal Dalton, and the rest of the Leon Schlesinger studio. Bugs became the cartoon star of the WWII era, a streetwise smart aleck who takes on any opponent and always comes out on top.

Woody Woodpecker
(Walter Lantz/Walter Lantz Productions/1940)
Legend has it that a woodpecker disrupting the honeymoon of Lantz and his wife, Gracie, inspired this batty bird. Mel Blanc originated the voice and distinctive laugh, writer Ben "Bugs" Hardaway and Grace Lantz succeeded Blanc in voicing the character. His theme, "The Woody Woodpecker Song," became a number-one hit record in 1948.

Tweety
(Bob Clampett/Warner Bros./1942)
"I Tawt I Taw a Puddy Tat" is Tweety's famous phrase, usually heralding another assault on Sylvester's senses. The innocent little canary was responsible for two Academy Awards in the Warner Bros. camp. As usual, Mel Blanc originally provided the voice.

Mr. Magoo
(John Hubley/ UPA/1949)
Based on Director Hubley's bull-headed father, the near-sighted Mr. Magoo was the most popular of UPA's cartoon characters. Jim Backus provided the hilarious wordplay, mumbles, and cackles. Pete Burness directed the funniest episodes, including Academy Award-winners *When Magoo Flew* (1954) and *Magoo's Puddle Jumper* (1956).

The Road Runner and Wile E. Coyote
(Chuck Jones/Warner Bros./1949)
Chuck Jones based the Coyote's problems with Acme roadrunner traps on his own inability to use hammers, screwdrivers, and most household tools. The Road Runner, object of his aim, whizzes by with a "Beep-Beep," occasionally stopping to hold up a picket sign with his intentions spelled out for us to read. A speaking Wile E. Coyote also appears with Bugs Bunny in a handful of hilarious cartoons.

Yogi Bear
(Hanna-Barbera/1959)
TV star Yogi began his career as the middle cartoon on "The Huckleberry Hound Show," but became so popular that he was spun off into his own series in 1961. A freeloading inhabitant of Jellystone National Park, and "smarter than the average bear," Yogi is assisted in his picnic-basket snatching by cub Boo-Boo and thwarted at every turn by Ranger Smith. He starred in a feature-length movie, *Hey There, It's Yogi Bear,* in 1964.

Rocky and Bullwinkle
(Jay Ward and Alex Anderson/Ward Productions/1959)
Crazy characters, limited animation, and hilarious dialogue have sustained the popularity of the flying squirrel and the dimwitted moose from Frostbite Falls, Minnesota, for more than thirty years. Pursued by Russian spies Boris and Natasha, Rocky and Bullwinkle were voiced by June Foray and Bill Scott, respectively.

Fred Flintstone
(Hanna-Barbera/1960)
"Yabba-Dabba-Doo!" Fred is the head of network television's first prime-time animated sitcom, "The Flintstones." Originally voiced by Alan Reed, Fred was featured along with his wife, Wilma; neighbors Barney and Betty Rubble; daughter Pebbles; and pet, Dino, in hundreds of episodes, as well as their first animated feature, *The Man Called Flintstone* in 1966.

Pink Panther
(Friz Freleng/DePatie Freleng/1964)
This cool cat was created for the animated opening titles in *The Pink Panther,* Blake Edwards's 1963 feature film starting Peter Sellers. The character was so appealing that United Artists commissioned a series of pantomime theatrical shorts, the first of which, *The Pink Phink,* won an Academy Award. Henry Mancini composed the popular theme music.

The Simpsons
(Matt Groening/Gracie Films/1990)
This popular dysfunctional family began its Emmy-winning weekly series in 1990, but first appeared in short segments on "The Tracey Ullman Show" (1987). The stories revolve around nuclear power plant worker and donut afficionado Homer Simpson; his housewife, Marge; and their three kids, Bart, Lisa (whose favorite TV shows are "Krusty the Clown" and Itchy and Scratchy cartoons), and baby Maggie.

Ren and Stimpy
(John Kricfalusi/Nickelodeon/1991)
"Happy Happy, Joy Joy!" An asthmatic Chihuahua and a hairball-hurling cat make an unusual series of cartoons. Yak-Shaving Day, the History-Eraser Button, the Happy Helmet, a toy called Log, and Powdered Toast Man are but a few of the nutty concepts that made this show an instant success among children and adults.

What Makes a Cartoon Great?

The fifty short films presented in this volume share a unique bond. Each has moved us with its humor or drama, touched us with its beauty or its charms, or enthralled us with its display of skill and art. Most of them were produced within an assembly-line system, under strict budget and time constraints, and with a single mandate: to entertain. But these extraordinary films are the ones that reached beyond those bounds; they were loved when they were first seen and have stood the test of time. They aren't just fifty great cartoons, but fifty great films, period, on par with any live-action counterparts. And they prove that great animation can affect us the same way any great filmmaking can.

So what makes cartoons great? Usually they are marked by a combination of factors, including concept, artwork, music, innovation, quality of animation, humor, and dialogue. It is as difficult to compare the primitive but charming *Gertie the Dinosaur* with the wacky *Quasi at the Quackadero* as it is to compare the films of Charlie Chaplin with those of Howard Hawks, but the genre is wide enough to encompass them both. Both accomplish what their artists set out to do with the skill and talent that set them apart. In the case of *Gertie*, it is the creation of a new type of animation no one had ever attempted before, along with the distinct personality of the character. In *Quasi*, it is a brilliant graphic style combined with offbeat and memorable humor.

ORIGINALITY

In some films, originality is the main claim to greatness. Without ignoring its intrinsic value, we can recognize that *Gertie the Dinosaur* would not be as admired and prized today had it come in the middle of a long line of similar cartoons; it was startling because it broke new ground. Similarly, *Gerald McBoing Boing* redefined an art form in seven minutes—because of its instant success, critical and popular, its style was copied by every studio. *Steamboat Willie* might not be the best of Disney's shorts, but it was the first to use sound. And Chuck Jones's *The Dover Boys* earned a place because its graphic style paved the way for clever use of limited animation.

ARTISTRY

In many more cartoons, skillful artistry is more important than originality. It was Walt Disney who brought fine art to the world of animation, who moved it away from cartoonists and comic strip producers and brought European artistry to the field. *The Old Mill* is an example of this approach; when the Mama bird places her wing over her chicks, you can feel her emotion in the finely drawn scene; when the rope on the mill breaks, you feel its tension. The bird looks like a real bird, but more so—the essence of the bird is captured in the drawings in a way that could never be achieved with photographs of a single bird. In *Clock Cleaners*, Disney's artists captured perspective and depth of field, creating intricate cities that heightened the comic effect of the almost-falling feeling.

Expert drawing ability was used to very different effect in *Coal Black*, where wild, exaggerated drawings convey everything from manic energy to total exhaustion. In *The Tell-Tale Heart*, limited movement and stylized paintings take the audience into the mind of a madman—the cartoon's color scheme and gothic heaviness perfectly mirror the tone of the story and the madman's thoughts. *Superman* presents a totally different type of drawing: more literal and less cartoony, with characters that seem almost real.

ANIMATION

Animation drawings are more than just ink or paint on paper; they are created to produce motion, and their excellence is judged in relation to their conveyance of motion. Winsor McCay's success was seen in his ability to make us see Gertie swallow and "feel" the weight of her jaws on a tree trunk. The animators of *The Band Concert* managed to make a tornado spin in time to music, with musicians and various inanimate objects, such as trees and laundry, joining in the frenzy. In *Brave Little Tailor*, two distinct types of animation excellence are shown: the dramatic action of Mickey sewing up the giant's sleeve and the simple dialogue of Mickey relating the tale are both riveting. *The Man Who Planted Trees* is a tour de force of fluid animation, with one scene flowing into another; although the design is restricted, there are no cuts in this elaborate story.

MUSIC

Music is often an important component of cartoons, ranging from classical (*Corny Concerto, The Skeleton Dance,* and *What's Opera, Doc?*) to jazz (*Minnie the Moocher, Rooty Toot Toot*); cartoons are successful when animators are able to create the perfect visual images to match the music, the exact story that brings the music into focus.

HUMOR

Even if we recognize and admire the artistry behind cartoons, it is usually their humor that we truly love. Often it is the humor of the unexpected: the gruff bulldog of *Feed the Kitty* falling in love with the ultra-cute kitten, Elmer Fudd in *What's Opera, Doc?* appearing on stage in Viking garb. In *Der Fuehrer's Face*, it is the constant repetition of the swastika theme, which appears in clouds, telephone poles, and weathervanes. Several directors perfected the humor of excess. In *Bad Luck Blackie*, Tex Avery took a normal idea—a black cat crossing a dog's path—and expanded it until it achieved the hilarious: Each time the cat pops out, a larger and more ridiculous object falls on the dog's head.

Often a single image captures an entire scene. When Daffy Duck turns into an eyeball in *Book Revue*, it is not a random image; Clampett has found the one image that captures the character's state of mind. The scene is funny because the image is so wonderfully apt. Dialogue sometimes provides the fun, as in Jack Mercer's mumblings in *Popeye* or Chuck Jones's immortal "Pronoun Trouble" sequence in *Rabbit Seasoning*.

Humor often revolves around adult themes. Tex Avery, of course, is famous for bringing sex into cartoons, basing a series of cartoons (two of which, *Red Hot Riding Hood* and *Rural Red Riding Hood*, are among the top fifty) on a wolf's pursuit of a beautiful woman. In truth, these cartoons, made in the 1940s, were preceded by several Fleischer cartoons filled with sexual innuendo: *Bimbo's Initiation* is regarded by many as purely a tale of sexual pursuit, and Betty Boop herself was sufficiently blatant that the Hays Commission decided she needed to be censored. UPA's *A Unicorn in the Garden*, based on a James Thurber story about a married couple, makes another kind of adult statement.

PERSONALITY

Some cartoons convey the personality of their animated stars with astonishing force. Perhaps none is as successful as Chuck Jones's *Duck Amuck*, which explores the slightly schizophrenic personality of Daffy Duck as he attempts to cope with the crazy world Bugs Bunny creates for him; the cartoon is almost stream-of-consciousness. *The Big Snit* brings us another married couple whose foibles and bickering, so obviously a part of their personalities, make us recognize their humanity.

CONCEPT

In some cases, it is the concept behind the cartoon that attracts us—reminding us that there are often ideas behind cartoons, that they are not simply random gags. *Peace on Earth* uses the medium to present a strong antiwar message. *One Froggy Evening* is a profound statement about man's inability to communicate and connect with other humans. And *Bambi Meets Godzilla* is all concept; it's genius lies in its ability to surprise us with its very simple idea in less than two minutes.

Many of the cartoons in this book are really not so very different from others made at about the same time; they use the same techniques, styles, and even characters. But something about them manages to do that same thing much better, putting the elements together with a kind of artistic integrity, or adding some extra ingredient—or so much more of the same ingredients—that they achieve that rare essence, the wholeness that makes them truly great.

The Fifty Greatest Cartoons

What's Opera, Doc?

WARNER BROS., 1957

CREDITS

A Merrie Melodies Cartoon

Directed by Chuck Jones

Story: Michael Maltese

Animation: Ken Harris, Richard Thompson, Abe Levitow

Effects animation: Harry Love

Layouts: Maurice Noble

Backgrounds: Philip DeGuard

Film editor: Treg Brown

Voices: Mel Blanc

Musical direction: Milt Franklyn

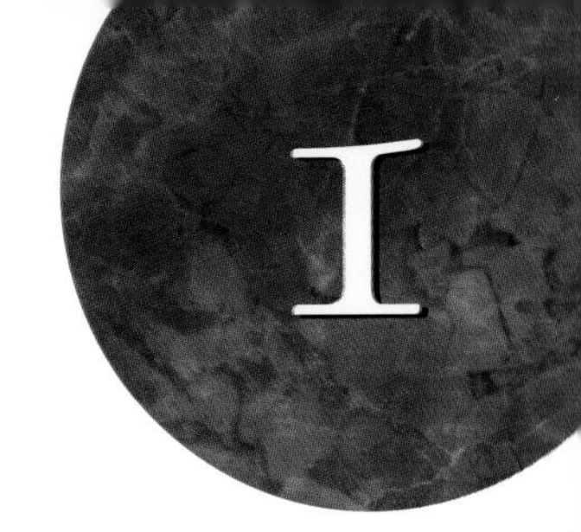

In *What's Opera, Doc?*, Chuck Jones compresses the entire fourteen hours of Richard Wagner's four-opera *Der Ring des Nibelungen* cycle into a six-minute cartoon. He manages to skewer classic opera traditions and Disney's *Fantasia* at the same time, with Bugs and Elmer singing most of their lines—with accents and speech impediments—in a stylized Valhalla. As the cartoon begins, Elmer Fudd, hunting rabbits in costume as a Teutonic knight, sings "Kill the Wabbit" to the Valkyries' theme and explains his mission to Bugs. Bugs transforms himself into a pigtailed Rhinemaiden on a white pony, and Elmer falls in love with him/her. They dance, and Bugs runs to the top of a tall, dizzying tower. There Elmer serenades the sexy blond Bugs with the melancholy "Return My Love," and they resume their dance until Bugs's wig slips and Elmer realizes he's been duped. Fudd unleashes his wrath, conjuring up the north wind and a lethal smog, and kills the rabbit. As Fudd mourns this tragic death, Bugs turns to the audience and asks, "What did you expect in an opera? A happy ending?"

Jones's vision caused this cartoon to transcend the ordinary. It contains 106 shots, a record. Animators pored over footage of the Ballets Russes de Monte Carlo to keep the ballet scene accurate as well as looney. Maurice Noble contrived a unique color scheme for the cartoon, dousing Elmer in bright shades. Ken Moore developed a technique to highlight the meeting on the top of the tower by cutting holes in specialty set-design materials. The entire staff doctored their time cards, stealing time from a less complicated Road Runner cartoon. Obviously, they all knew they were working on a masterpiece.

RETURN MY LOVE

ELMER: *O Brunhilda, you're so lovely.*

BUGS: *Yes I know it, I can't help it.*

ELMER: *O Brunhilda, be my love. [They dance]*

ELMER: *Return my love, our loving burns deep inside me.*

BUGS: *Return my love, I want you always beside me.*

ELMER: *Love like ours must be*

BUGS: *Made for you and for me . . .*

ELMER AND BUGS: *Return, won't you return my love For my love is yours. [They dance some more]*

LYRICS BY MICHAEL MALTESE

For sheer production quality, magnificent music, and wonderful animation, this is probably our most elaborate and satisfying production.

—*Chuck Jones*

CHUCK JONES

Charles Martin Jones, director of nine of the fifty great cartoons in this volume, was born in Spokane, Washington, in 1912 and grew up in Southern California, working as an extra in silent films as a child. Jones trained at the Chouinard Art Institute (now the California Institute of the Arts) and with Disney art instructor Don Graham and entered the animation field in the early 1930s as a cel washer for the Ub Iwerks studio. He joined Warner Bros. in 1933 and climbed through the ranks as inker, painter, in-betweener, animator, and finally director in 1938. His earliest films were slow-paced Disneyesque adventures featuring such characters as Sniffles the Mouse and Two Curious Dogs. He also directed some of the first Bugs Bunny cartoons and was instrumental in creating Private Snafu for the armed services during World War II. Jones, the most intellectual of the Warner crowd—he quoted G. K. Chesterton and George Santayana and based a cartoon on the writings of Eisenstein—was one of the first cartoon directors to experiment with stylized backgrounds and animation techniques, and his cartoons are noted for their highly artistic look and comic timing. He created Pepe Lepew, Marvin Martian, the Road Runner, and Coyote, and many memorable Bugs and Daffy cartoons, delving into his characters' personalities by drawing hundreds of poses for each. "I'm principally concerned with character," Jones says. "Not with what Bugs Bunny is, but with who he is. I want to get inside him, to feel him from my viewpoint."

The greatest cartoon of all time? The point remains debatable. Nevertheless, Chuck Jones's splendiferous *What's Opera, Doc?* has emerged as the clear, sentimental favorite of the largest assemblage of animation fans, practitioners, critics, and general cartooniacs ever polled. The fact that this fabled film is a work of stunning beauty, great humor, and masterly execution only serves to make the choice seem eminently reasonable.

Yet perhaps the reason that *What's Opera, Doc?* has consigned all other cartoons to the status of also-rans is that it mirrors, in significant ways, several of the attitudes central to many animation lovers' experience of watching cartoons. And it accomplishes this by bringing together a roster of seeming opposites. The film both exalts its characters and remains joyously aware of their lowdown Toontown roots. It illustrates our sense of the quasi-mythic nature of these characters, but it also provides a singular example of why these characters are loved in the first place—because their actions and personalities, whether sassy or simpleminded, pull us into intimate touch with them, and thereby provide the pleasure of breaking down our sense of the cold remoteness of mythic figures. Indeed, the film almost invites us to serve as coconspirators with its characters against the bombast and intimidation of the Wagnerian universe. With artful adroitness, *What's Opera, Doc?* blurs some of the boundaries between spectacle and spectator. High and low are here deliciously intermixed.

Also, as we do, the film, with its emphasis on spectacle, revels in the richness available to animated filmmaking, yet takes equal delectation in cartoon's tradition of razzing everything in sight—first and foremost, in this case, the casting of Bugs Bunny and Elmer Fudd as bedizened Wagnerians. From its first images, that of the would-be awesome *Fantasia*-like figures devolving into the shadow of puny lisping Elmer Fudd, the film piles up pretensions only in order to mow them down. Gloriously overbaked, the film reveals that ultimately, it was only cooking up fodder for satire. By reducing Wagner's *Ring* into a subtext for an archetypal Bugs and Elmer chase, *What's Opera, Doc?* pulls off a dazzling mingling of reverence and ridicule.

—*Steve Schneider*

It is one of a handful of American animation masterpieces, and likely the most cerebral of them. Daffy makes the most of his opportunity for a definitive solo tour de force. It is at once a laugh riot and an essay by demonstration on the nature and condition of the animated film and the mechanics of film in general.

—*Richard Thompson, Film Comment, 1975*

Duck Amuck

WARNER BROS., 1953

Stand back, musketeers! They shall sample my blade," exclaims Daffy, dressed as a dashing swordsman and surrounded by suitable scenery. But after a few thrusts, he notices he's out of background scenery. When he asks, "Where's the scenery?" a paintbrush appears and fills in a farmyard setting, ending the suitability of the musketeer costume. He changes into overalls and gets a hoe, but now the scenery presents the North Pole. "Would it be too much to ask if we could make up our minds? Hmmm?"

In *Duck Amuck*, something has gone terribly wrong, and Daffy finds himself in a surreal send-up of all cartoon conventions—and his own worst nightmare. The scenery, colors, and sound effects are clearly in the hands of a fiend, and although Daffy does his best to adapt to the story suggested by each background, his woes only increase. The bewildered duck talks back to the animator, but his requests are met with cruel caprice.

A character breaking the fourth wall was not a new idea—Felix the Cat and Koko the Clown did it frequently in the 1920s—but Chuck Jones used it to explore the limits of Daffy Duck's schizophrenic mood swings, creating a hilarious, animated, one-man show of desperation. The cartoon was created in a free-form, stream-of-consciousness style. Recalls Jones, "We started out, I sat down and started drawing, and I came up with the opening, and it was just the idea that he runs out of background. From that point on it happened right on the board. We didn't even have a story as such, we made one afterward, but there wasn't one at the time we were making it. The Bugs Bunny ending was not hit upon until the last week of layout."

CREDITS

A Merrie Melodies Cartoon

Directed by Charles M. Jones

Story: Michael Maltese

Animation: Ben Washam, Ken Harris, Lloyd Vaughan

Layouts: Maurice Noble

Backgrounds: Philip DeGuard

Voices: Mel Blanc

Musical direction: Carl W. Stalling

DAFFY DUCK

Daffy Duck has a split personality. In the 1930s and 1940s the duck was a total screwball. Jumping, laughing, and instigating mischief, he was a complete lunatic and public nuisance. In the 1950s and 1960s, Daffy matured into an egotistical foil for Bugs Bunny and Elmer Fudd. As the foolhardy hero of a dozen movie spoofs, Daffy got laughs playing the self-centered, greedy slob most of us are but are afraid to reveal.

First appearing in Tex Avery's 1937 cartoon *Porky's Duck Hunt*, he became an immediate star. The character alternated between starring roles in the color Merrie Melodies series (*Daffy Duck and Egghead, Daffy Duck in Hollywood*) and lead supporting roles in Porky Pig's black-and-white Looney Tunes cartoons (such as *The Daffy Doc* and *You Oughta Be in Pictures*).

Mel Blanc, trying to differentiate Daffy's voice from that of Disney's famed Donald Duck, chose to roll his *r*s and lisp—not unlike the actual speaking voice of producer Leon Schlesinger. The voice was sped up to make it zanier. Sylvester the cat has exactly the same voice, but it is not sped up.

By the time *Duck Amuck* was created, Daffy had been transformed by Chuck Jones into his new persona as the frustrated egomaniac. The other directors had just as much fun using this character in a variety of situations: Friz Freleng's *Show Biz Bugs* (1957) cast Daffy as a wanna-be celebrity trying to outwit superstar Bugs Bunny, and Robert McKimson's *Fool Coverage* (1952) put Daffy in the most "dethpicable" role of his career: insurance salesman.

"Stand back, Musketeers . . ."

(Layout drawing by Chuck Jones)

"Oh, brother, I'm a Buzz Boy."

. . . . *they shall . . .*

. . . *sample my blade?"*

"Not me, you slop artist!"

"What are you doing down there?"

"Under the spreading chestnut tree . . ."

"Ain't I a stinker?"

The Band Concert is a perfectly realized cartoon that manages to blend music, comedy, personality animation, dramatic action, and storytelling into a seamless whole. I've always felt that it was the natural drama of *The William Tell Overture* that inspired Walt Disney and his staff to such incredible heights. It's certainly one of their finest achievements—a great, great cartoon.

—*Leonard Maltin*

The Band Concert

WALT DISNEY, 1935

CREDITS

Directed by Wilfred Jackson

Animation: Jack Kinney, Gerry Geronimi, Ugo D'orsi, Cy Young, Louis Schmitt, Dick Williams, Frenchy DeTrémaudan, Huszti Horvath, Les Clark, Dick Huemer, Wolfgang Reitherman, Archie Robin, Roy Williams, Johnny Cannon

The *Band Concert* was an ideal vehicle for the first color Mickey Mouse cartoon. Designed to be something special, the film fulfilled its promise. As the film opens, a crowd cheers bandmaster Mickey Mouse and his five park musicians on their performance of "Selections from Zampa." Next is *The William Tell Overture*, and the band—responsive to every move of Mickey's baton—plays in fine form until Mickey hears snack vendor Donald Duck hawking his hot dogs and lemonade. Delighted by the music, Donald pulls out a fife and starts playing "Turkey in the Straw." The musicians change tunes and join him. Mickey breaks Donald's fife, but the duck produces more of them through magic tricks performed for the audience.

Mickey chases the duck away, and the trombone player shakes a dozen flutes out of him, but Donald always has another and resumes his melody. Then a bee disturbs the performance. It lands on Mickey's head, Donald tosses a scoop of ice cream at it, the ice cream lands in the trumpet's mouth and is blown back onto Mickey. The movements Mickey makes as it slides down his back change the tempo and tune of his band's music.

When Mickey turns to the next page of music—"The Storm"—leaves begin swirling around, and the sky darkens. Soon a tornado enters the park, literally sucking up the scenery. Mickey and his band members are swept up in the twister, with Mickey waving his baton and the musicians playing as they spin, their music stands remaining in front of them. Mickey and his band reach a musical climax at the height of the storm and then fall back to land in a tree, each loyally performing his part of the finale. Mickey turns to take his bow, but the only applause is from Donald.

It has comedy of detail, such as the sleeve of Mickey's oversized uniform continually slipping down to conceal his baton; it has comedy of structure based on the duck's persistent attempts to break up the concert by playing a competing tune on the flute—a tune to which the band, against its will, has to turn; it has comedy of character in the stern artistic devotion of Mickey contrasted with the unmotivated villainy of Donald; it has comedy of action when the tornado twists the entire concert into the air and then reverses itself and brings the players back to the grandstand. In no other picture have I observed so many flashing details—during the tornado itself there is the general line of comedy that in the whirlwind, or caught on treetops, all the players continue to follow their music, but there are moments in this scene when the screen seems to be animated by dozens of separate episodes. They are miraculous if you catch them, and even if you do not, the total effect is miraculous still.

—*Gilbert Seldes,*
The Saturday Review, 1961

DISNEY ANIMATION

The release of *The Band Concert* was a watershed in the history of Disney animation. The studio was now squarely on course for bigger and better things. The Mickey Mouse cartoons, beginning with this one, were now in full Technicolor, and the series would play an important part in the growth and maturity of Disney's art form. Each new Silly Symphony, as well, was a subtle experiment in story, design, technique, or animation; experiments which culminated in the release of the studio's first feature-length film, *Snow White and the Seven Dwarfs*.

Walt Disney's goal was to have the best cartoons on the market, and, to that end, he established a private school of animation. In 1932, nighttime art classes taught by Don Graham, a top instructor at the Chouinard Art Institute, were established for students to study action, practice life drawing, and analyze animation. Students like *The Band Concert* animators Les Clark (whose intuitive character animation of Mickey dates back to *Steamboat Willie,* 1928) and Wolfgang Reitherman (a specialist in action sequences and personality) went on to become two of the Nine Old Men, the elite team of artists who set the standards known as Disney classic animation.

From the outset, Disney strove for realistic personality animation. "I definitely feel that we cannot do the fantastic things based on the real, unless we first know the real," Walt said. "The closer the cartoon characters behaved like us, the more the humor and drama could connect with the audience."

The Disney studio not only conquered personality animation, but, in its quest for realism and maximum entertainment, made pioneering use of music and sound, depth and color, as well as action and special effects. Disney's strides during the 1930s were followed by most of his competitors, improving the quality through the entire industry and influencing animators around the world.

The [cartoon] in main outline would be very little, if it weren't for the way every incident, every foot of film, is given a solid basis in observation, so that natural action is caught and fixed in a typical gesture rendered laughable through exaggeration or through transference into the unfamiliar; and for the swift way all the incidents pile up on one another. No one ever saw a band so busy, proud, and full of troubles as this, from the virtuoso swapping of hands in the flute duet to the hard-pressed air of the brass section.

—*Otto Ferguson,*
<u>*The New Republic*</u>, 1935

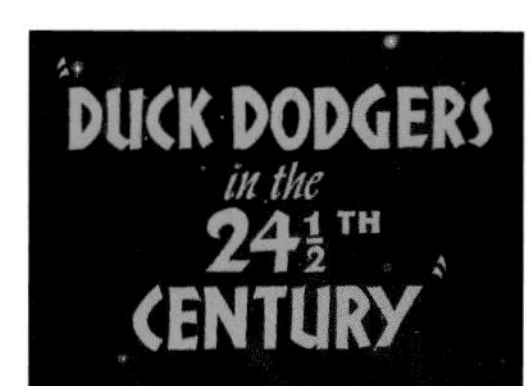

Buck Rogers, Captain Video, and the various other space cadets crisscrossing the intergalactic void during the 1950s were not alone: Also aloft in a spaceship were Duck Dodgers (Daffy Duck) and his "eager young space cadet" (Porky Pig).

"No one knows his way around outer space like Duck Dodgers in the 24½th century!" announces Daffy. His mission: Find Planet X, source of "aludium fozdex, the shaving-cream atom." With the aid of his loyal cadet (who calls him "Your Heroship"), he locates the planet (it comes right after Planet W and before Planet Y) and claims it for Earth until Marvin Martian lands and claims it as well. The planet—which only Maurice Noble could have envisioned—isn't big enough for both of them, so they set about exchanging ultimatums and other unpleasantries, making use of various up-to-date products of the ever-present Acme Co. The conflict between Martian and earthling escalates until they finally blow the planet to a single bit, barely big enough for Daffy to stand on.

By 1953, Daffy Duck and Porky Pig were stars with thoroughly defined personalities. Jones had taken Daffy from his screwball origins and developed him into an egotistical foil for Bugs Bunny and Elmer Fudd. And Porky, who now enjoyed the status of a regular supporting player, had become a smarter, more aware character, with tongue planted firmly in cheek. This was the Martian's third screen appearance (his first two were opposite Bugs Bunny in 1948's *Haredevil Hare* and 1952's *Hasty Hare*).

Film producer George Lucas is particularly fond of this cartoon, and many theaters booked it alongside his movie *Star Wars*.

Duck Dodgers in the 24½th Century

WARNER BROS., 1953

CREDITS

A Merrie Melodies Cartoon

Directed by Charles M. Jones

Story: Michael Maltese

Animation: Lloyd Vaughan, Ken Harris, Ben Washam

Layouts: Maurice Noble

Backgrounds: Philip DeGuard

Effects animation: Harry Love

Voices: Mel Blanc

Musical direction: Carl W. Stalling

PORKY PIG

A popular supporting player in many Daffy Duck cartoons of the 1950s, Porky Pig was in fact the biggest Warner Bros. cartoon star of the 1930s. Porky was first seen in a small part in Friz Freleng's 1935 *Merrie Melodie: I Haven't Got a Hat.* Tex Avery developed Porky further in a series of Looney Tunes in 1936: *Gold Diggers of '49, The Blow Out,* and *Plane Dippy* among others.

Mel Blanc began doing Porky's voice with *Porky's Duck Hunt* (Daffy Duck's debut film) in 1937. Blanc took the character's annoying stutter and made it entertaining and comic, without being offensive. Porky's popular signature line "That's all folks!" has since become the trademark of Warner Bros. cartoons.

It's always amazed me that the Warner Bros. cartoons could manage to be both timeless and topical. If they'd relied too heavily on current events and fads in the 1930s, '40s, and '50s, they might not have survived, particularly as entertainment for kids. But if they hadn't reflected the times in which they were made, they wouldn't be quite so much fun for the grownups. *Duck Dodgers* was Warner's principal entry in the science-fiction sweepstakes of the 1950s, and I daresay it's as great as any of the bigger, more ambitious live-action films of the period.

—*Leonard Maltin*

THE WARNER BROS. STUDIO

The Warner Bros. cartoon department began as an independent studio owned by Leon Schlesinger and led by Disney renegades Hugh Harman and Rudolph Ising. Looney Tunes, starring Bosko, began in 1930 and the miscellaneous musical series Merrie Melodies started in 1931. When Harman and Ising left the studio in 1933, Schlesinger promoted Friz Freleng to director. Tex Avery joined the studio in 1935, and along with fellow animators like Bob Clampett and Chuck Jones, musician Carl Stalling, and voice actor Mel Blanc, gave the studio its own identity as the home of funny cartoons.

This team knew how to develop funny characters and situations. Avery introduced Daffy Duck (1937), Clampett created Tweety (1942), and Chuck Jones debuted the Road Runner (1949)—just a few of the cartoon superstars who, along with the incomparable Bugs Bunny, formed the Warner Bros. stable. By the 1940s, Warner Bros. cartoons were the most popular in America.

During World War II, Warner cartoonists contributed cartoons about Private Snafu, the dumbest soldier in the army, to the war effort. In 1944, Schlesinger sold his studio to Warner Bros. The cartoon department won its first Oscar in 1947 for *Tweetie Pie,* the first cartoon to team Tweety and Sylvester, and the studio went on to win a total of six Academy awards under the 1950s and 1960s triumvirate of Chuck Jones, Friz Freleng, and Robert McKimson.

Warner Bros. animation has continued to be an active division of the studio, producing TV specials, feature films, occasional theatrical shorts, TV commercials, public service spots, and merchandising artwork. Today, the studio produces the highly successful "Tiny Toon Adventures" and "Batman, the Animated Series," among many others.

"ONE FROGGY
EVENING"

SINGING FROG!
HERE!
FRANTIC
TONITE
IT SINGS!
DANCES
IT'S WONDERFUL
OPENING TONITE
GRAND OPENING
8:30
NOW
THE
of the

One Froggy Evening

WARNER BROS., 1956

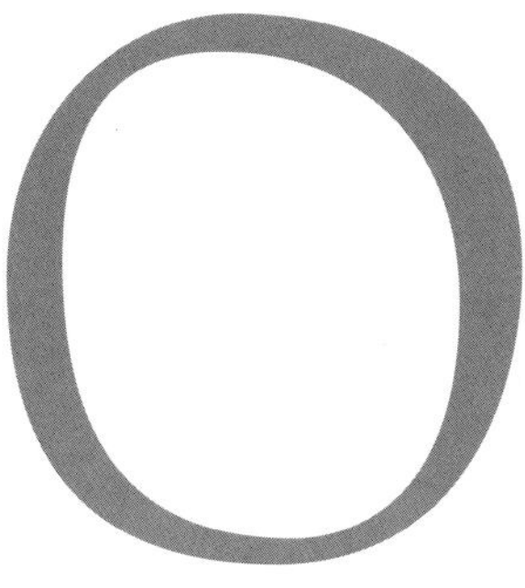

One of the most famous Hollywood cartoons ever made, *One Froggy Evening,* has the simplicity of a parable, and its fame is all the more remarkable because the cartoon is silent—except for a singing frog. The story begins with the demolition of an old building. Opening the building's cornerstone, a construction worker finds the dedicatory documents, dated April 16, 1892. Also in the cornerstone is a frog, who greets the worker with a rendition of "Hello, My Ragtime Gal." A singing frog! Imagining the wealth soon to be his, the man takes the frog home.

Far from riches, the man gets only frustration and financial ruin, for the frog will perform only for him; in the company of others, it's simply a humdrum ribbiting frog. This becomes painfully clear when he takes the frog to a theatrical agency—a scene viewed from outside the agency's windows—and uses his life savings to rent a theater for a frog performance (he even offers free beer to fill the house). Rendered penniless by his efforts, the man ends up on a park bench on a cold winter night. The frog sings for him, a policeman hears, and when the man explains it was his frog, he finds himself in a psychiatric hospital (entertained by the frog, of course). Released, he sees a building about to be dedicated and puts the frog in the cornerstone. The next scene takes place in A.D. 2056: A worker with the Acme Building Disintegration Co. opens the cornerstone, finds the frog, the frog sings for him, and . . .

Much of the cartoon's humor comes from Chuck Jones's decision to tell the story without dialogue, and from the expressive animation of the frog (animators studied *New Yorker* cartoons before they started). "It was a difficult film to do," he said, "but I think of all my pictures, I like it best."

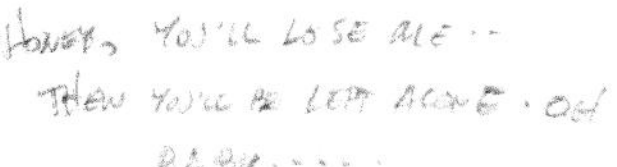

CREDITS

A Merrie Melodies Cartoon
Directed by Charles M. Jones
Story: Michael Maltese
Animation: Ken Harris, Abe Levitow, Richard Thompson, Ben Washam
Layouts: Robert Gribbroek
Backgrounds: Philip DeGuard
Music: Milt Franklyn

There are only a few enduring silent-screen comics who still have impact today, and among them I'd number Chaplin, Keaton, Laurel and Hardy, and Michigan J. Frog. With simplicity and economy of drawing, the frog foils the plans of his would-be marketer with increasing sophistication. The hat and cane give way to a high-wire act and then a vocally demanding aria; the frog's talent expands exponentially as his owner's mental health deteriorates, the frog remaining cheerfully oblivious to his owner's plight. The frog's cultured tenor voice and lithe movements are directly and uproariously juxtaposed with his public persona, that of a lumpen, limp-limbed frog whose only sound is an impolite "ribbit."

The story is classical in structure, a departure from the peripatetic zaniness of the typical Warner Bros. cartoon, and paints a familiar scenario of the dreamer who, unable to share the brilliance of his dreams, is gradually destroyed by them. The cartoon is enduring enough to have been imitated in *Spaceballs* (imitating *Alien*), in which the alien pops out of a stomach to perform "Ragtime Gal" on a diner counter. Even those in the audience who had never seen *One Froggy Evening* laughed at the sheer ludicrousness of it. Michigan J. Frog is timeless and eternal.

—*Jami Bernard*

. . . as close as any cartoon has ever come to perfection.

—*Time* magazine, 1973

MICHIGAN J. FROG

Chuck Jones discussed his decision to eschew dialogue in *One Froggy Evening* in an interview with Joe Adamson: "I decided that the picture would be funnier if that discipline was imposed. For one thing, it had an explosive quality. You never knew when the son of a bitch frog was going to sing, but you always knew that nobody was going to hear it except the poor guy."

This is the only cartoon featuring the singing frog (later dubbed Michigan J. Frog), who warbles eight tunes: "Hello, My Ragtime Gal," "Come Back to Erin," "I'm Just Wild About Harry," "McCluskey's Fight," "Won't You Come Over to My House," "Please don't talk about me when I'm gone," and a Jones/Maltese/Franklyn original, "The Michigan Rag."

Winsor McCay is a major figure in the history of American animated cartoons. McCay, a popular newspaper cartoonist during the first decade of the twentieth century, also appeared in vaudeville doing "chalk talks."

Inspired by flip books, McCay began, in 1909, to experiment with animating his comic strip character Little Nemo. Two years later he startled his vaudevillian audiences, which were used to seeing cartoonists doing static "lightning sketches," with moving drawings of his most famous creation. McCay followed up that film with a more ambitious subject, *The Story of a Mosquito* (1912), but it was *Gertie the Dinosaur* that truly astounded his audiences.

Two falsehoods have become attached to *Gertie the Dinosaur* over the years: that it was the first animated cartoon and that it was Winsor McCay's first animated cartoon. And though both are wrong, *Gertie* is still a milestone in animation history, if only because Gertie is the first cartoon character with a true personality. Previous film animation, most notably by pioneers J. Stuart Blackton and Emil Cohl, were essentially "trick films," presenting as novelty the magic of moving drawings. For *Gertie*, McCay developed "The McCay Split System," an early version of the process of animating extreme poses to be filled in by "in betweens" later—a system all Hollywood cartoon studios adopted by the 1930s. (Most mass-produced cartoons until then were animated straight ahead—one drawing at a time, each movement drawn in succession.) This process allowed for the development of character animation. *Gertie* also thrilled audiences by being the first "interactive" cartoon. McCay talked to Gertie, and she responded—obeying his commands, catching a pumpkin thrown by McCay, and even carrying the artist in her mouth!

John Canemaker, McCay's biographer, wrote: "Where McCay differed from his predecessors was in his ability to animate his drawing with no sacrifice of linear detail; the fluid motion, naturalistic timing, feeling of weight, and eventually, the attempts to inject individualistic personality traits into his characters, are qualities that McCay first brought to the animated film medium."

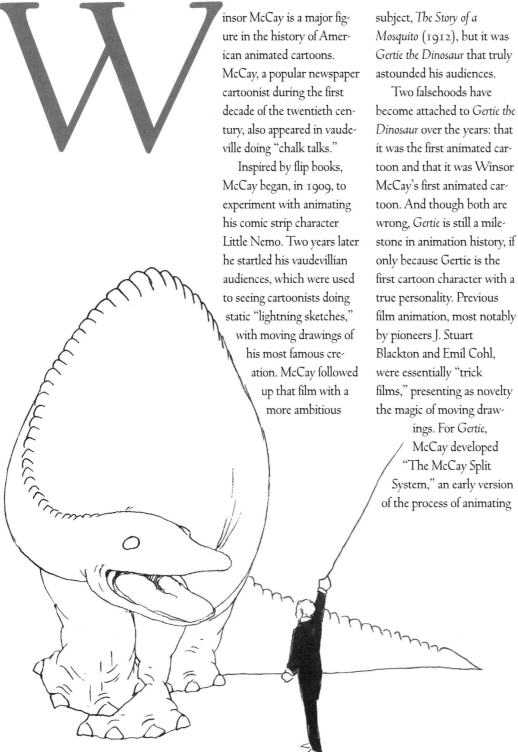

6

Gertie the Dinosaur

CREDITS

Written, directed, animated, and produced by Winsor McCay

Winsor McCay's endearing Gertie, the petulant, childlike diplodocus who cries when admonished, is a masterpiece of personality animation created twenty years before the Walt Disney studio hit its stride.

Drawn in McCay's elaborate close-line, realistic style, the animation of Gertie imparts an illusion of weight through subtle means: When Gertie drinks an entire lake, her belly does not bulge in a cartoonish manner; instead, part of the cliff on which she stands gives way beneath her feet. Another weighty example: When she attempts to toss a boulder at a mischievous mastodon, the rock slips twice from her jaw's grip.

Gertie is also a thinking character who takes time to consider her options. She is a dimensional personality: shy and also a show off, headstrong and defiant, yet sensitive enough to be provoked to tears.

Gertie's tears are, in fact, a baptism, consecrating a new kind of animation that led to a now-familiar cartoon pantheon of personality kids, including Felix, Mickey, Bugs, Grumpy, Dopey, Happy, et al.

—*John Canemaker*

RED HOT
RIDING HOOD
Something New
has been added –

Red Hot Riding Hood

MGM, 1943

CREDITS

An MGM Cartoon

Directed by Tex Avery

Producer: Fred Quimby

Animation: Preston Blair and others

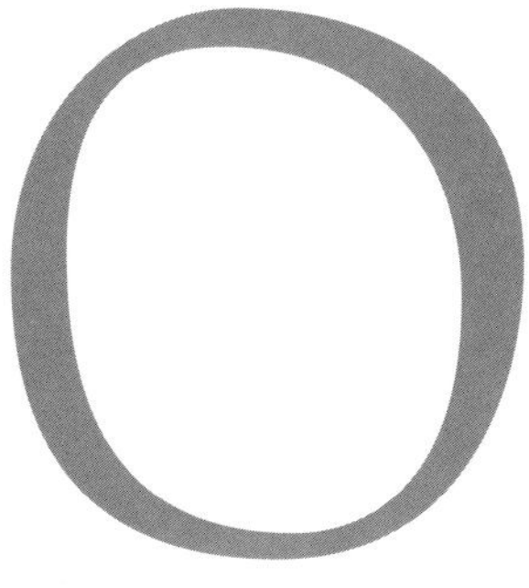

nce upon a time, Little Red Riding Hood was skipping through the woods." So begins the narrator, but the Wolf interrupts. "Aw, stop it!" he complains, "I'm fed up with that sissy stuff. It's the same old story, over and over! If you can't do this a new way, bud, I quit!" Red joins the protest and makes an important point: "Every cartoon studio in Hollywood has done it this way!"

So the narrator reintroduces the characters. The Wolf is now a girl-crazy playboy, Red is a nightclub singer, and Grandma is a man-hungry spinster with a neon sign on her downtown skyscraper: "Grandma's Joint—Come up and see me sometime." The Wolf arrives at the nightclub to catch Red's act, a lively number ("Hey, Daddy") that drives him crazy. He drags her to his table and invites her out, but she resists his promises of diamonds, pearls, ermine, and a new set of sidewall tires and hurries off to Grandma's. The Wolf pursues her but is soon trapped by the sex-starved granny. He tries to escape through doors, but finds brick walls (with Avery-esque signs like "Imagine That, No Door!") or nothing. The Wolf finally dives out the window and lands on the street lamp of Hollywood and Vine. Fed up, he vows to kill himself before he'll "look at another babe." When Red appears onstage, the Wolf blows his brains out, and his ghost emerges to whistle and stamp his feet for the sexy singer.

Preston Blair designed and animated Red, a character so immediately popular that finished animation cels were grabbed by cartoon department employees even before they were shot. Red and the eye-popping Hollywood Wolf (or some variation of them) appeared five more times during the 1940s, in *The Shooting of Dan McGoo* (1945), *Swing Shift Cinderella* (1945), *Wild and Woolfy* (1945), *Uncle Tom's Cabana* (1947), and in a super sequel, *Little Rural Riding Hood* (1949).

FOR THE BOYS

Actually, we were thinking of the army when we made the first in the *Red Hot Riding Hood* group . . . the sergeant [stationed at MGM to plan training films] spotted the thing and roared. . . . When the censor saw it . . . we had to trim and juggle and cut back. It got back to Washington, to some colonel or whatnot, that the censor had cut out quite a bit from us. Finally, Louis B. Mayer got a telegram from the colonel saying that he wanted an uncut version of a *Red Hot Riding Hood* cartoon for his personnel overseas. The studio dug around, and I don't know how many prints they gave him, but, man, it went over great overseas.

—*Tex Avery, interviewed by Joe Adamson*

AUDIENCE REACTION

In 1943, the manager of an Iselin, New Jersey, theater noticed that one of his short subjects was getting whistles and wild applause, and when the short was over, the audience shouted to see it again. The manager wanted to oblige them, but also felt obligated to stick to his existing schedule—so he cancelled one of the other scheduled shorts to clear time for a second running of *Red Hot Riding Hood*. Reaction was just as enthusiastic during the second running, and instead of being satisfied, the audience demanded to see it again. Though a full evening of features and other attractions was booked, the manager screened the cartoon yet again for anyone who cared to stay; 150 fans stuck around long enough to whistle and cheer it on for a third time.

An animation business that was working hard to catch the dating crowd (only to be branded "kid stuff" during a postwar baby boom) was being geared more and more toward teenagers, soldiers, and in this case, randy sailors, with less and less concern for whether the small fry were going to get all the jokes or not.

Red Hot Riding Hood shares many of its stylistic characteristics with Tex Avery's other early MGM cartoons—*Who Killed Who?*, *The Early Bird Dood It*, *Dumb-Hounded*, and *The Blitz Wolf*: elaborate visuals; full, flowing animation by Irven Spence, Ed Love, and Preston Blair in the pseudo-Disney MGM "production value" style established by Harman and Ising; and, tucked in Avery's briefcase the day he left Warner Bros., an insistent, almost self-conscious sense of humor that drew attention to the fact that it was shattering cartoon shibboleths. Although this dates *Red Hot* and sets it apart from the more pared-down, stylized, nearly effortless effects Avery achieved at his peak in the late 1940s, it allows for moments of subtlety and character illumination less possible in the later gag-fests and more striking in the overall pattern of directorial intensity. When the Wolf, who's supposed to pounce on Red Riding Hood, reacts instead to the gushy narrator by turning to him with that unexpected "What the hell planet are you from?" expression on his face, he effectively becomes a critic of the very film we had up to that moment presumed him to be a character in—a distancing effect achieved with a single shading of inflection.

In the same way, when the Wolf interrupts the flow of his suave Charles Boyer lovemaking with a backwoods "What's yer answer to that, babe?" the contrast is adroitly consummate—absurd in its abruptness and at the same time deadly accurate in capturing the uncertainty of tone inherent in nearly everyone's relations with the opposite sex.

The shock once achieved by these effects has worn off a trace in the intervening years, and anyone familiar with Avery's style will find little to surprise him in the brassy, insistent '40s way this film has of rubbing your nose in its own hipness. What saves this cartoon today is the indomitable humor of its dominant contrast between the animated fantasy world it keeps one foot in and the sophisticated adult world it simultaneously kicks its way into with the other foot. We keep thinking "OK, we get the joke already," and *Red Hot Riding Hood* keeps reminding us that, as long as we think sex is something we're able to be adult about, it's got another joke up its sleeve—and it's probably on us.

—*Joe Adamson*

Porky in Wackyland

WARNER BROS., 1938

Welcome to Wackyland. It can happen here." Inspired by a *Los Angeles Times* article about an expedition to Africa in search of the rare dodo bird, Bob Clampett decided to send Porky Pig to African Wackyland (as opposed to Alice's Wonderland), home to some of the zaniest denizens ever devised, paying homage to such diverse influences as artist Salvador Dalí and cartoonist Milt Gross. Aviator Porky is hunting the rare dodo, believed to be extinct, and worth so much that the zeros in its monetary value don't fit in a newspaper headline.

The bird is truly a rare one, with a bird head, banana feet, and arms that appear and retract as needed. It uses wacky logic to avoid capture: It can draw a door to exit through whenever it chooses and can lift the backdrop and replace it with a brick wall for Porky to crash into. The other characters of the Wacky landscape include a goon in convict stripes who holds a prison window in front of his face and demands to be freed; a cross-eyed rabbit that sways on a swing suspended by its own ears; a peacock with playing-card plumage; and a three-headed weirdo (his mama was scared by a pawnbrokers sign). Using his own disguises, Porky finally catches the dodo—but was it really the last of them?

CREDITS

A Merrie Melodies Cartoon

Directed by Robert Clampett

Animation: Norman McCabe, I. Ellis

Musical direction: Carl W. Stalling

CLICK!
OH BOY! THE LAST
OF THE DODO'S

8

STAFF REACTION

Porky in Wackyland was screened for the entire Leon Schlesinger Studio on August 1, 1938. The staff was routinely asked to write their comments on each new picture—and *Porky in Wackyland* got some of the best reactions ever:

As far as I'm concerned, it was swell. . . the animation is tops—better than from the other units.

—*Frank Tashlin*

One of Clampett's best. It's just too bad such a good story wasn't done in color.

—*Lee Larson*

Keep this up and we'll all be candidates for Wackyland.

—*Michael Maltese*

The sign at the beginning of *Wackyland,* stating, "It can happen here," proved to be Clampett's mantra for the rest of his career. Perhaps Clampett wasn't just artist with pencil when Porky crossed that line into Wackyland, but his soulmate as well. By stretching and squashing the characters in an exaggerated way, toying with space and time, and altering the audience's relationship to the film, Clampett and his team created a wacky new style of cartoon. Their enthusiasm was unstoppable, despite some studio resistance to what is now called the "Warner Style." By 1938, with Avery, Clampett, and others heading their own units, the new wave was building up a head of steam. Everything from the speeded up "Merry-go-round broke down" theme music to Porky Pig's embarrassing stutter proved nothing was sacred to this bunch.

—*Bob Clampett, Jr.*

YEAH-MAN!
YEAH- I'M THE LAST OF THE DODOS
AIN'T I, FELLERS?

BOB AND PORKY

By the time he made *Porky in Wackyland*, Bob Clampett had been doing black-and-white Porky Pig cartoons for more than a year and had made ten funny films, including *Porky's Hero Agency* (1937) and *Porky's Party* (1938). His trademark was placing the pig in outrageous situations with equally outrageous costars, such as Daffy Duck, Gabby Goat, and even a drunken dog named Black Fury. In this, his eleventh cartoon, Clampett indulged in outrageous screwiness for its own sake, creating what he knew would be a masterpiece. Originally, Porky was accompanied on his hunt by Injun Joe, his adversary in a previous film, *Injun Trouble*, but when the storyboards became top-heavy with looney characters and crazy gags, Joe's part was eliminated.

Gerald
McBoing boing
color by Technicolor

Gerald McBoing Boing

UPA, 1951

CREDITS

Columbia Pictures/Jolly Frolics

Directed by Robert Cannon

Supervising director: John Hubley

Production manager: Adrian Woolery

Story: Dr. Seuss

Adaptation: Bill Melendez, Ruddy Larriva, Pat Matthews, Willis Pyle, Frank Smith

Backgrounds: Jules Engel

Color style: Herb Klynn, Jules Engel

Music: Gail Kubik

Story told by: Marvin Miller

The story of "Gerald McCloy and the strange things that happened to that little boy" is a landmark in the history of animated films, for it proved that the Disney style was not the only path to follow. With such cartoons as *Gerald McBoing Boing*, the "UPA look" became the new standard for cartoons in the 1950s.

When the infant Gerald opens his mouth, he doesn't speak works, but "goes 'boing boing' instead." His distressed parents call a doctor who examines the boy but declares, "I've no cure for this, I can't handle this case." With time, Gerald's sound repertoire increases, including the noise of traffic and trains. When he makes the sound of an explosion, his father decides it's time for him to go to school, but the teacher sends him home. The neighborhood children don't want Gerald around and taunt him with the nickname "Gerald McBoing Boing, the noisemaking boy."

Downhearted, Gerald runs away from home and is about to board a freight train when a radio-station owner appears. He needs someone to make the sounds for his shows, and soon Gerald becomes the star of the "Silent Sam Steelheart" western show. Before his admiring parents, he demonstrates his talents by making the sound effects for a classic western showdown. A crowd of autograph seekers awaits Gerald and his parents outside the studio, and the narrator ends the story, "Now Gerald is rich, has friends, is well fed, 'cause he doesn't speak words, he goes 'boing boing' instead."

Not since the days of Disney's *Three Little Pigs* has any cartoon occasioned such dancing in the streets. Based on a story by Dr. Seuss, its revolutionary distinction lies in its appeal to the adult mentality and imagination. Its drawing is spare and clean, its backgrounds are mere rough sketches and outlines. Color is applied loosely and suggestively, not realistically. The music, composed by Gail Kubik, is daringly modern, completely in keeping. And this economy of means has produced a picture far richer in humor and spirit than all the fussily detailed conventional cartoons. Not the least delight of this little film is the absence of cut animals. Even the people are different. They look like cartoon characters, which, after all, is what they are.

—*Arthur Knight*, *The Saturday Review*, 1952

Gerald
Mcboing-boing
color by Technicolor

DR. SEUSS

Gerald's tale is told in the distinctive rhyming lines of Theodor Geisel, better known as Dr. Seuss. Geisel wrote the story and showed it to Stephen Bosustow, UPA's cofounder and producer, who saw it as the perfect vehicle for his innovative animators. Dr. Seuss, who had written the story as a children's phonograph record, was not convinced that the tale, which relied heavily on sound effects, could work visually. But he was more than pleased with the finished film. "It started a revolution in animation," he proudly declared later. Supervising director John Hubley told the *New York Times* in 1952, "We proved with *Gerald* that a short can cut across the whole of the audience and can be made attractive and entertaining to both adults and youngsters."

King-Size Canary

MGM, 1947

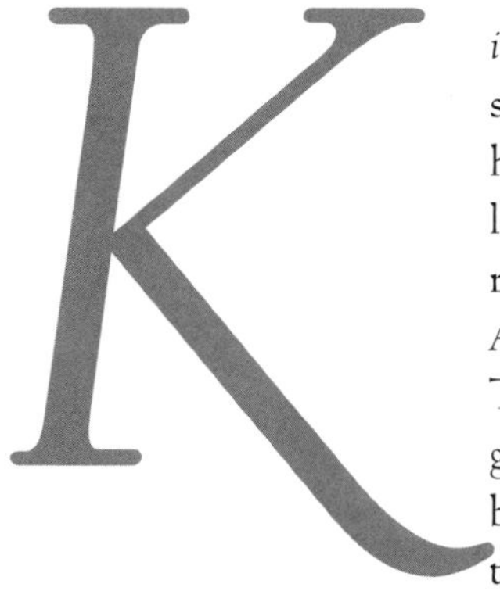

ing-Size Canary opens like a standard cartoon about a hungry alley cat but quickly leaps into the impossible and reveals itself as one of Tex Avery's wildest creations. The cat is about to investigate a refrigerator when a bulldog charges. The cat tosses sleeping pills down the dog's throat, but finds the refrigerator bare. There's nothing in a sardine tin, but a can of "Cat Food" contains a live mouse. The mouse sidesteps doom by offering advice: "I've seen this cartoon before, and . . . if you're smart you won't eat me . . . 'cause before this picture's over, I save your life!" The mouse recommends the cat eat the canary, but the poor bird is emaciated. Then the cat spots a bottle of "Jumbo-Gro" plant food and gets an idea.

With that bottle, the cartoon departs the merely wacky and begins an exploration of maniacal animation. The bird, cat, bulldog, and mouse all drink the potent mixture, growing larger with each sip. The cat chases the king-size canary but is stopped by the bulldog—now a good thirty feet tall. The dog chases the cat but is soon scared off by the now-giant mouse. (The cat and mouse shake paws: "I told you I'd save your life.") Still hungry, the cat takes another swig of "Jumbo-Gro" and goes after the mouse. The mouse gets the bottle and grows even larger, then the cat swipes it back and gets taller. The cat and mouse keep drinking until there's none left. "Ladies and gentlemen," announces the mouse, "we're gonna have to end this picture. We just ran out of the stuff. Goodnight." The pair embrace and wave goodbye as the camera pulls back to reveal the monsters standing atop a tiny planet Earth.

CREDITS

An MGM Cartoon

Directed by Tex Avery

Producer: Fred Quimby

Story: Heck Allen

Animation: Robert Bentley, Walter Clinton, Ray Abrams

Music: Scott Bradley

10

King Size
CANARY
156
RACING FORM
COLOR SEPARATION AROUND EYES
FORMULA ON MOUSE.
POT BELLY
CHART #1
PIC #156
FORMULA ON DOG
PROPERTY OF
M-G-M CARTOON DEPT.
1-30-46
SHAGGY TOOTH
LOOSE VEST ON NORMAL CAT.
BANDAGE ON TAIL
FORMULA ON CANARY HEAD
BIG HEAVY SHOULDERS ON BULL DOG
TRAMP CAT
HAT OPEN ON TOP
HEAVY CHEST
BACK LEGS THIN AND WEAK
NORMAL CAT 2 WHISKERS ON EACH SIDE.
FORMULA ON CAT

I'm not here to proclaim *King-Size Canary* a cold-war allegory, Freudian phallic fantasy, or surrealist simulacrum—not because it isn't (numerous critics, theorists, and French have beat me to it), but mainly because it deserves comment on its own terms: a 1947 MGM cat-and-mouse cartoon not starring Tom and Jerry in which the characters become really, really big (i.e., very, very funny).

Numerous animators mined this premise as early as Winsor McCay's 1921 *The Pet*, but no one ever did a more thorough job of it. No characters ever got as big as Avery's, and Tex Avery knew that if big is funny, then biggest is funniest. And Avery's agenda was making the quantitatively funniest cartoons in the industry.

In character animation, a prime pleasure for the artist and audience alike seems to be in the definition and subsequent distortion of the cartoon character they've created and accepted, from Disney's subliminal squash and stretch to Clampett's gnarled hyperthyroid histrionics. But only in *King-Size Canary* is character distortion the driving force of the cartoon's plot. Avery's 1947 MGM standard-issue cat, mouse, canary, and bulldog exist only to distort, distend, and gloriously mutate for our entertainment and amusement. And the manner in which Avery has delineated their plight is singularly demented; while their salami torsos expand heavenward, their hands, legs, and heads remain puny and disproportionate. Not merely scaled-up cartoon designs, they become freakish victims of poisoned metabolisms suggesting very real human glandular disturbances. These mean, funny drawings are at the core of what makes *King-Size Canary* so perversely appealing. They function as subversive graffiti superimposed upon our normal expectation of what a cartoon character should look like: the same dynamic that packed our grandparents into freak shows and today racks up ratings for Oprah, Sally, and Geraldo.

—*Mark Newgarden*

TEX AVERY ON HIS HUMOR

A lot of it comes from those old slapstick comedies. You can see some of the things they contrived with wires and so forth to get impossible gags—Mack Sennett with his Ford that goes between two trolleys and comes out squashed. We found out early that if you did something with a character, whether animal or human, that couldn't possibly be rigged up in live action, then you'd have a guaranteed laugh. If a human can do it, it isn't always funny in animation; or if it's funny, a human could do it funnier. . . . We used any kind of distortion that couldn't possibly happen, like a character getting stuck in a milk bottle. You couldn't get Chaplin in a milk bottle."

© The Walt Disney Company

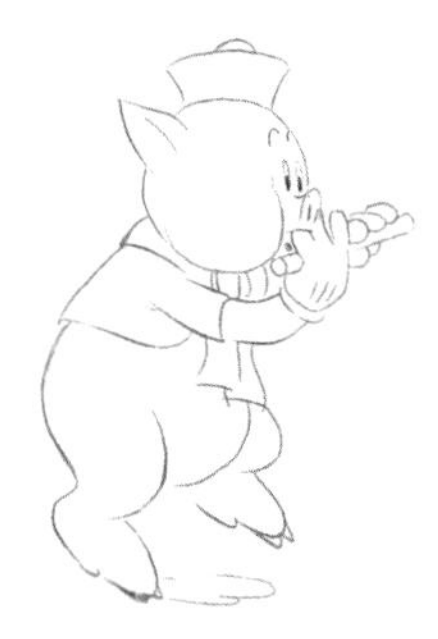

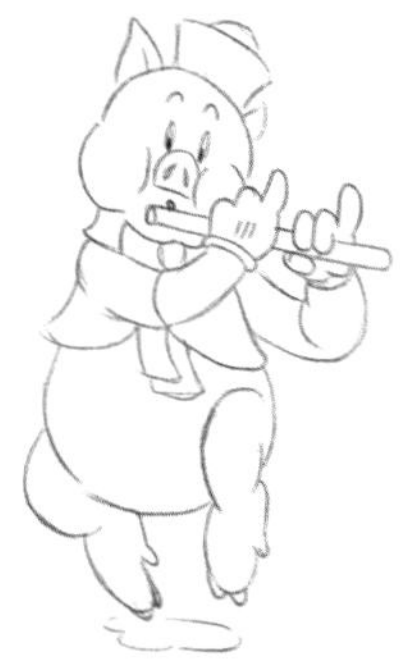

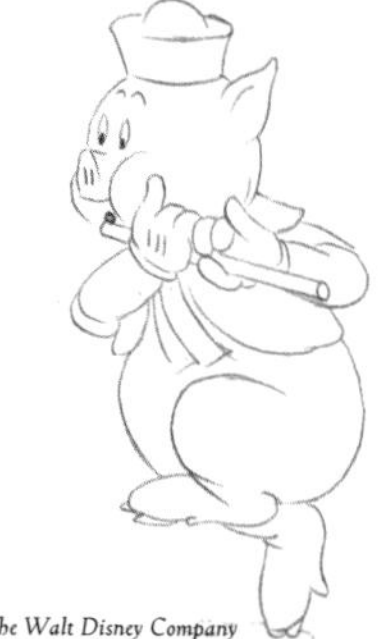

Three Little Pigs

WALT DISNEY, 1933

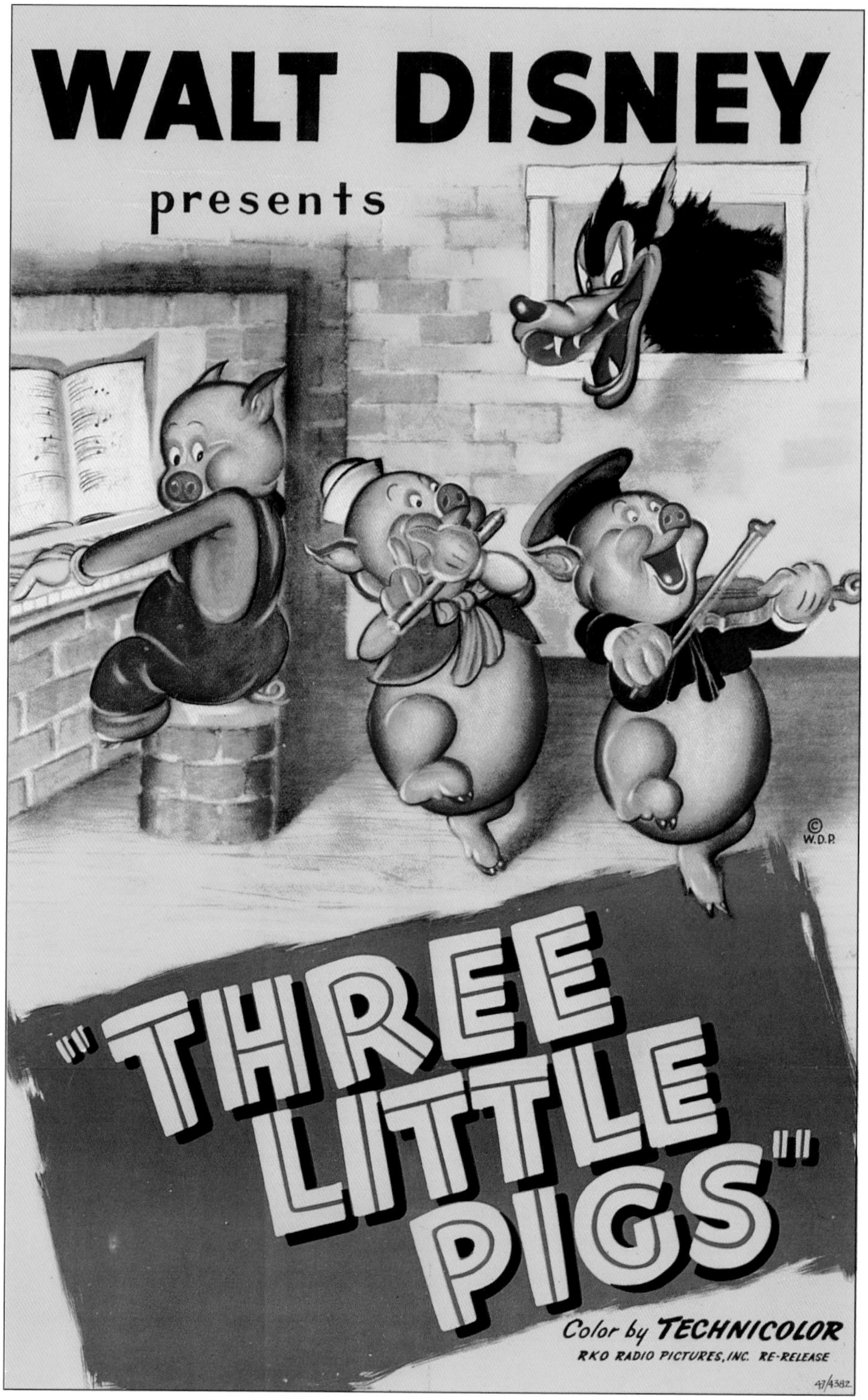

CREDITS

Directed by Bert Gillett

Animation: Fred Moore, Dick Lundy, Art Babbitt, Norm Ferguson, Jack King

Voices: Pinto Colvig, Billy Bletcher, Mary Moder, Dorothy Compton

© The Walt Disney Company

One of the most popular cartoons ever made, *Three Little Pigs* is also historically significant as a milestone in the art of animation. Although physically similar, each of the little pigs has a distinct personality, seen in their movements as well as their dialogue; the cartoon is a breakthrough in "personality animation." Disney had begun to "cast" his animators, and in this film, Fred Moore was principal animator of the pigs, Norm Ferguson (best known for his work on Pluto) did the wolf, and Dick Lundy, who specialized in dance animation, drew the opening jig. *Three Little Pigs* was Disney's most sincere effort to combine a standard folk tale with music, gags, and bright colors. Its main song, "Who's Afraid of the Big Bad Wolf?," written by Frank Churchill, Ted Sears, and Pinto Colvig, became a national anthem, hailed in *Time* magazine as "the tune by which 1933 will be remembered."

A flute-playing little pig builds a house of straw and hay; his violin-playing friend uses sticks. They sing and dance to a third little pig, hard at work building his house of stone and brick. When the third pig warns, "I'll be safe and you'll be sorry when the wolf comes to your door," the first two laugh, and with gleefully squealing voices, sing, "Who's Afraid of the Big Bad Wolf?"

Tattered and scraggly, the wolf is indeed nearby. At the straw house, when the pig refuses to let him in—"Not by the hair on my chinny chin chin"—the wolf threatens, "I'll huff and I'll puff and I'll blow your house in." That's just what he does, and then repeats the process at the stick house. The two pigs flee to the brick house of the third pig: The bricks hold. The wolf then goes down the chimney, lands in a boiling kettle, and is sent howling into the sky, then skulks down the road as the three little pigs reprise their theme song.

Released during the height of the depression, *Three Little Pigs* provided a pertinent warning to Americans: Economic survival depends on building a strong house of bricks to ward off the threat of foreign forces intent on undermining national self-sufficiency. It also gave Americans an affirmative theme song with which to confront the wolf of poverty and hunger scratching at the door: "Who's afraid of the big bad wolf?" The film earned $125,000 in the first years of its release.

—M. Thomas Inge

© The Walt Disney Company

Rabbit of Seville

WARNER BROS., 1950

he directors at Warner Bros. were given a great deal of autonomy over their productions. As Chuck Jones said, "These cartoons were never made for children. Nor were they made for adults. They were made for me." Since Jones was fond of music, and had very sophisticated taste, it's not surprising that he made a series of Bugs Bunny musical spoofs (others are *Long-Haired Hare, Baton Bunny*, and *What's Opera, Doc?*).

Although fond of classical music, Jones was fully aware of animated-film potential. "Some music has a comedic quality if you put something funny in front of it. In all the musical films I did, including *Rabbit of Seville* the music is always played straight. It's what the characters do that makes it a comedy." Thus the music in *Rabbit of Seville* is the original Rossini score for *The Barber of Seville*, but the cartoon shows respect for absolutely nothing else.

Elmer Fudd's endless hunt of the rabbit Bugs takes them across the stage of the Hollywood Bowl just as the orchestra tunes up for *The Barber of Seville*. The rising curtain reveals the rabbit as barber, with the hunter as his customer. In tempo with the overture, Bugs gives Elmer a close shave. He then massages Fudd's bald scalp and tosses a fruit salad on it, shines the hunter's pate, grows and mows a beard on his face, gives him a cement mud-pack, and uses "Figaro Fertilizer" to grow hair on his head that blossoms into flowers. This is enough for Fudd, who faces off with the rabbit, and the two confront each other with larger and larger axes and guns until Bugs offers flowers and a ring. He marries Fudd and dumps him into a cake. Having finished with him, he calls out, "Next!"

CREDITS

A Looney Tunes Cartoon

Directed by Charles M. Jones

Story: Michael Maltese

Animation: Phil Monroe, Ben Washam, Lloyd Vaughan, Ken Harris, Emery Hawkins

Layouts: Robert Gribbroek

Backgrounds: Philip DeGuard

Voices: Mel Blanc

Musical direction: Carl Stalling

MICHAEL MALTESE

name that appears over and over among credits for great cartoons is that of storyman Michael Maltese, of whom Chuck Jones said, "The quirky brilliance of his ready wit was never, never neutral. He disdained facts as useless—only the odd, the unusual, the hilariously peculiar interested him." Maltese's Lower East Side-New York origins found their way into the personalities of many Warner characters. He was responsible for writing the stories for *What's Opera, Doc?, Rabbit Seasoning, Rabbit of Seville, Duck Dodgers in the 24½th Century, One Froggy Evening, For Scentimental Reasons*, and *Fast and Furry-ous*, among many other hits.

12

© 1950 Warner Bros., Inc

RABBIT OF SEVILLE SONG

How do
Welcome to my shop
Let me cut your mop
Let me shave your crop
Daintily . . . daintily.
Hey, you–
Don't look so perplexed.
Why must you be vexed
Can't you see you're next
Yes, you're next
You're so next
How about a nice close shave
Teach your whiskers to behave
Lots of lather
Lots of soap
Please hold still
Don't be a dope
Now we're ready for the scraping
There's no use to try escaping
Yell and scream and rant and rave–
There's no use, you need a shave.
There–you're nice and clean
Although your face looks like it might have gone through a machine.

One obvious distinction between *Rabbit of Seville* and other previous Warner forays into the realm of cartoon slapstick synched to classical music is that Jones's film, from beginning to end, is anything but a "one-shot"; instead it is very much in the ongoing tradition of the tried and true Bugs Bunny/Elmer Fudd hunting cycle. As a personality specialist, Jones made certain that the different rules and "disciplines"—the peculiar narrative and structural elements—that he applied to all his Bugs Bunny films would still hold sway here, even in a work with as intricate a musical agenda of its own as *Rabbit of Seville*. One rule of thumb that Jones chose to use for his Bugs Bunny pics is that the character must first be introduced in an environment indigenous to rabbits, and another, that Bugs's enormous anarchic energy must be kept in check until the character is outrightly provoked by an antagonist. Jones accomplishes both in one fell swoop at the beginning of the film as the camera picks out flashes of gunfire in the distant hills, and with effortless economy, pans from left to right as Bugs, pursued by Elmer, races into the foreground and toward the nearest available sanctuary—the backstage of an outdoor amphitheater. It isn't long before we get a close-up shot of Bugs's gloved hand oh-so casually flicking a switch to raise the curtain, thus initiating the rabbit's revenge. Jones's keen deliniation of character attitude through facial expression is working overtime: Priceless is Elmer's expression as the curtain rises, the orchestra strikes its first heavy chord, and it dawns on Fudd that he's not in Kansas anymore but caught on the fully dressed set of an opera in progress.

—*Greg Ford*

BUGS BUNNY

Bugs Bunny is one of the most popular cartoon characters because he does and says things we all wish we could get away with. He's brash, smart, funny, heroic, and clever—an underdog we can identify with, intelligent enough to defy any opponents.

Bugs was developed over a series of cartoons made in the the 1930s. Tex Avery's success with a screwball duck-hunting cartoon (*Porky's Duck Hunt*) in 1937 prompted animators Ben "Bugs" Hardaway and Cal Dalton to follow up with an even screwier rabbit-hunting opus (*Porky's Hare Hunt*) in 1938. The "Bugs" Bunny character was brought back twice in 1939. Chuck Jones modified him a bit in *Presto-Chango*, while Hardaway and Dalton revised him further in *Hare-um Scare-um*. It was Tex Avery's 1940 cartoon, *A Wild Hare*, that solidified the personality we know today as Bugs Bunny. Mel Blanc's Brooklyn-Bronx accent, Arthur Q. Bryant's Elmer Fudd, and the catch phrase "What's up, Doc?" became the trademarks and the blueprint for the direction of the series.

Bugs became the symbol for the American spirit during World War II, appearing in such cartoons as *Hare Meets Herr* and *Bugs Bunny Nips the Nips*, as well as in a bond-selling trailer singing Irving Berlin's "Any Bonds Today?" A Bugs Bunny short, *Knighty Knight Bugs*, directed by Friz Freleng, won the Oscar for Best Animated Short in 1958.

The self-reliant personality of Mickey Mouse, his smiling face, and jaunty figure made an image of resourceful optimism that is probably recognized globally more than any other image in history. According to Ub Iwerks, he designed the original Mickey and animated all of *Plane Crazy* to a story by Walt Disney and animated *Steamboat Willie* with help from Les Clark, Johnny Cannon, and Wilfred Jackson. Disney, influenced by fellow Missourian Mark Twain, cast Mickey as a gallant riverboat pilot who cranes Minnie aboard when she arrives late. Disney devised the cartoon's great originality of having Mickey perform an unorthodox rendition of "Turkey in the Straw" using cooking utensil drumbeats, duck quacks, and pig squeals. The consonance of cartoon personality on the screen with music, dialogue, and sound effects is the key to the great success of Disney animation from then until now. Oh, yes: Walt also spoke for the parrot.

—*James Culhane*

Steamboat Willie

WALT DISNEY, 1928

Today's viewers of *Steamboat Willie* delight at seeing Mickey in his tender youth, but earlier audiences were thrilled by the first combination of animation and sound. Disney used the new "talkie" craze that was sweeping the nation to introduce his new character with voice in the third short in a series of Mickey Mouse cartoons. "Ironically, in 1928, just when I had put the finishing touches on my first Mickey cartoon [*Plane Crazy*] the talkies came in," said Disney. "My silent Mickey was a dead dodo. I hurried to New York . . . and recorded a soundtrack for a new Mickey Mouse cartoon." The cartoon is a paean to synchronized sound, but, as noted by Russell Merritt and J. B. Kaufman in *Walt in Wonderland*, "it was Disney's visual and storytelling skills that sustained Mickey's extraordinary popularity." Mickey first appears at the steamboat's helm, whistling, tapping his foot, and thoroughly enjoying himself; the boat moves to his rhythms. Cranky Captain Pete ends these diversions. Minnie's "Turkey in the Straw" sheet music is eaten by a goat. Mickey opens its mouth, Minnie cranks its tail, and out comes "Turkey in the Straw," including musical notes that spill from the animal's mouth. The boat offers other opportunities for carrying on the tune, and Mickey gleefully explores them all. The orgy of sound is ended by Captain Pete, who banishes Mickey to the galley to peel potatoes. When Pete's parrot tries to get the last laugh on Mickey, the mouse knocks the bird out the porthole with a potato.

Steamboat Willie was first shown on November 18, 1928 (Mickey's official birthday), at New York's Colony Theater. As Disney said, "We discovered we didn't have just a cartoon toy to amuse children, we had a unique medium that delighted whole families. We had an art form and an impressive illusion."

CREDITS

Directed by Walt Disney

Animation: Ub Iwerks, Les Clark, Johnny Cannon, Wildred Jackson

The *Old Mill* was made for two reasons: It was an experiment to see if effects animation, music, and color design alone could engage an audience for ten minutes, and it was a test of Disney's new multiplane camera, a device that added three-dimensional depth to the flat world of cartoons. The cartoon has no stars; as storyman Dick Rikard explained, "Our story is the wind and the windmill."

From a distance, the camera slowly moves in toward the mill at sunset. Cows return from pasture, ducks leave the pond, and a bluebird flies into the mill. The camera follows the bluebird as he joins his mate and then explores the mill, which is inhabited by mice, doves, bats, and an owl that seems aware of the intruder. As evening grows, the bats fly off, water lilies curl up, and frogs come out to croak. Crickets and fireflies join in the soundmaking.

Blowing leaves signal wind; a storm arrives, and the ancient mill machinery begins to move. The mother bluebird panics when her nest is endangered by the turning gears; the owl seeks a dryer location. At the height of the storm, lightning strikes the old mill, making it totter.

The next morning the bats return, the pigeons continue to coo, and the owl turns away from the camera's prying. The bluebird's eggs have hatched: Life goes on within the mill. The camera moves back as the cows go out to pasture and the ducks return to the water. The film ends from the distance where it began, just as a new day begins.

The suspense in *The Old Mill* is splendid, even for the viewer who knows the endangered momma bird is destined to ride out a night of terror with a safely hatched nestful. The bravura orchestral scoring, as compelling as the multiplane pictorial sweep, retains a measure of surprise by grace of its very appropriateness. And a leavening of comedy—a startled frog, blissfully oblivious doves—punctuates the prevailing tone of vast menace. But beyond its power to thrill and inspire dread, *The Old Mill* works as a vivid example of entropy, of Nature's reclaiming her own from an industrial encroachment. It is a tremendous example of its category.

—*Michael H. Price*

Disney devised the multiplane camera, and Bill Garity built it for use on *Snow White*. Disney animators Frank Thomas and Ollie Johnston recalled, "Our eyes popped when we saw all of *The Old Mill*'s magnificent innovations—things we had not even dreamed of and did not understand." The film won an Academy Award for Best Animated Short in 1937, and the studio won an Oscar for the camera.

14

© The Walt Disney Company

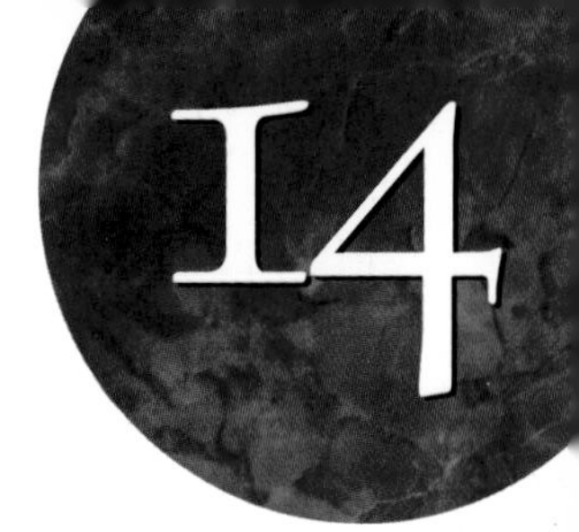

The Old Mill

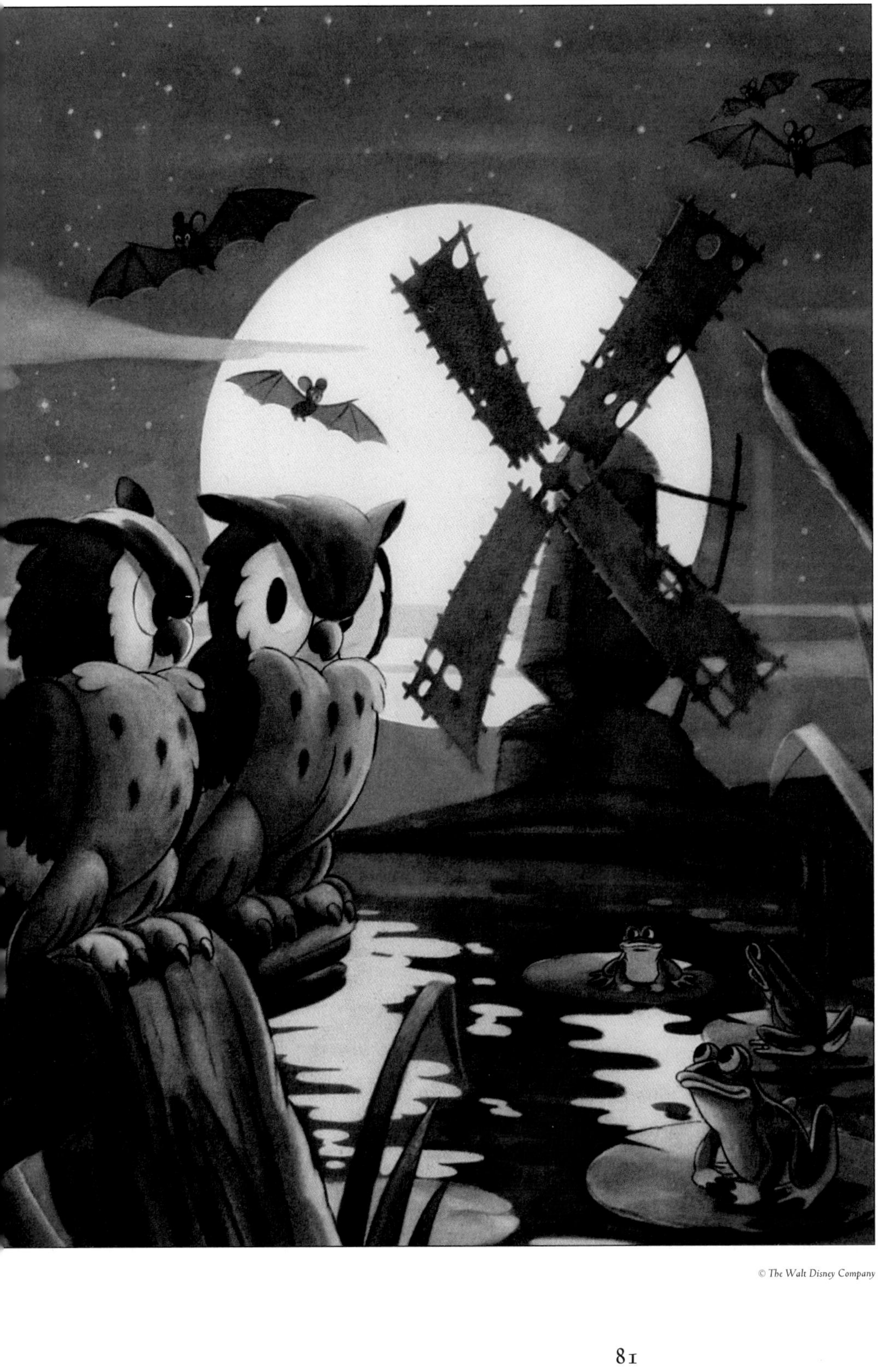

WALT DISNEY, 1937

CREDITS

A Walt Disney Silly Symphony

Directed by Wilfred Jackson

Animation: Ugo D'Orsi, Ralph Somerville, Jack Hannah, Tom Palmer, Robert Stokes, George Rowley, Josh Meador, Bob Wickersham, Dan McManus, Stan Quackenbush, Robert Martsch

"Bad Luck
Blackie"
Directed by
Tex Avery

Bad Luck Blackie

MGM, 1949

Like all of Tex Avery's best MGM films, *Bad Luck Blackie* takes a simple premise—in this case, black cats and bad luck—and animates it beyond the realm of the possible. The story begins with a cute white kitten (designed and animated by former Disney animator Louis Schmidt) being terrorized by a sadistic, laughing bulldog. The kitten meets a streetwise black cat named Blackie, who offers to help by simply crossing the dog's path. The first time Blackie crosses the dog's path a flowerpot falls from the sky and knocks the dog out. Blackie gives the kitten a whistle to blow whenever he is needed. When the bulldog revives, the kitten blows the whistle, and Blackie instantly appears, crosses the dog's path, and another flowerpot bashes the dog.

No matter how impossible the situation—in a dead-end alley, on high telephone wires, or in a narrow drainpipe—when the kitten calls, Blackie appears and saves its life by crossing the dog's path. And each time, the dog gets hit with a larger and heavier object: a trunk, a cash register, a fire hydrant, a piano. The dog carries a horseshoe for good luck, but when he tosses it in the air, four horseshoes hit him on the head—followed by the entire horse.

Tex Avery recalled to animator Nancy Beiman: "We built the picture so that it went from the bulldog getting hit by a flowerpot to the kitchen sink, to a battleship . . . Finally, we couldn't think of anything else to drop on him. How do you end it? Well, you're obliged to come back to the hero at the end of the cartoon. So you pull a switch—the kitten turns nasty and laughs like the bulldog did all through the picture."

Tex Avery, duly adored for his pliable and pitiless anarchy, hits his highest note by accepting for *Bad Luck Blackie* a bedrock premise whose formalist symmetry would have pleased the play-by-play structuralists at Warners.

A man who would cheerfully end a piece in a galaxy three distant from the one in which he began lashed himself to a device which returned him again and again to The Rule: A black cat crosses your path, something bad will happen to you. Only after he narrows the parameter still further—something will fall on you—does Avery feel that his imagination is sufficiently challenged. Then he makes the customary Averian transposition of the sweet into the perverse and the villainous into the victim. And he begins.

—*Jeff Miller*

CREDITS

An MGM Cartoon

Directed by Tex Avery

Producer: Fred Quimby

Story: Rich Hogan

Animation: Grant Simmons, Walter Clinton, Preston Blair, Louis Schmidt

Music: Scott Bradley

The Great Piggy Bank Robbery

WARNER BROS., 1946

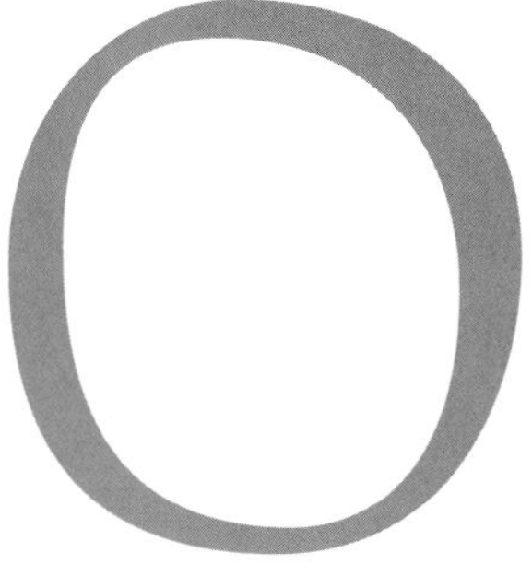ut on the farm, comic-book maniac Daffy Duck is elated by the arrival of the latest issue of *Dick Tracy* ("I love that man!"), but knocks himself out in his excitement and dreams he's "Duck Twacy." Phone calls arrive about stolen piggy banks ("It looks like a piggy bank crime wave!")—even his is missing. Magnifying glass in hand, detective Daffy takes a streetcar (with Porky Pig in a walk-on role as conductor) to the gangster's hideout. There he encounters such characters as Mouse Man, Snake Eyes, 88 Teeth, Hammer Head, Pussycat Puss, Bat Man, Double Header, Pickle Puss, Pumpkin Head, Neon Noodle, Jukebox Jaw, Wolf Man, and Rubber Head. Rubber Head tries to "rub" Daffy out. The duck then tangles with Neon Noodle and twists him into an "Eat At Joe's" sign. Daffy mows them down with a machine gun and finds the piggy banks, including his own. He kisses the bank only to wake up back on the farm kissing a sow. "I love that duck!" says the pig.

Daffy was the perfect star for this cartoon. His neurotic behavior, from anxiously awaiting the arrival of his comic books in the mail to frantically gunning down two dozen archcriminals, perfectly fits his zany character. *Dick Tracy*'s characters, such as Pruneface, the Brow, and Flattop, were ideal inspirations for Clampett. An earlier version of the story featured such evildoers as Dandruff Dome, Snow Coat, Slot Face, and the Nostril ("You mugs stay here. I got to blow!").

DICK TRACY

The popular *Dick Tracy* comic strip, created in 1931 by Chester Gould, was a perfect inspiration for Clampett. Characters such as Pruneface, the Brow, and Flattop were perfect for parody (Flattop's head makes a brief appearance as an aircraft runway). Sherlock Holmes, the most famous fictional detective of all time, also appears in a cameo gag that was originally planned to be a running gag in which Sherlock keeps bumping into Daffy throughout the cartoon.

CREDITS

A Looney Tunes Cartoon

Directed by Robert Clampett

Story: Warren Foster

Animation: Rod Scribner, Manny Gould, C. Melendez, I. Ellis

Layouts and backgrounds: Thomas McKimson, Philip DeGuard

Voices: Mel Blanc

Musical direction: Carl W. Stalling

16

Robert Frost said that the poet's principal mission is to come up with words that stick—to conjure those visions and constructions that, somehow, stay with people, making of ephemeral language something enduring and strong, with the power to change lives. Applying this principle, Bob Clampett's forever priceless *The Great Piggy Bank Robbery* is clearly a work of the highest cinematic poetry, for prompting the film's manic hilarity are a sequence of images that remain among the most indelible in cartoon history. Scene after scene resonates with moments that, courtesy of Clampett's visionary brilliance, are well nigh impossible to forget: Daffy doing Duck Twacy, or agonizing over his purloined bank, or smacking into Sherlock Holmes, or mock-sidestepping the trap door into the gangsters' lair, or stalking along the ceiling. And then there are the bad guys themselves, inspired by Chester Gould (creator of *Dick Tracy*), but here transformed into incomparable cine-surrealism: from Mouse Man, Jukebox Jaw, and 88 Teeth to Pickle Puss, Hammer Head, and Pumpkin Puss. In the final minutes of this masterwork, animation achieved its finest mélange of unhinged terror and inspired silliness. Indeed, the film represents a rare synthesis of animation's capacity for hallucinatory visuals and the very apogee of classic character comedy. Realized with immense wit, dash, and high spirits, this cartoon is one of the real cherishables, and the one that, of all animated films, I hold dearest. Even after innumerable viewings, it remains unbelieva—and I don't say this lightly—ble.

—*Steve Schneider*

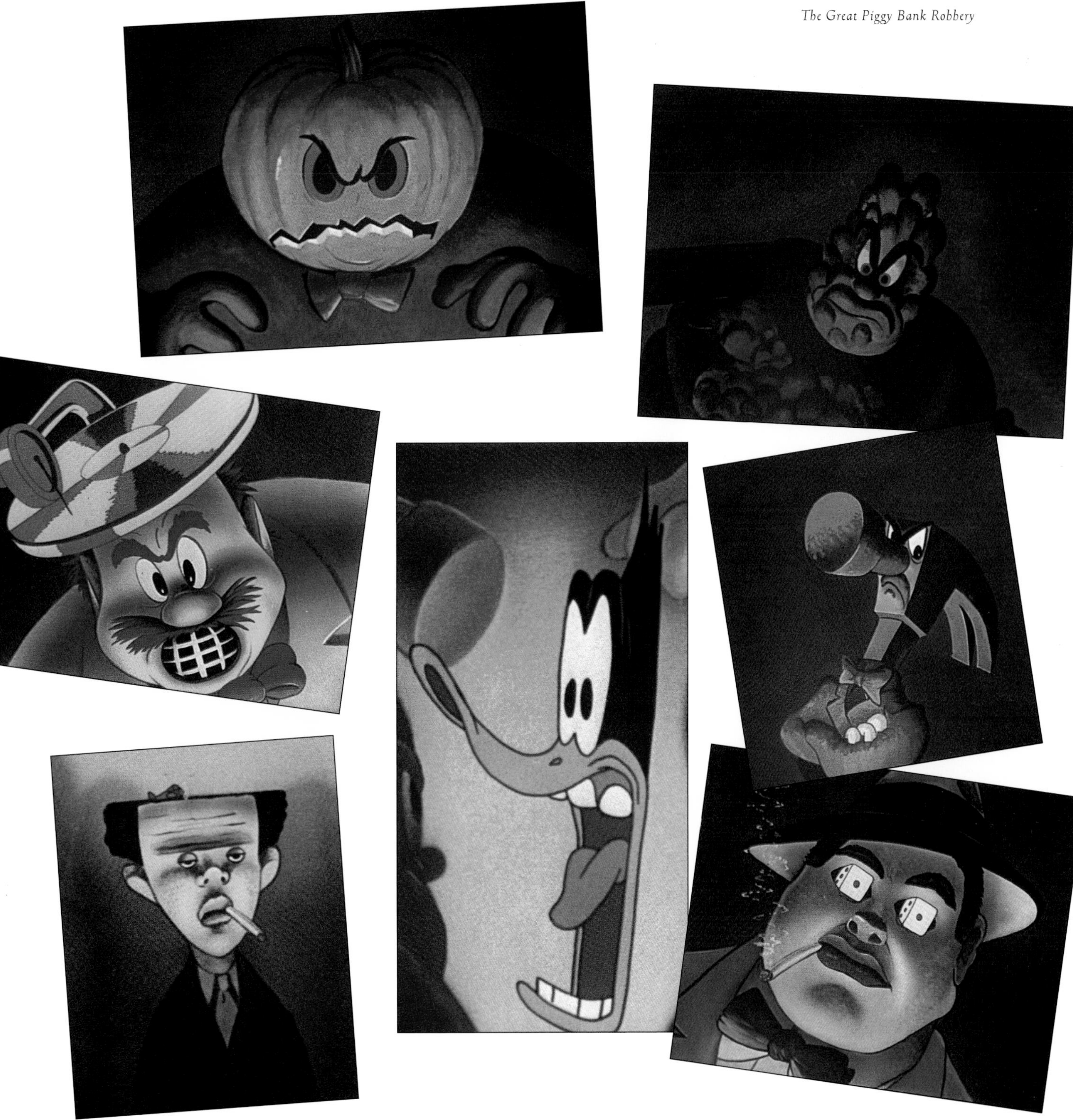

One weekend they ran a Bob Clampett cartoon, and when his name came on, I thought, "Oh, he's the guy who does those old ones." And then I saw it, and I was floored. It was the *The Great Piggy Bank Robbery*, and it was instantly my favorite. I thought it was the best cartoon that man had ever produced. There was Daffy Duck reading a Dick Tracy comic book, and he manages to knock himself out cold and have a dream about being "Duck Twacy." All the Chester Gould villains are there; it was totally surreal and bizarre. And Daffy Duck was actually daffy.

—*John Kricfalusi*

FLEISCHER'S BACKGROUNDS

The lush, feature-film quality of Sindbad's cave and island result from the Fleischer studio's use of three-dimensional sets. The technique involves constructing miniature sets on a twelve-foot circular turntable mounted in front of an animation camera. Between the camera and the turntable, cels are hung vertically on a glass plate and shot one frame at a time. The set is rotated incrementally, frame by frame, so that foreground props move at different speeds than background elements, giving a realistic sense of dimension.

ADOLPH ZUKOR presents

POPEYE THE SAILOR MEETS SINDBAD THE SAILOR

A Max Fleischer Cartoon

By arrangement with King Features Syndicate, Inc. and Segar

A PARAMOUNT PICTURE

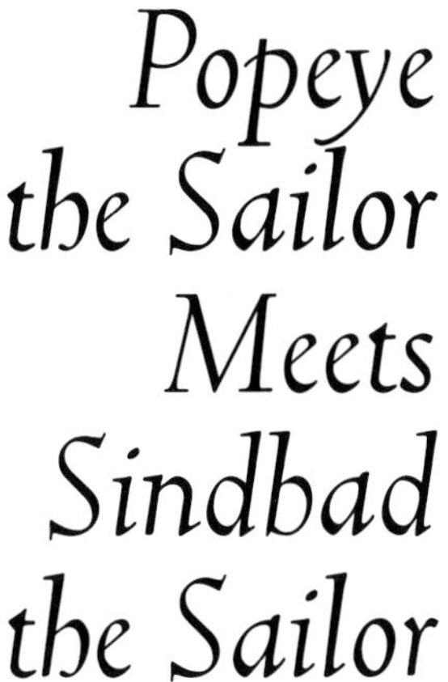

Popeye the Sailor Meets Sindbad the Sailor

FLEISCHER, 1936

As Popeye's popularity soared during the 1930s—he was Mickey Mouse's greatest rival—the Fleischer brothers decided the sailor deserved to be showcased in a special film. Seventeen minutes long—more than twice the running time of an average cartoon—this was also the first Popeye cartoon in Technicolor, the first to use Fleischer's unique 3-D backgrounds, and the first Max Fleischer cartoon nominated for an Academy Award.

The cartoon answers the question: "Who's the most remarkable, extraordinary fellow?" Sindbad the Sailor (Bluto) asks this question musically, singing his personal theme song to himself as he strolls around the Isle of Sindbad, which is home to a menagerie of beasts, dragons, apes, and snakes. Also on hand are prizes from past adventures: the two-headed giant Boola and Rokh, an airplane-size bird.

On a boat out at sea is Popeye the sailor, singing his own song, with Olive Oyl and Wimpy. Sindbad spots them and commands Rokh, "Wreck that ship, but bring the woman to me!" The bird obeys, but Popeye, saving Wimpy along the way, soon arrives on the island in search of Olive. He outroars a pair of lions and smashes through a stone wall to find Olive slavishly dancing to Sindbad's tune. Popeye makes short work of Rokh and Boola, then goes for his spinach and takes on Sindbad, finally conquering him with a "twister punch" that spins him around like a propeller. The island's animals declare him "the most remarkable, extraordinary fellow" and the new king of the island.

The cartoon was so popular that the studio produced two follow up specials, *Popeye the Sailor Meets Ali Baba's Forty Thieves* and *Aladdin and His Wonderful Lamp*.

It's classic wish fulfillment: Somehow eating a can of spinach miraculously gives you the strength to beat your burly opponents. Let's face it: The funniest moments in the early Popeye cartoons are the hilariously clever ways Popeye knocks the stuffing out of of Bluto. Those action scenes (or "funny beatings," as John Kricfalusi calls them) are key to *Popeye Meets Sindbad*. And this film has more than usual: "Twister punches," electric generator arm muscles, violent mayhem timed to patriotic music, 3-D sets, and brilliant Technicolor, all topped off by Mercer's witty ad-libs make this the best Popeye ever.

—*Jerry Beck*

CREDITS

Alfred Zukor Presents a Max Fleischer Cartoon

Directed by Dave Fleischer

Animation: Willard Bowsky, George Germanetti, Edward Nolan

Music and lyrics: Sammy Timburg, Bob Rothberg, Sammy Lerner

NACH

POPEYE'S ORIGINS

Popeye first became a star in comic strips. Created in 1929 as a supporting player in E. C. Segar's *Thimble Theater*, Popeye quickly stole the show, and by 1930 the comic strip was completely centered around the gruff one-eyed sailor. Max Fleischer, a fan of the comics, approached the King Features Syndicate about bringing the character to the screen. Popeye was introduced in a Betty Boop cartoon (*Popeye the Sailor*, 1933) and was an immediate hit; within a few months he was appearing monthly in new cartoons.

Matching a voice to the gruff comic-strip sailorman was difficult, but the ultimate choice was inspired. Ironically, if it were not for Cliff "Ukelele Ike" Edwards (later the voice of Jiminy Cricket) there would be no Popeye as we know him today. Throughout the 1920s, Edwards (1895–1971) was a major star of vaudeville, Broadway, and records; he spawned a number of imitators, among them Billy "Red Pepper Sam" Costello (1898–1971), whose earliest recordings featured scat singing nearly identical to that of Edwards (at least two of his records were miscredited to Ukelele Ike). One ingredient that separated Costello from Edwards was the strange, guttural bass that occasionally peppered his falsetto scat solos. This voice (known as "lower throat vocalization" to speech pathologists) had been employed on stage for years by vaudevillian Gene Green (1877–1930). Music historian Mike Kieffer recently recovered a Green recording which appears to be the earliest recorded example of the "proto-Popeye" voice. Traces of the Popeye voice can be heard in Billy Costello's first record "You're Nobody's Sweetheart Now," which was used in the soundtrack of *Betty Boop, M.D.* (1932). Costello, who also voiced Gus the Gorilla, remained Popeye's voice for only one year, at which point studio artist Jack Mercer took over. Mercer's zany sense of humor fit the unique post-production recording of cartoons; he added numerous mumbles and asides, which are cherished by fans today.

—*Will Ryan*

The Skeleton Dance was the first of the Silly Symphonies, a series without leading characters that Disney used for experiments to expand the horizons of cartoons.

Having added music to underscore the action in the the first Mickey Mouse pictures, Carl Stalling (Disney's first musical composer) suggested to Disney that the reverse could be done: adding animated action to a musical score. "I told him I was thinking of inanimate figures, like skeletons, trees, or flowers coming to life and dancing and doing other animated actions fitted to music in a more or less humorous and rhythmic mood. He became very interested." Disney saw this as an opportunity to push the combination of animation and music even further.

The Skeleton Dance opens on a spooky night in a graveyard, full of wind and flying leaves; even an owl is frightened by a blowing branch. At the stroke of midnight, bats fly out of a belfry, a spider drops by, and a dog howls at the moon. Two black cats atop tombstones stop their spat when a skeleton rises from its grave. The skeleton prowls around the graveyard, is momentarily frightened by the owl, and is then joined by three other skeletons. The four dance, obviously enjoying themselves and exploiting their articulated bones. They make their own music: One skeleton uses another's vertebrae as a xylophone, another skeleton uses a cat as a fiddle.

A rooster alerts the skeletons to the coming dawn. In a panicky rush to get back to their coffins, they smash into one another, creating a single four-skulled skeleton that dives into a tomb.

In 1929, cartoons were usually just strings of gags held together by a vaguely defined story: *Skeleton Dance* was an eerie musical fantasy with few real jokes. The image of four skeletons dancing in a graveyard sounds gruesome, but Ub Iwerks's animation has an ingenuous appeal that makes the most grisly characters seem benign and playful. They dance jauntily, wriggle like rubber Halloween toys, and play tunes on each other's bones. (The corresponding xylophone figures in the score have led many writers to misidentify the music as Saint-Saëns's *Danse Macabre*; it's Grieg's *March of the Dwarfs*.) The film is more sophisticated than most silent-era cartoons. The skeleton that dives at the screen and almost swallows the camera seems like an ordinary visual today, but in 1929, only Otto Messmer's Felix the Cat cartoons offered comparably imaginative touches.

—*Charles Solomon*

18

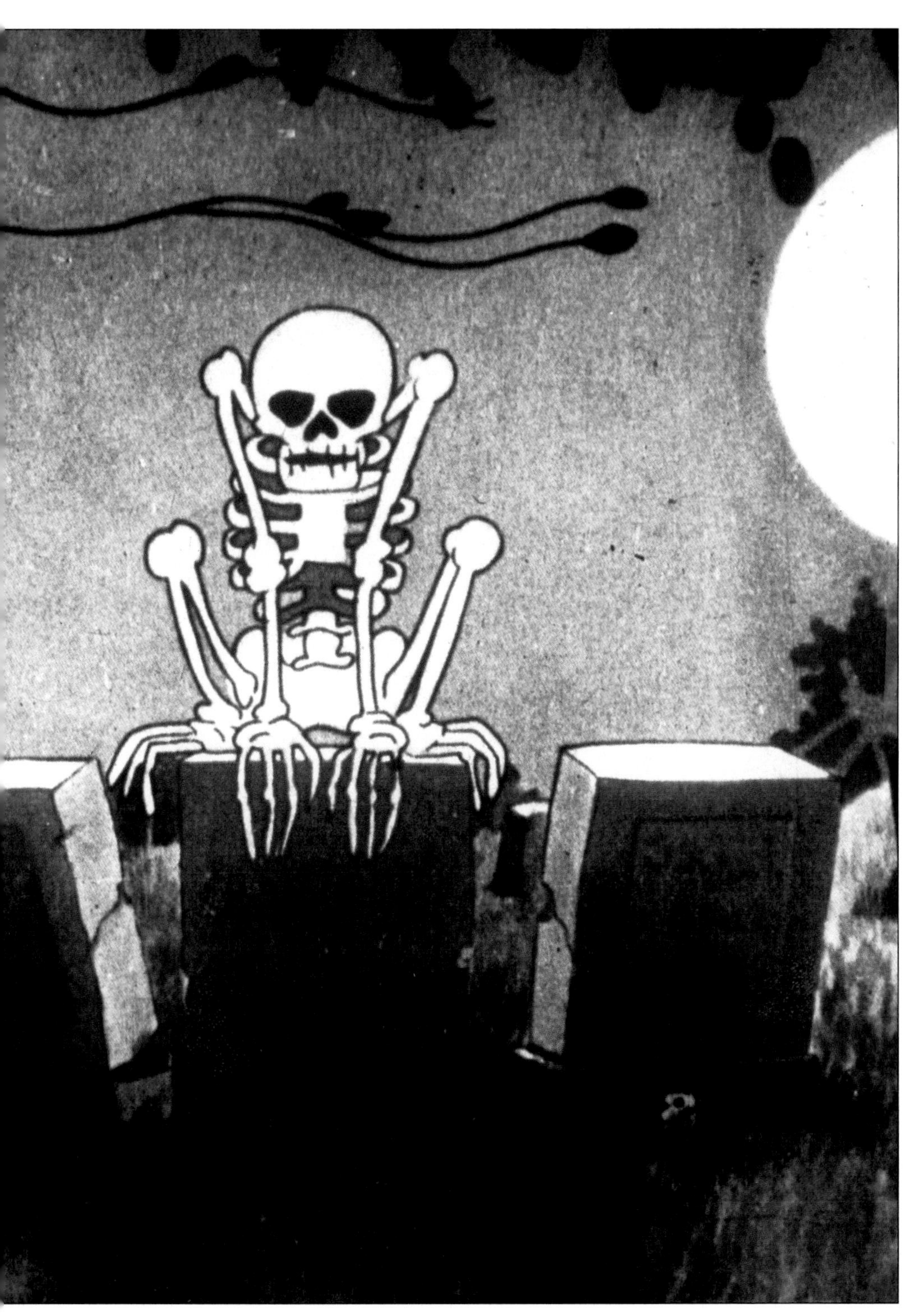

The Skeleton Dance

WALT DISNEY, 1929

CREDITS

A Silly Symphony

Directed by Walt Disney

Animation: Ub Iwerks

Music: Carl W. Stalling

Snow White

PARAMOUNT, 1933

CREDITS

A Paramount Cartoon

Directed by Dave Fleischer

Animation: Roland C. Crandall

Vocals: Cab Calloway

"Who's the fairest in the land?" asks the Wicked Queen of her magic mirror, and this time it's Betty, just arrived at the castle to visit "stepmama." The Queen consults the mirror again (as do Bimbo and KoKo); all agree that Betty is now the fairest. The Queen orders the knights to behead Betty, who bemoans her fate in a song ("Always in the Way") and makes them junk their axes and fake her grave. Betty gets locked in an ice coffin that slides into the cottage of the Seven Dwarfs, who accompany the coffin to the Mystery Cave. The Queen shows up as a witch and changes KoKo and Bimbo into frozen statues. The magic mirror explodes, thawing Betty, Bimbo, and KoKo, and transforming the Queen into a dragon. Bimbo pulls the dragon's tongue and turns the creature inside out, and the film ends with the three heroes dancing in a circle.

Of Cab Calloway's three Betty Boop cartoons, *Snow White* is probably the best. A quick run-down of the story reveals how meaningless conventional plot lines are in the visually surreal Fleischer cartoons.

Calloway said that the cartoons in which he appeared played in each city a week or two prior to his live engagements. With Betty as his "advance woman" he found ticket sales significantly increased.

Snow White is said to have been animated by one man, Roland (Doc) Crandall, over a six-month period. Crandall had resisted the urge to head west to the land of sunshine, palm trees, and Disney, a situation which had stripped the Fleischer studio of many top people; perhaps this solo gig was his reward for staying. The consistency and beauty of the cartoon, along with the attention to detail, support this supposition. Crandall was adroit with fairy tale settings, which show up in the details of the Wicked Queen's castle and the mysterious cave of the Seven Dwarfs. There, a long-legged cartoon Calloway sings the mournful "St. James Infirmary Blues" —another tale of sex, drugs, and rock 'n' roll. As he sings, Calloway's animated figure transforms itself to describe the lyrics, at one point into a watch chain and a bottle of boo-oo-ooze. As if such dazzling rotoscoped animation weren't enough, a background filled with macabre images slides steadily by, fighting for attention with the action in the foreground. Here is a cartoon making full use of the medium of animation, and a model of the classic "rubber hose" cartoon style of the early 1930s.

—Leslie Cabarga

19

THE FLEISCHERS

Max Fleischer, cartoonist and inventor, pioneered animated films with his invention of the Rotoscope in 1917. Using this unique device to trace live-action film for creating lifelike animation, Max and his brother Dave went into business making clever animated films, eventually becoming Walt Disney's greatest rival. In the 1920s, the Fleischer studio had great success with KoKo the Clown, who cavorted in the "real" world through clever animation tricks. The Fleischers introduced the sing-along cartoon, the famous "bouncing ball," and were the first to make sound cartoons (in 1924), years ahead before Disney synchronized sound and animation. With the advent of sound, the studio came up with Betty Boop and licensed Popeye from King Features, embellishing his personality with a unique voice. Another innovation of the studio was three-dimensional backgrounds that gave the early Fleischer cartoons a feeling of depth that Disney would achieve years later with his multiplane camera.

The Fleischers released five extra-length cartoons and two feature films, *Gulliver's Travels* (1943) and *Mr. Bugs Goes to Town* (1941), and were nominated for an Oscar for *Superman* (1941), the first in a series of realistically drawn adventure cartoons.

In a move still controversial today, Paramount Pictures took control of the studio in 1942 and ousted the Fleischer brothers. Max continued his role in animation with an association with the Jam Handy industrial film company; Dave went to Hollywood, producing animation for Columbia Pictures, Republic Pictures, and Universal Studios.

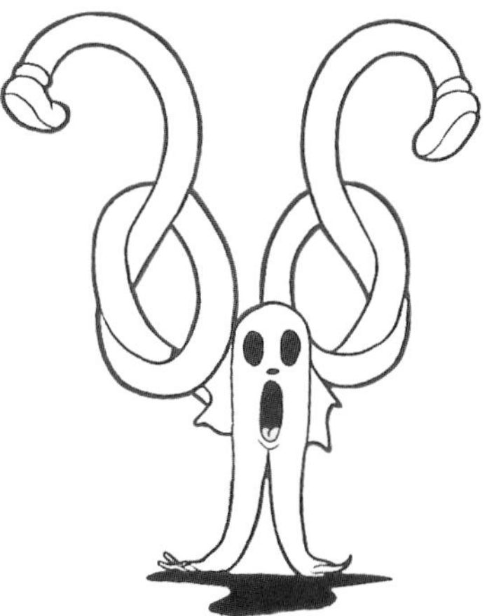

Minnie the Moocher

PARAMOUNT, 1932

This cartoon opens with a live-action clip of singer Cab Calloway and his orchestra. It then goes to Betty Boop seated at the dinner table being berated by her parents: "Why won't you eat your hassen-feffer?" Betty leaves the table in tears and decides to run away, singing, "They'll all be sorry that they picked on me." She packs her toothbrush, pens a farewell note, and calls her dog, Bimbo, who meets her beneath the window. As it gets dark, the pair hide in a cave, where they meet the Walrus (Cab Calloway) who recalls the sordid tale of Minnie the Moocher. The Walrus dances in front of an ever-changing cave wall of bizarre images. All manner of ghosts and goblins chase Betty and Bimbo from the cave. Back home in her room, Betty finds her farewell note mysteriously torn up, leaving the words "Home Sweet Home."

"Minnie the Moocher" was a hit recording in 1931 and made Calloway a star. His "Hi-de-ho" lyrics became his trademark, and his swaying and strutting style of bandleading was so unique that Fleischer rotoscoped his movements. *Minnie the Moocher* was the first of three Boop cartoons to feature Calloway (*Snow White* and *The Old Man of the Mountain*, both released in 1933, were the others). The film enjoyed a revival as a "head film" in the 1960s.

CREDITS

Max Fleischer Presents a Talkartoon

A Paramount Pictures Release

Directed by Dave Fleischer

Animation: Willard Bowsky, Ralph Sommerville

Vocals: Cab Calloway

For the first time, Betty is shown in a plausible setting: She is a young girl, probably seventeen or nineteen, involved in the inevitable parental conflict. Mae Questal, who provided the voice for Betty, always claimed the animators based the character's mannerisms and personality on hers. This film would seem to bear her out. Just seeing the young Calloway performing on film at the beginning of *Minnie* should be enough to have the film classified a national treasure. His appearance seems at first incongruous until, midcartoon, his dancing is beautifully traced over (rotoscoped) into animation. Use of Calloway's theme song, "Minnie," is one of the great enigmas of cartoondom. Was the song's sordid subject matter —drug addiction, maybe even prostitution—acknowledged by the Fleischers?

—*Leslie Cabarga*

BETTY BOOP

The Fleischer studio's most famous original character, Betty Boop, began life as a singing dog. Designed by animator Grim Natwick, she first appeared in *Dizzy Dishes* (1931) as a canine crooner performing a parody of novelty singer Helen Kane.

Originally, the studio, in need of a starring character to compete with Disney's Mickey Mouse, had begun to feature a nondescript dog character named Bimbo in a series of cartoons. When a crooning "Boop-oop-a-doop" character stole one of the films, the Fleischers increasingly featured her in the Talkartoon series—eventually, this character, Betty Boop, was starring in the cartoons, and Bimbo had supporting roles.

Helen Kane, herself a Paramount contract player, decided in 1934 to sue the studio when the cartoon version became more well known than her. Unfortunately for her, Paramount and the Fleischers were able to prove that her style of singing had been around longer than her career.

Betty Boop's most interesting cartoons were produced during 1932 and 1933, during the heyday of inspired lunacy at the Fleischer studio. This was also before the Hays Office Motion Picture Production Code took effect in 1934, effectively "cleaning up" Hollywood. These pre-Code cartoons were pretty racy: from Cab Calloway's soundtracks, which made reference to drugs, alcohol, and sex, to lecherous villains who threaten to take Betty's "Boop-oop-a-doop" away.

After the Code took effect, Betty's skirt was lowered to her knees and she began costarring in stories with the likes of Grampy, an eccentric inventor, and Pudgy, her cute little dog. Betty also starred in Fleischer's first color cartoon, *Poor Cinderella* (1934).

The Fleischer studio retired Betty in 1939, but her popularity has lasted without the assistance of new cartoons for more than fifty years. Only in the last decade or so has any effort been made to revive Betty's career. An appearance in *Who Framed Roger Rabbit?* (1988) and two recent TV specials (produced by Bill Melendez and Colossal Pictures) have kept her name alive, ensuring that Betty will boop well into the next century.

GRIM NATWICK

Mention must be made of Myron "Grim" Natwick, the original designer of Betty Boop. At the time he animated *Dizzy Dishes*, Natwick was already an animation veteran, having begun his career in 1916. After studying at the Chicago Art Institute, Natwick became a prolific illustrator of sheet music. Looking for more work, he joined his fellow art school graduate, Gregory La Cava, who was in charge of Hearst's animation shop (producing films like *Krazy Kat* and *Bringing Up Father*) in New York.

After a brief stint in Vienna studying art, Natwick returned to New York and joined the Fleischer studio just as talkies were taking over the industry. He left in 1931 to join Ub Iwerks in Hollywood, where he designed and animated many Flip the Frog and Willie Whopper cartoons. He was soon working for Walt Disney, primarily animating *Snow White*. Natwick rejoined the Fleischers in the late 1930s, where he designed and animated Princess Glory for the feature film *Gulliver's Travels*. Thereafter he was the preeminent specialist in animating the female form.

His skill led him to many diverse assignments: animating Woody Woodpecker for Walter Lantz, creating art for the first TV cartoon, "Crusader Rabbit," doing commercials and theatrical shorts for UPA (including *Rooty Toot Toot*), and teaching his craft to a younger generation while working for Richard Williams (*Raggedy Ann and Andy*, *The Thief and the Cobbler*). Grim Natwick died at age one hundred in 1990.

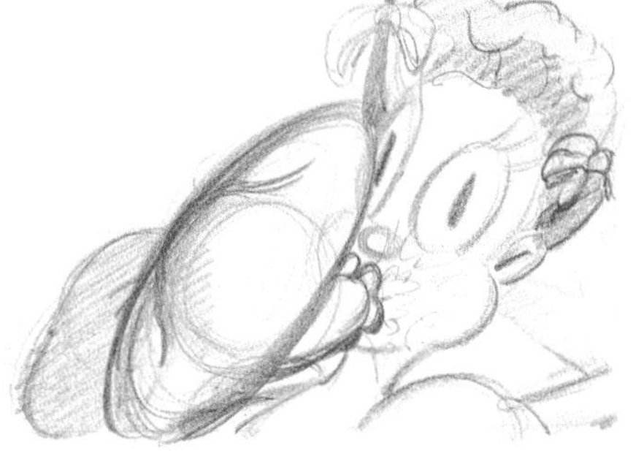

Coal Black and de Sebben Dwarfs

WARNER BROS., 1943

CREDITS

A Merrie Melodies Cartoon

Directed by Robert Clampett

Story: Warren Foster

Animation: Rod Scribner

Musical direction: Carl W. Stalling

This rhyming parody of Disney's *Snow White*—with wartime themes, sex, and jazz—begins with a mother telling her child the story of So White. The Wicked Queen (a hoarder of rationed goods) asks her magic mirror for a prince. To Prince Chawmin', the queen "sure is a fright/ but her gal So White is dynomite!" Murder, Inc., called by Queenie to "blackout So White," leaves the girl in the woods where she joins the Seven Dwarfs at their army camp. The Queen arrives with a poisoned apple that puts So White to sleep. The Prince can't awaken her with his "Rose-bud" kiss, but a dwarf succeeds with his special hot kiss "that is a military secret!"

Black caricatures and references to WWII date this cartoon, but its animation, musical score, and comic timing make it a classic. Clampett took his animators out to Hollywood's black nightclubs for inspiration, and performers loaned their voices and authenticated the work: Ruby Dandridge (the Queen), Vivian Dandridge (So White), and Zoot Watson (Prince Chawmin'). Eddie Beale and his band augmented Carl Stalling's score, particularly the impressive trumpet acting during the kiss.

Bob Clampett's *Coal Black and de Sebben Dwarfs* is, of course, a twist on the Grimms' story—Clampett originally planned to call his film *So White*—but it pokes fun only tangentially at Disney's *Snow White*. And despite the caricatured blacks who make up its cast, *Coal Black* is not really about race, either; as outlandish as most of the black characters are, they're no more grotesque than, say, the middle-aged white men Clampett lampooned in cartoons like *Draftee Daffy* and *The Wise Quacking Duck*. The characters are black because the idea for this cartoon was born when Clampett saw the Duke Ellington revue *Jump for Joy* in 1941. During work on *Coal Black*, as animator Virgil Ross recalled, "we went over to the east side of town, in the black district, to go through the nightclubs and the dancing." What Clampett found in those black performers and dancers was the real subject of his film: energy. He translated their exuberance into animation whose vitality was unprecedented then and has never been equaled since.

—*Michael Barrier*

"COAL BLACK
AND DE
SEBBEN DWARFS"
— BOB CLAMPETT — DIRECTOR —
gh
©
LEON SCHLESINGER PRODUCTIONS
1351 No. Van Ness Av
HOLLYWOOD, CA
QUEENIE
COAL BLACK
DE PRINCE

CONTROVERSIAL CARTOONS

Everyone who knows and loves cartoons knows two things: that *Coal Black* is certainly among the greatest cartoons ever made, and that it certainly is offensive to many people. Bob Clampett's 1942 masterpiece is perhaps the ultimate example of a cartoon of its time, and like most cartoons from Hollywood's golden age of animation, it is rife with racist, sexist, and violent content, material that would be totally unacceptable in cartoons produced today. Clampett's film is a particularly obvious example of racial parody, and it is difficult for most audiences to see past its stereotypes. But it is not an isolated case: Among many other examples are Betty Boop's Jewish parents in *Minnie the Moocher* and Native Americans in Tex Avery's *Big Heel-watha.*

Cartoons are not the only form of entertainment involved either; it is difficult to find a black person in a movie, play, or book before the 1960s in any but a menial position. Thus, today *Huckleberry Finn* is banned from some libraries for its racial content, Stepin' Fetchit's supporting roles are removed from movie prints, and radio's Amos and Andy are remembered as the epitome of racist stereotyping. There is no question as to whether or not some vintage cartoons are racist (they are) or that they did do harm. The only question is if these cartoons should be removed from view and excluded from books such as this one.

There is a growing inclination to do just that. Disney no longer shows *Song of the South*; the company would not grant permission to use certain illustrations from *Der Fuehrer's Face* because Donald appears in Nazi uniform. Similarly, *Birth of a Nation* can no longer be viewed at the Library of Congress except under special conditions.

No one would suggest that cartoons depicting sexist or racist stereotypes should be shown indiscriminately on Saturday morning children's shows. But it seems just as foolish to sanitize our history and make believe these cartoons—and that era—never existed. One of the values of the trove of animated cartoons is the depiction of their times; every national event, trend, and fad is reflected in them, from the Depression to gas rationing, from censorship to the liberation movements. The cartoons are racist because the country was racist. To remove any material that is now seen as objectionable would be to divorce the cartoons from their very identity, and to remove one of the most important features of the genre as a whole.

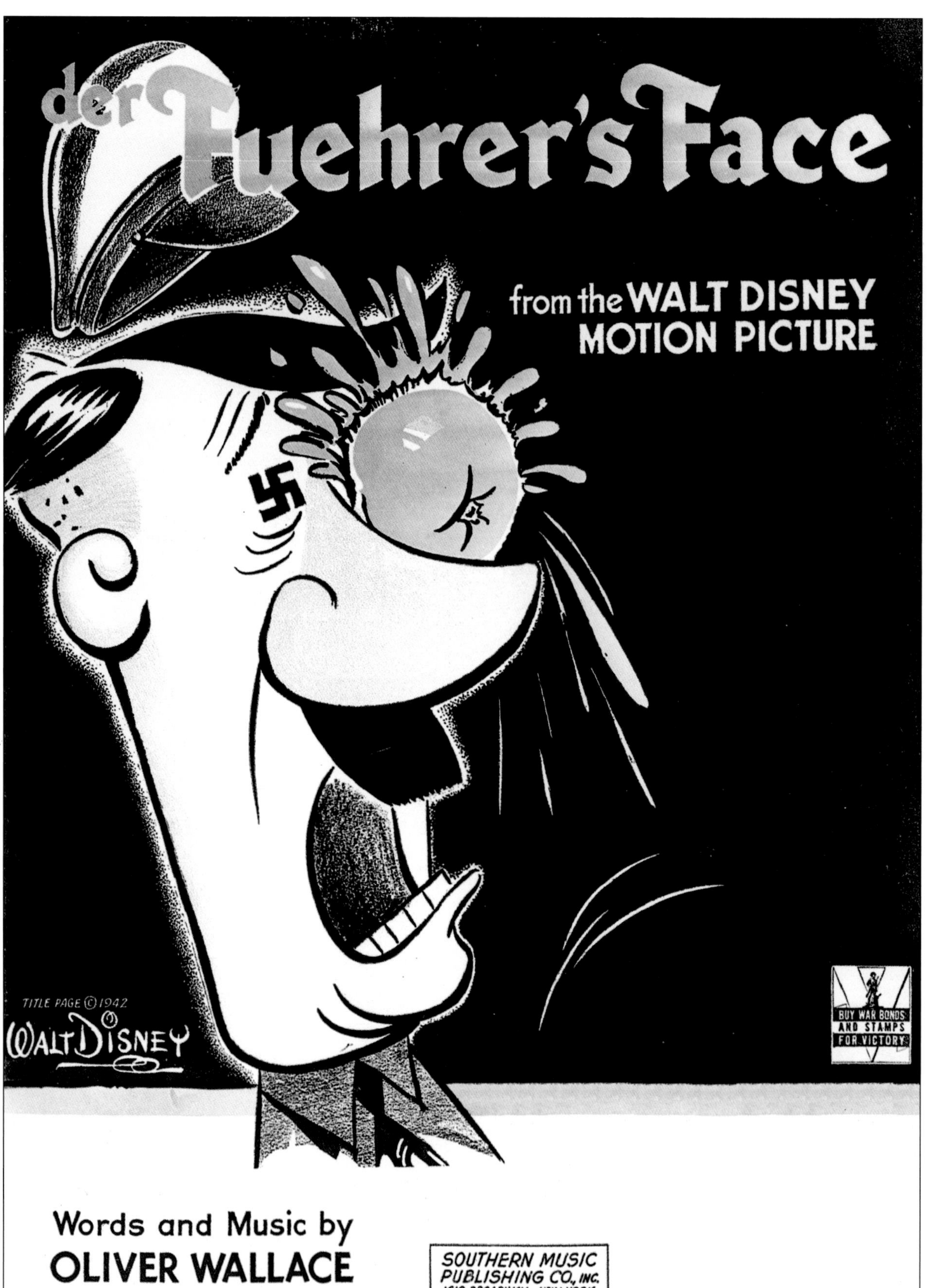
der Fuehrer's Face
from the WALT DISNEY
MOTION PICTURE
TITLE PAGE © 1942
WALT DISNEY
BUY WAR BONDS
AND STAMPS
FOR VICTORY
Words and Music by
OLIVER WALLACE
SOUTHERN MUSIC
PUBLISHING CO., INC.
1619 BROADWAY, NEW YORK

Der Fuehrer's Face

WALT DISNEY, 1943

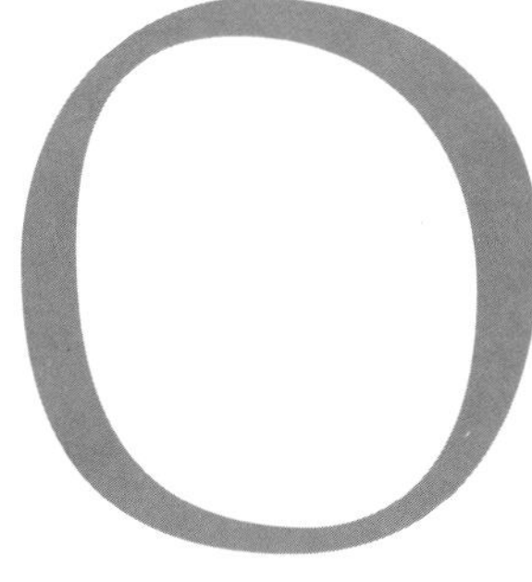

One of four anti-Nazi cartoons the Disney studio released in 1943 (the others were *Chicken Little*, *Education for Death*, and *Reason and Emotion*), this cartoon was written by Dick Huemer and Joe Grant for a series of shorts commissioned by the U.S. government, which turned it down. But Disney liked the idea and produced the film as a special Donald Duck cartoon.

A German marching band, playing "Der Fuehrer's Face" as it parades through Nutziland, whisks Donald off to a munitions plant to his usual "48-hour" day of labor. His job is closing shells—and "heiling" the Fuehrer's face whenever it appears. Forced to work faster and faster, Donald goes mad and hallucinates that the shells are attacking him. He finally awakens in his bedroom, in red-white-and-blue pajamas. He begins to salute a "heiling" shadow on the wall, but it turns out to be his Statue of Liberty. Nightmare over, he hugs the statue, grateful "to be a citizen of the United States of America." The film ends with a caricature of Hitler struck by a tomato thrown from the audience.

Released on New Year's Day 1943, *Der Fuehrer's Face* became one of the most famous cartoons of the war years and earned Disney his tenth Oscar. Jack Kinney wrote of the film in his memoirs, "Prints were sent all over the world, even to Russia, which used its propaganda message to encourage the troops. I don't think it was very popular with the Nazis. In fact, we heard that Hitler burned every copy he could find. We loved that."

CREDITS

A Walt Disney Donald Duck Cartoon

Directed by Jack Kinney

Layouts: Don DaGradi

Animation: John Sibley, Bill Justice, Milt Neil, Andy Engman, Les Clark, Charles Nicholas, Robert Carlson

Walt Disney's most significant contribution to American propaganda in the Second World War—and to the art of graphic satire—*Der Fuehrer's Face* satirizes Adolph Hitler, Hitler's Nazi regime, and totalitarianism in general. Originally called *Donald Duck in Nutziland*, Disney changed the title when peppery, spirited Ollie Wallace (composer of the "Pink Elephants" music for that surrealistic sequence in *Dumbo*) wrote words and music for a song called "Der Fuehrer's Face." The song's basic structure was a "raspberry" or Bronx cheer. "I built that cartoon around the song," said director Jack Kinney. In a masterpiece of satirical design, everything in *Nutziland*, from the trees and hedges to the houses whose chimneys seem to give the Nazi salute, is shaped like the swastika, the symbol of Nazism. A caricature of Hitler's face glares down on Donald as he struggles to keep up with inhuman quotas on making shells for Hitler's war machine. Les Clark animated the surrealistic depletion of oppression with panache.

—*John Culhane*

Little Rural Riding Hood

MGM, 1949

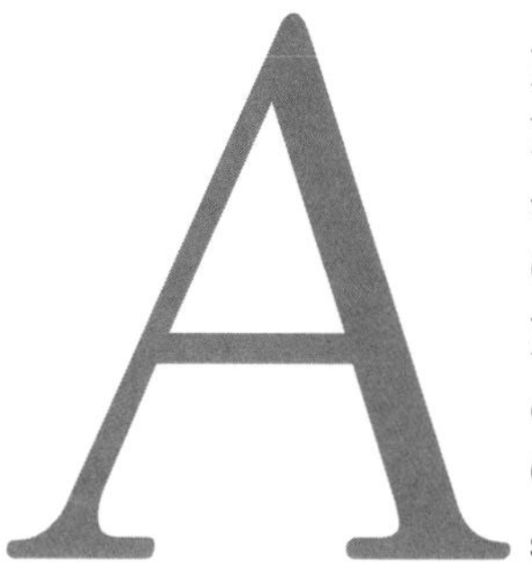

A hillbilly version of Red Riding Hood is skipping through the forest to Grandma's house, bringing her some nourishment, a jug of whiskey. Meanwhile, at Grandma's, a country version of the Wolf (voiced by Pinto Colvig) informs us that "Of course, I'm supposed to eat Red Riding Hood all up, but I ain't a-gonna do it. All I'm gonna do is chase her and catch her and kiss her and hug her and love her . . ."

When Red arrives, the amorous Wolf chases her all over the house, but succeeds in kissing only a cow. He catches her at last, but is interrupted by the arrival of a telegram from his city cousin: "Quit wasting your time on the country gal. Come to the big city and I'll show you a real Red Riding Hood!" The enclosed photo of a sexy Red has the Wolf's eyes popping out of his head.

When Rural Red demands, "Kiss me, my fool!" the Wolf shoves the cow at her lips and takes off for the city. He arrives, hootin' and hollerin' for the city Red Riding Hood. His sophisticated city cousin sedates him with a baseball bat.

Decked out in tails, the country Wolf watches Red perform her number ("Oh, Wolfie!" a repeat of the musical sequence from *Swing Shift Cinderella*) and makes such a fuss with whistles, cat-calls, and eye-pops, that the city Wolf knocks him out again with a mallet. "I'm afraid this city life is a bit too much for you," he tells his relative. "I shall motor you back to the country."

Once there, however, the city Wolf gets a look at the hillbilly Red Riding Hood and goes gaga, mimicking many of his country cousin's previous eye-popping takes. The country Wolf happily takes his cousin back to town.

CREDITS

An MGM Cartoon

Directed by Tex Avery

Producer: Fred Quimby

Story: Rich Hogan, Jack Cosgriff

Animation: Grant Simmons, Walter Clinton, Bob Cannon, Michael Lah

Music: Scott Bradley

23

Tex Avery's unerring timing and effortless effect were not achieved without painstaking craftsmanship. Veterans of his unit have claimed that Avery, dismayed over the fact that the perception of his timing was altered as a scene moved from the animators' pencil tests to the final inked-and-painted Technicolor photography, would actually trim frames out of the negative of a completed scene.

Little Rural Riding Hood is well constructed, its three big comedy scenes serving as foundation, and each one a tour-de-force of ingenious, hyperbolic, explosive, but immaculately timed animation:

1) The country Wolf racing around a farmhouse in genuinely hot pursuit of a country Red Riding Hood.

2) The country Wolf reacting to his city cousin's notice that the Red Riding Hoods are more plentiful in the city, where he repairs on the instant, not having any great success in keeping his enthusiasm in check.

3) The country Wolf taken by his cousin to a nightclub to witness the city's version of a Red Riding Hood and proceeding with appropriate showmanship to provide the topper for all his previous reactions.

In the third of these scenes, the country Wolf rushes pell-mell toward the stage, accompanied by a collage of bells and percussion effects, only to be stopped before he can touch Red (and incur the wrath of the Hays Office) by a mallet strung in his suspenders by the city Wolf. He is wheeled away on his rotating head like a hand truck with one wheel squeaking. This is repeating a gag straight out of "Fido the Dog Director," a mid-twenties Bray Studios cartoon by Walter Lantz that Tex must have seen in his adolescence and never forgotten.

The massive master shot that climaxes the first of these sequences, in which one poor victimized door is slammed in and around a single room, helplessly creating doorways wherever it lands—on the floor, on the ceiling, next to the original doorway, across the room—is retraced from Avery's 1945 Screwy Squirrel cartoon *The Screwy Truant*. When the city's version of Miss Riding Hood appears in the the third sequence, she is performing a reprise of her hit, "Oh, Wolfie!" from *Swing Shift Cinderella*, and the animation (generally the most expensive single element in cartoon production) is again a repeat. With the resources remaining in the schedule and budget of an ordinary 1940s theatrical short subject, Avery was able to create an extraordinary film.

What appears on the screen as manic energy, spinning out of control in all directions at once, off the screen and in the audience's lap, was in reality carefully built up out of a multitude of small effects, each as perfectly realized as a detail in a Persian rug.

—*Joe Adamson*

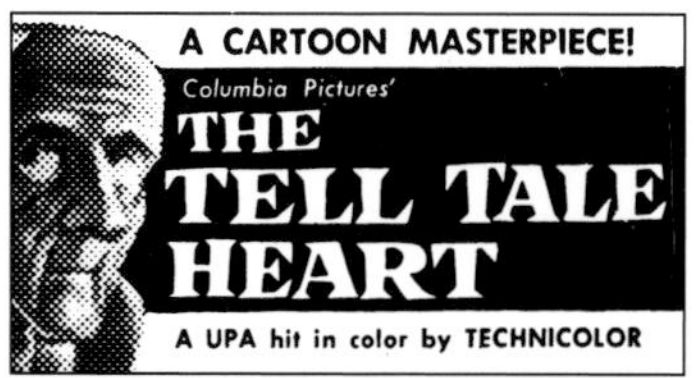
A CARTOON MASTERPIECE!
Columbia Pictures'
THE TELL TALE HEART
A UPA hit in color by TECHNICOLOR

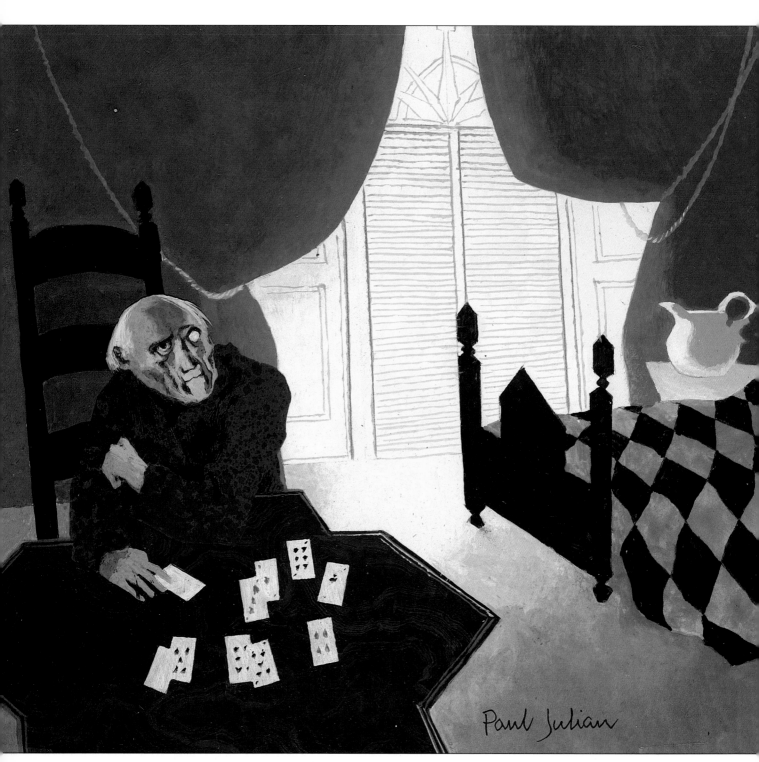

24

The Tell-Tale Heart

UPA, 1953

Based on a short story by Edgar Allan Poe and narrated by actor James Mason in a voice on the verge of frenzy, *The Tell-Tale Heart* was one of the first uses of the animated cartoon to tell a psychological horror tale. The film uses modern, Dalí-esque images to create a dreamlike atmosphere perfectly suited to Poe's chilling tale of murder by a madman.

"True, I'm nervous, very dreadfully nervous, but why will you say that I am mad?" So begins the narrator, who goes on to explain how he was disturbed by the milky-white blind eye of his older housemate. "Of course," he explains, "I had to get rid of the eye."

He waited seven days for the right moment—"I could feel the earth turn"—and on the fateful night hid in the old man's room. In the darkness, he could hear the beating of the man's heart growing louder and louder. "So strong for such an old man." He had to stop it. "Then it was over. The heart was still, the eye was dead, I was free." He then carefully buried the old man beneath the floorboards in his room.

The police arrive—neighbors had heard a scream—and inspect the premises. But all is quite in order, nothing amiss. They are about to leave when the madman insists they stay for tea. Then he hears it, softly at first, then louder and louder. "It was the beating of his hideous heart!" The madman breaks down and confesses his crime, removing the floorboards to reveal the corpse.

"True, I'm nervous, very dreadfully nervous, but why will you say that I am mad?" So ends the madman from within his prison cell.

CREDITS

Columbia Pictures Presents a UPA Production

Directed by Ted Parmalee

Producer: Steven Bosustow

Design and color: Paul Julian

Story adaptation: Bill Scott, Fred Grable

Animation: Pat Matthews

Camera work: Jack Eckes

Production manager: Herb Klynn

Music: Boris Kremenliev

Narrator: James Mason

The UPA fellows have gone ahead, breaking new ground with their extraordinary animated drawing based on Edgar Allan Poe's "The Tell-Tale Heart." You note we do not define it as an animated cartoon, since that suggests humorous treatment, which this piece of work does not have. It is a bizarre and eerie comprehension, in fitful images, of a madman's view of a murder he does and then fatefully rues. The style and design resemble Dalí's with all sorts of modern overtones. This is a highly commendable experiment in the field of animation.

—*New York Times*, 1953

UNITED PRODUCTIONS OF AMERICA

In 1944, a trio of former Disney animators—Steve Bosustow, Dave Hilberman, and Zack Schwartz—formed a small film studio called Industrial Films and Poster Service. Their first production, *Hell-Bent for Election* (a pro-Roosevelt campaign film sponsored by the United Auto Workers), and subsequent films (particularly U.A.W's *The Brotherhood of Man* and the Navy's *Flat Hatting*) explored the other end of the cartoon world as previously defined by Walt Disney, using abstract modern art and stylized graphics.

Hilberman and Schwartz sold out to Bosustow in 1946 (the pair soon began Tempo Productions in New York, succeeding in the new field of TVcommercials), while United Productions of America (as the company was officially renamed in 1945) continued to turn out innovative industrial films with production manager Adrian Woolery and supervising director John Hubley.

UPA signed a contract with Columbia Pictures in 1948, and for the next eleven years turned out unique short cartoons that won three Oscars, were critically praised, and influenced animators from Hollywood to Zagreb. UPA also created Mr. Magoo, a caricature of animator/storyman Leo Salkin; Magoo's personality was based on that of John Hubley's businessman father. In UPA, Bosustow had created a studio that gave his artists tremendous freedom. The range of subjects they tackled, from children's book adaptations (*Madeline*) to jazz updates (*Rooty Toot Toot*) were given innovative spins by a talented roster of directors: Robert Cannon, Art Babbit, William Hurtz, Ted Parmalee, and Pete Burness.

Paul Julian

The Big Snit

NATIONAL FILM BOARD OF CANADA, 1985

he film begins in the home of two unusual characters, a man and wife, who are playing Scrabble. The wife has a hard time keeping the pupils of her eyes straight, so she removes her eyeballs and shakes them into the correct position.

Her husband's mind is occupied with the game as he fumbles with Scrabble tiles—all *E*s. The wife gets up to vacuum while she awaits his next move. Frustrated, the man looks at his watch and discovers it's time for his favorite TV show; he pulls out his saw and tunes into "Sawing for Teens."

While his wife vacuums the bathtub, the sound of sawing from the TV puts the man to sleep, and both miss a newscast informing the public that nuclear war has just broken out. The housecat disconnects the television by chewing on the power cord.

Screams from the neighbors and a sudden traffic jam wake the man, who wonders, "Is there some kind of parade on?" When his wife returns to the table, the man is startled. "Were you looking at my letters?" she asks. He denies it and begins sawing the table (and denies doing that as well). A fight ensues, and the wife leaves the table in tears.

Picking up a photo of the couple taken at Expo 1957, the husband recalls happier days. He tries to get back into his wife's good graces by playing the accordion. Their love reignites and they embrace. Both of them have been so consumed by the argument and its resolution that they don't realize the world has come to an end.

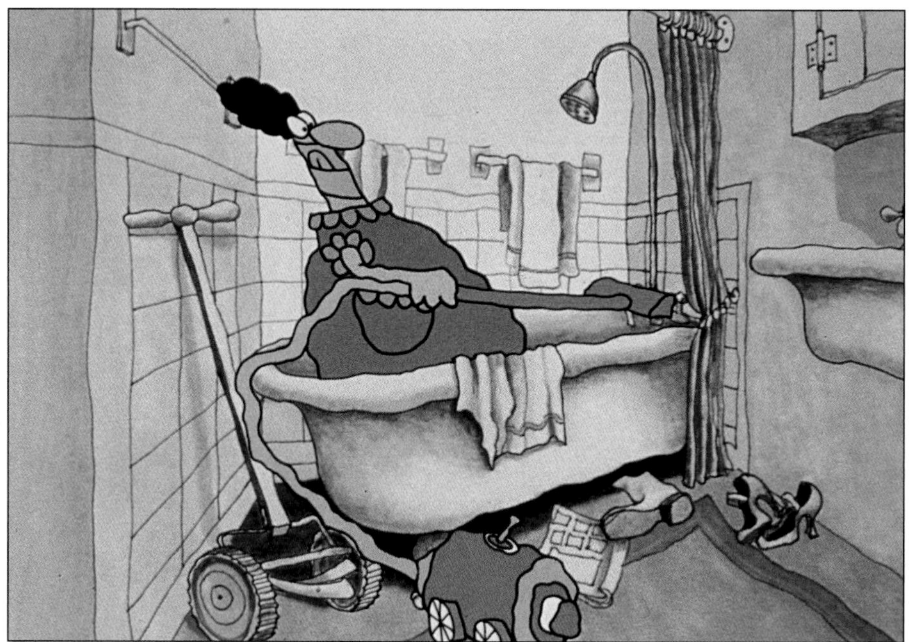

CREDITS

A National Film Board of Canada Cartoon

Story, direction, and animation: Richard Condie

Producers: Richard Condie, Michael Scott

Inking and backgrounds: Sharon Condie

Music: Patrick Godfrey

Voices: Jay Brazeau, Ida Osler, Randy Woods, Bill Guest

25

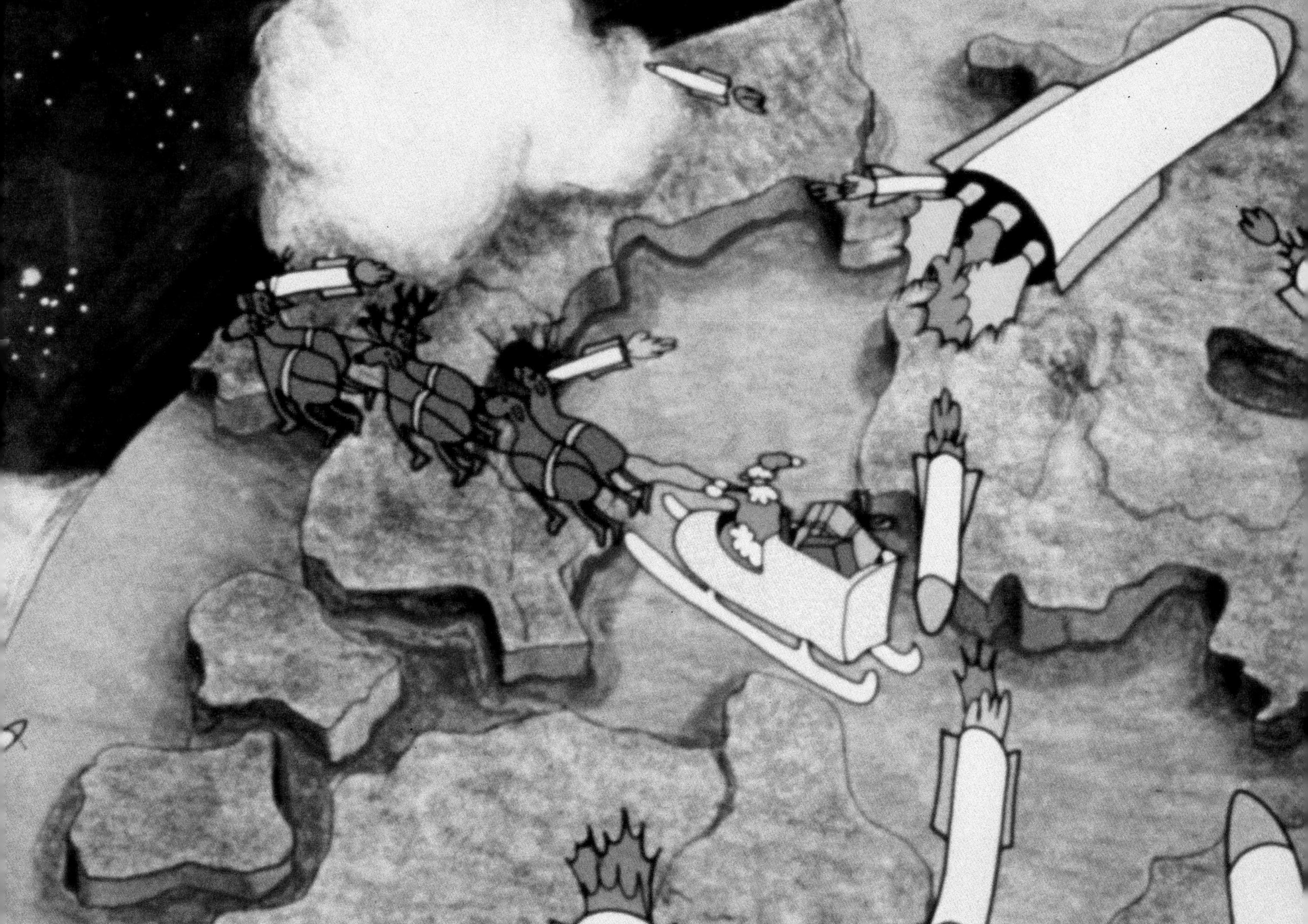

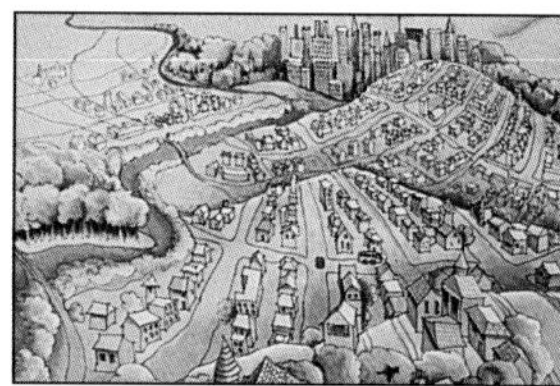

The Big Snit's appeal comes from its richness in humor and humanity. It is a simple story about a couple who do mundane things: They play Scrabble, clean house, watch TV, fight, kiss, and make up. Married for many years, they are still deeply in love and also totally oblivious to what is about to happen in the outside world. As the film and world end, all they want to do is finish their game. It is hard to imagine anyone not seeing a bit of themselves and people they know in this couple.

The laughs come from Richard Condie's attention to wonderful detail. The film opens with romantic violins and a tuba playing a strange bass line. The silly music sets the mood for the laughs to come. Another unexpected treat is the house's decor—as the couple wanders through their home, there is always something new that deserves a chuckle.

Condie is from Manitoba, Canada, where winters must seem to last forever; perhaps cabin fever is why Manitoba has produced some of the funniest animators working today. In any case, Condie has found the time and discipline to write great cartoon scripts, to create exceptional soundtracks, and to beautifully execute his visuals.

—*Karl Cohen*

The film remains with you long after the laughter because the message is strong. *The Big Snit* is a brilliant, worthy film about the fragility of life and is recommended for people of all ages who may at one time or another have wasted precious time being in a snit.

—*John Canemaker*

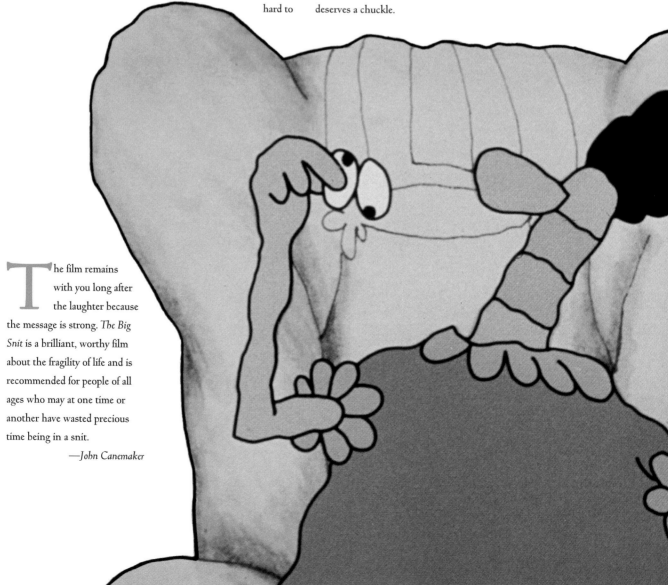

RICHARD CONDIE

Richard Condie was twenty-seven when he decided to make films; he cannot recall what triggered this idea. Aided by grants from the Canada Council, Condie became a filmmaker and found work on TV's *Sesame Street*. In 1978 he completed his first film for the National Film Board of Canada, *John Law and the Mississippi Bubble*. "We could have made it funnier, but we were lacking in experience," recalls Condie. "It was quite a jump from thirty-second non sequitur clips for *Sesame Street* to a ten-minute story."

His later films, *Getting Started* (1980) and *Pigbird* (1981), are well known for their humor and have won many international awards. *The Big Snit* took three years to make and it received the Hiroshima Award at the Hiroshima Festival, the International Critics Award at Annecy 85 in France, a Silver Prize at the Chicago Film Festival, Best Short Film at the Montreal World Film Festival, and an Academy Award nomination. "I tried to make it as funny as I could," says Condie. "Yet there's a serious undercurrent I can't explain."

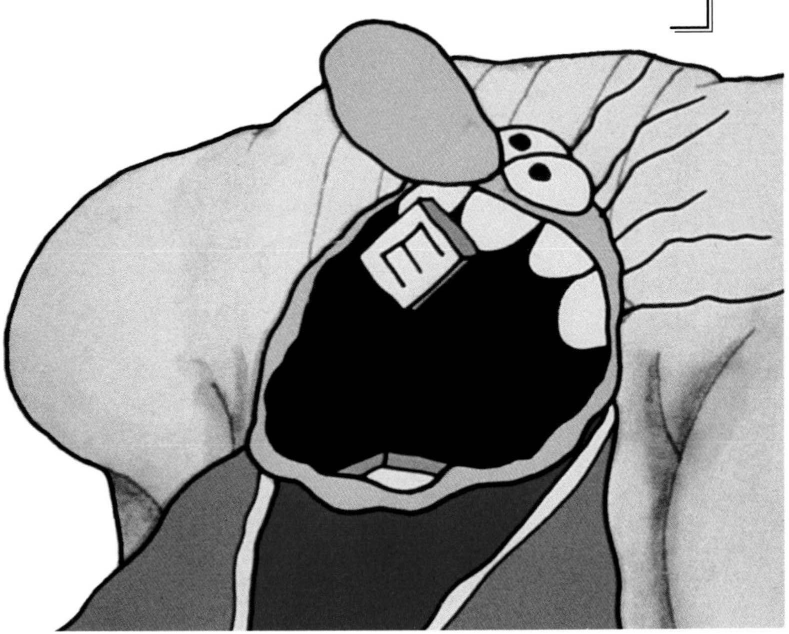

THE NATIONAL FILM BOARD OF CANADA

The NFBC was founded in 1939 by an act of Parliament, its official purpose being "to initiate and promote the production and distribution of films in the national interest and in particular . . . to interpret Canada and Canadians to other countries." Artist Norman McLaren founded the NFBC's animation unit in 1941. From the beginning, artistic freedom has been the trademark of the NFBC productions. Independence to create and experiment has led NFBC animators to produce a wide range of films that entertain, inspire, and pioneer while using every form of animation: from drawing on film, pixilation, and computer graphics to pinscreen, clay, sand, and cels. Four animated films from NFBC have won Academy Awards, and twenty others have been nominated.

BRAVE LITTLE TAILOR
FOR CAPTURE
GIANT
Color by TECHNICOLOR

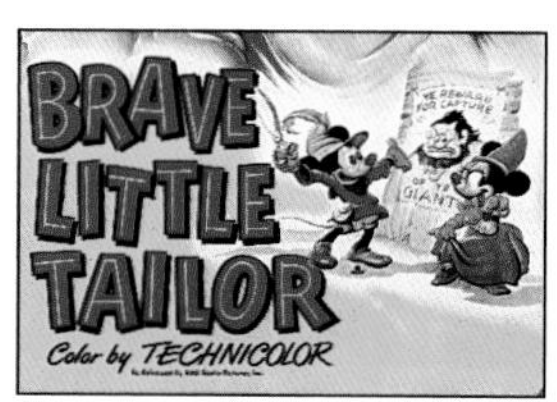

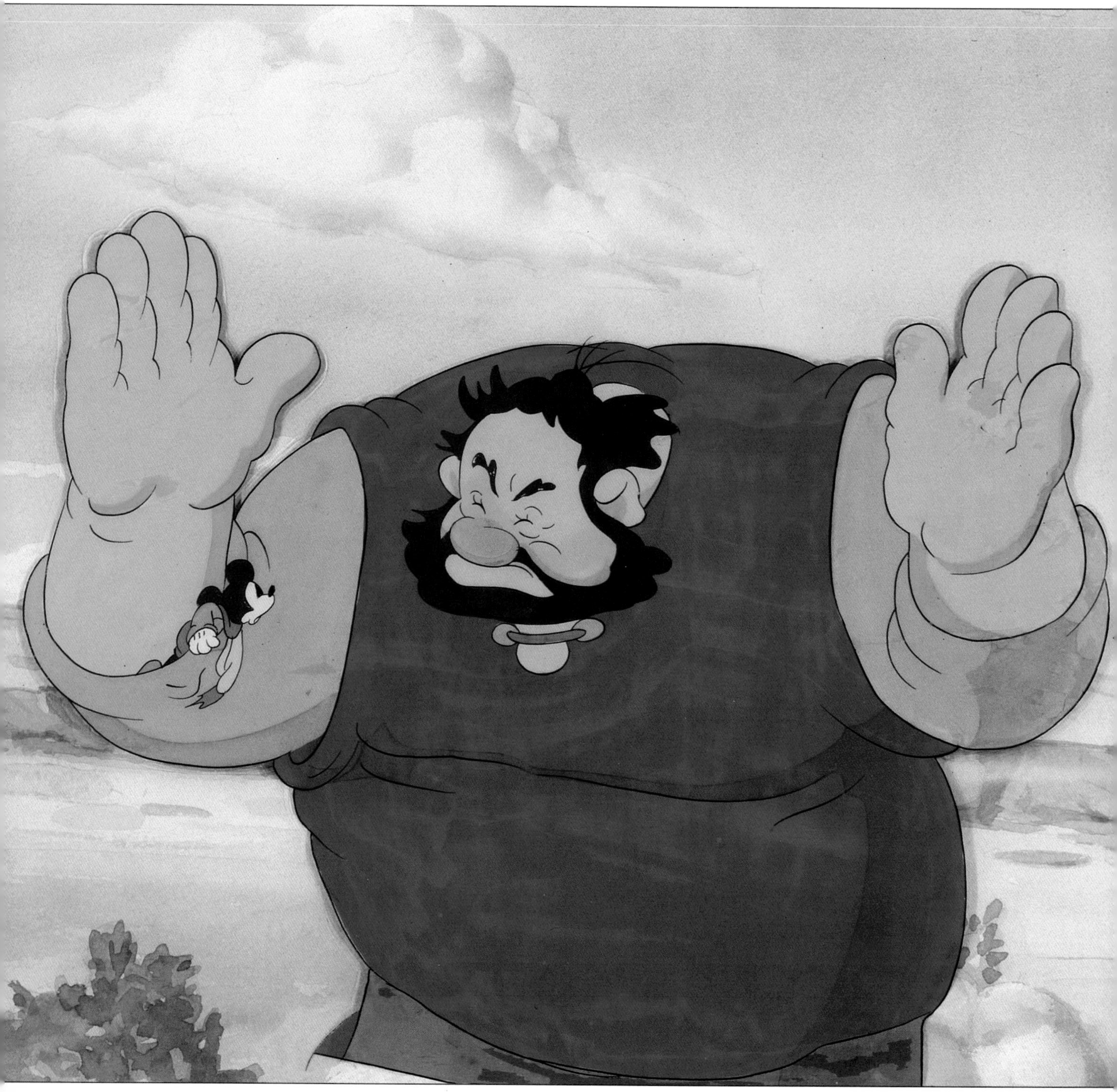

Brave Little Tailor

WALT DISNEY, 1938

CREDITS

A Walt Disney Mickey Mouse Cartoon

Directed by Bill Roberts

Animation: Frank Thomas, Bill Tytla, Riley Thomson, Ollie Johnston, Fred Moore, Roy Williams, Les Clark, Milt Schaffer, Cornett Wood, Frank Follmer, Archie Robin, Richard McDermott, Don Patterson, Jack Campbell

The tale begins in a medieval town abuzz with news that "the Giant is at large." Busy at work in his shop, Tailor Mickey Mouse is pestered by a swarm of flies, so he kills all seven by using two flyswatters.

Outside his shop three locals are discussing the Giant. Just as one asks, "Say, did you ever kill a giant?" the tailor throws open his window and proudly exclaims, "I killed seven with one blow." The misunderstanding spreads through town, and the king orders Mickey to appear before him. The tailor, wearing his scissors like a sword, dramatically describes his ordeal: He is talking about flies, but the king hears only giants and appoints Mickey Royal High Killer of Giants, offering him millions of "pazuzas" and Princess Minnie's hand in marriage. Mickey is delighted until the town's gates shut behind him.

As he worries, the Giant appears, crushing everything in his path. When the Giant drinks from an uprooted well, Mickey is thrown into his stomach. He escapes, but he catches the Giant's attention and has to climb up his face. Mickey uses his tailoring skill to sew up the Giant's sleeves, and in the final scene, Mickey and Minnie kiss on a carousel powered by the Giant.

The Disney Studio publicized *Brave Little Tailor* as a special cartoon, a virtual mini-feature, with lavish promotions and publicity. The *Mickey Mouse* Sunday comic strip featured an entire story continuity built around the filming of this short.

This high point in Mickey Mouse's long cinematic career stands out as a triumph of design and character animation. During the mid-thirties, animator Fred Moore redesigned Mickey's physical appearance, giving him his most appealing proportions. The interplay of circular forms within that design give Mickey an almost irresistible charm: To look at him is to like him. The fluid animation, largely done by Moore and Frank Thomas, is perfectly wedded to the design. Strong poses and vivid expressions capture Mickey's thoughts and emotions—the cocky stance he assumes balancing on his scissors, or the way his face falls and his shoulder sag when he reluctantly leaves to face the giant. Bill Tytla's animation of Willie the Giant conveys the ponderous weight of a great lumbering oaf: When Willie sets his foot down, the audience can feel his ponderous bulk settling into place.

—*Charles Solomon*

MICKEY MOUSE

Mickey Mouse is more than just the corporate symbol for the Walt Disney Company. His name has become a household word and his image is an internationally recognized icon of good will.

Walt Disney created Mickey on a fabled 1928 train ride back to California after a disastrous meeting in New York. Control of his then-current creation, Oswald the Lucky Rabbit, and his entire animation staff was being taken over by his producer and distributor. Walt needed a new character—fast. He decided on a mouse. Mrs. Disney came up with the name, and Ub Iwerks worked up the design. After unsuccessfully trying to sell Mickey in two completed cartoons (*Plane Crazy* and *Gallopin' Gaucho*), Walt decided to make one for theaters that were wiring up for sound. *Steamboat Willie* put Disney and Mickey on the map—and Walt never forgot it.

Some characters exist for a while and fade from view. This easily could have happened to Mickey throughout his long career, especially as characters like Donald Duck, Goofy, the Seven Dwarfs, and many others in the Disney stable became more popular. But Walt always kept Mickey alive, fresh, and in front of the audience.

Mickey starred in short subjects though 1952. One Mickey Mouse short won an Oscar (*Lend a Paw*, 1942) and many were nominated. Occasionally, Disney would cast him in special cartoons—as the Sorcerer's Apprentice in *Fantasia* (1940) and as Jack of the Beanstalk in *Mickey and the Beanstalk* (1947). When Walt entered television, "The Mickey Mouse Club" was created to reintroduce his star to a new generation of youngsters.

"I killed seven with one blow!"

Based on the Grimms' tale "The Gallant Tailor," *Brave Little Tailor* was Disney's first attempt to cast Mickey as a character in a classic story. As always, Disney was thinking about the future, and the success of this cartoon paved the way for *The Sorcerer's Apprentice*, *Mickey and the Beanstalk*, and *Mickey's Christmas Carol*.

Clock Cleaners

WALT DISNEY, 1937

Mickey, Donald, and Goofy are cleaning a giant clock atop a skyscraper. Mickey mops the numbers by riding the second hand. Inside the clockworks, Goofy brushes the teeth of gears while Donald becomes a prisoner of the mainspring. A stork is sleeping on one of the gears. Mickey tries to force it away, but the stork turns the tables, and soon Mickey is hanging out the window by a rope.

Donald tries pounding the mainspring back into place but ends up fighting with the spring's end coil. The duck has a verbal battle with the stubborn spring, which pushes him onto a balance wheel, making his head, legs, and hat do a tick-tock wiggle.

Goofy goes to work on the large chime on the ledge outside. Singing away, he dusts the bell from the inside, unable to see the mechanical Father Time figure who raps once, sounding the hour and giving Goofy a headache. Goofy continues dusting inside the bell, and then a mechanical Lady Liberty rings, adding to his confusion. He spots her about to ring again, but gets beaned on the head with her torch. Dazed, he walks around the clock tower, unaware he is inches from dropping to his doom.

Goofy falls from the ledge and lands on a rope which is about to give out. Mickey spots his pal and sends a scaffold trapeze to his rescue. Still dazed, Goofy continues walking unconsciously onto a ladder which Mickey gets under his feet. Goofy falls through a broken rung, bounces on a flagpole, and is sent straight to Mickey. Mickey and Goofy fly through the clock's innards, bouncing off Donald's just-repaired mainspring. The trio land in the balance wheel, their heads and backsides wiggling in time to the clock's ticking beat.

CREDITS

A Walt Disney Mickey Mouse Cartoon

Directed by Ben Sharpsteen

Animation: Chuck Couch, Bill Roberts, Al Eugster, Wolfgang Reitherman, Frenchy DeTremaudan

Layouts: Ken O'Connor

Music: Paul Smith, Oliver Wallace

Voices: Walt Disney, Clarence Nash, Pinto Colvig

Clock Cleaners crosscuts between three clutzy Mr. Fix-its at their three different posts, chronicling the separate snits that each manages to work himself into. What better way to stress the flesh-and-blood personalities of Disney's by-now well-rounded and identifiable characters—Mickey, Goofy, and Donald Duck—than to have the star trio cope with the impertinent impersonality of a big machine? Mickey dutifully polishes the clock's colossal digits, and Goofy confronts the mechanical statuettes that come clickety-clacking out to toll the hour, while the big mainspring gives Donald Duck an argument—getting itself uncoiled, rearing up cobra-like and insolently talking back—boingingly mimicking Donald's squawk in a smartly animated scene by New Yorker Al Eugster.

Future Disney director Woolie Reitherman impressively animated Goofy's stuporous tightrope walk at the climax of *Clock Cleaners,* credibly adapting basic physical principles like weight and gravity, inertia, and momentum. The sequence, staged over stunningly executed, perspective background art, evokes past silent Harold Lloyd masterworks like *Safety Last* and reminds us that when live-action comedies of the decade had resorted to the non-stop talk of screwball farce, Disney's cartoons were there to pick up the slapstick slack.

—*Greg Ford*

Northwest Hounded Police
Directed By
TEX AVERY

28

Northwest Hounded Police

MGM, 1946

Like all the arts, cartoons come in genres, and the genre here is wild, eye-popping double takes. That genre's maestro was Tex Avery, and this is his magnum opus. At Alka-Fizz Prison, the Wolf, a prisoner, draws a door in his cell, opens it, and effects his escape. He then heads north into "Mounty County."

At police headquarters, the top sergeant assigns Sgt. McPoodle (Droopy) to bring in the convict. The Wolf soon finds himself warned by a series of road signs: "Don't Look Now; Use Your Noodle; You're Being Followed; By Sgt. McPoodle." He runs at super speed to a cabin in the mountains, slams a dozen doors shut behind him, and swallows the key—only to be shocked to find McPoodle in the easy chair, reading the Sunday funnies.

Everywhere the Wolf runs or hides he finds McPoodle: in an eagle's egg; swimming underwater; inside a snowball; driving a cab, co-piloting an airplane; on the screen of a movie theater; in a lion's stomach. The Wolf goes to plastic surgeon Dr. Putty Puss to get a new face and ends up with McPoodle's. (The doctor, too, turns out to be McPoodle.)

Finally captured, the Wolf wonders "if there could have been more than one of those little guys." A chorus of hundreds of Droopys responds, "What do you think, brother?"

Avery made Droopy's first cartoon, *Dumb-Hounded*, in 1943; by the time he made *Northwest Hounded Police*, he had hit his stride at MGM. *Northwest Hounded Police* takes its premise from *Dumb-Hounded*, but the pace is faster and the "takes" are wilder. The humor is based on funny drawing—the loony, exaggerated takes that have become "Tex Avery clichés" in modern animation. But in 1946, Avery's brand of visual humor was new and original and quite "eye-popping" to audiences.

The part I remember best about *Northwest Hounded Police* is the wolf's screaming. Tex would use it often, but each time it got more extreme, to the point where it became completely abstract and ultimately a new art form. This, I think, is essential to great humor. You take a truth—fear, which manifests itself in a scream—and exaggerate it. And that makes truth fresh, different, and surprising. And that makes people laugh. And Tex was the master at it.

—*Bill Plympton*

CREDITS

An MGM Cartoon

Directed by Tex Avery

Producer: Fred Quimby

Story: Heck Allen

Animation: Walt Clinton, Ed Love, Ray Abrams, Preston Blair

Music: Scott Bradley

DROOPY

Tex Avery developed Daffy Duck and Bugs Bunny while at Warner Bros., but during his MGM years his penchant for funny gags and outrageous situations outweighed his desire to create enduring characters. Droopy was his most successful attempt. Droopy's personality and voice were based on Wallace Wimple, a character portrayed by Bill Thompson on the radio show "Fibber McGee and Molly," and Avery hired Thompson to voice his stone-faced basset hound. Droopy debuted in *Dumb-Hounded* (1943) and went on to leading roles in more than twenty-five theatrical cartoons, but the character never achieved stardom during Avery's lifetime. Television showings of Droopy cartoons and his appearance in *Who Framed Roger Rabbit?* and later Roger Rabbit shorts have given him a newfound celebrity.

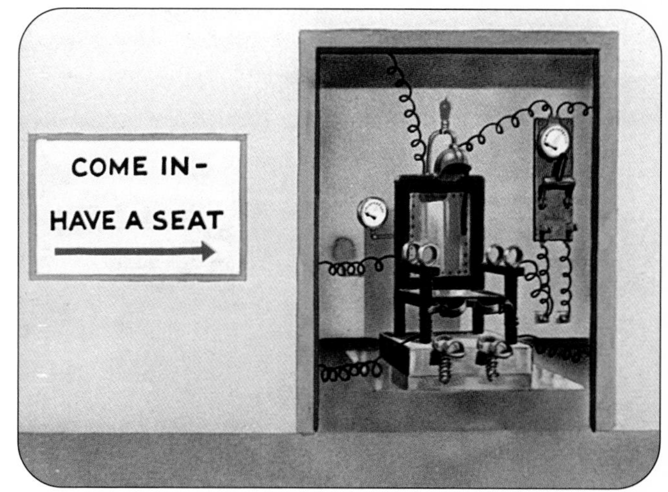

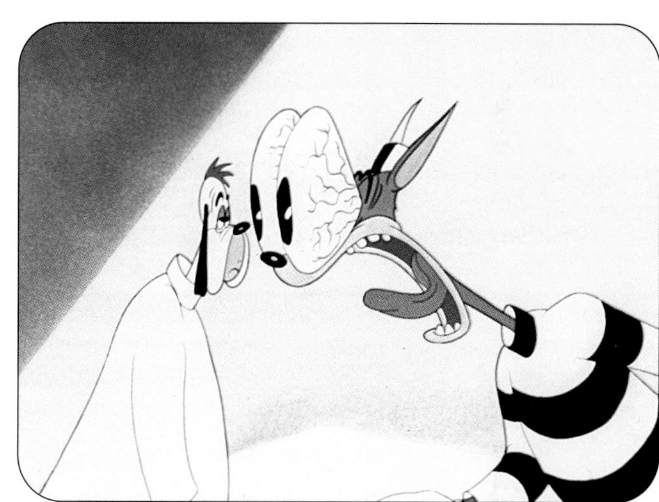

MGM ANIMATION

In the 1940s, under producer Fred Quimby's leadership, a group of talented directors, including Tex Avery, George Gordon, Robert Allen, and the team of Hanna and Barbera, turned out a solid supply of quality cartoons.

Toot, Whistle, Plunk and Boom

WALT DISNEY, 1953

By 1953, Disney was facing competition from UPA, the cartoon studio founded in 1943 by former Disney animators. The liberated graphic style and whimsical, sophisticated themes of UPA's cartoons were attracting attention and winning Oscars with stylized films like *Gerald McBoing Boing*. Disney fought back by changing the movie screen.

First came 3-D. In May 1953 Disney released the first Adventures in Music short, *Melody*, in which Professor Owl and his students recite stories to music, which are visualized in bold, modern-art styles that literally jumped off the screen.

3-D was only a passing fad, however, and Disney next turned to CinemaScope, a process that projects a picture over a wider area than the normal motion-picture screen. Six months after *Melody*, Disney released the first CinemaScope cartoon, *Toot, Whistle, Plunk and Boom*, which has highly stylized graphics that depart from Disney's usual naturalistic designs.

The cartoon presents Professor Owl teaching his feathered students the history of musical instruments, demonstrating how each began with a toot, whistle, plunk, or boom. The musical lecture shows how each of these sounds began with the cavemen and evolved into today's instruments: A caveman's whistling through a blade of grass eventually became the modern jazz saxophone; tooting through an animal's horn led to today's brass instruments; plunking rhythmically on a primitive bow was the basis for today's string instruments; and booming on his big belly was the earliest form of percussion sound.

The cartoon made a big impression on moviegoers and critics alike, and Disney topped UPA when the cartoon won the 1953 Academy Award for Best Animated Short, the studio's eleventh Oscar for a short cartoon.

Fresh and funny stylized graphics that depart from Disney's usual naturalistic designs offer an irreverent "history of music" from cave to concert hall. Ward Kimball, one of Disney's legendary Nine Old Men and a past master of full "personality animation" (in *Pinocchio, Dumbo, Fantasia*, etc.), championed the use of minimal animation used extensively in WWII propaganda films by Hollywood Animation studios, including Disney.

—*John Canemaker*

CREDITS

Walt Disney Presents Adventures in Music

Directed by C. August Nichols and Ward Kimball

Story: Dick Huemer

Animation: Ward Kimball, Julius Svendsen, Marc Davis, Henry Tanous, Art Stevens, Xavier Atencio

Character styling: Tom Oreb

Music: Joseph Dubin

Art direction: A. Kendall O'Connor

Assistant: Victor Haboush

Color styling: Eyvind Earle

Songs: Sonny Burke, Charles Elliott

29

RABBIT
SEASONING

30

Rabbit Seasoning

WARNER BROS., 1952

There are lettered signs in the woods: "If you're looking for fun; You don't need a reason; All you need is a gun; It's rabbit season." Those four signs lead to hundreds of others announcing "rabbit season" and pointing to the home of the rabbit Bugs. It is the duck Daffy who's nailing up the signs. "Awfully unsporting of me, I know," he confides, "but, hey, I've got to have some fun. And besides, it's really duck season."

The congenial hunter Elmer Fudd is soon blasting away down Bugs's hole, and when Bugs himself appears, the tiny cast—duck, rabbit, hunter—engage in a series of verbal duels. The invariable question is who'll get shot by the overeager Elmer, and the inevitable answer is Daffy. It's rabbit season, and Bugs is indeed a rabbit, but Elmer is impatient, Daffy is excitable, and Bugs has a way with words. So Daffy gets blasted twice.

Then Elmer's basic urges take over. "I'm sorry, fellas," he says, "but I can't wait any longer." He shoots at both of them. They hide in Bugs's hole, but Bugs decides to resolve the issue solo. Dressed in a Lana Turner sweater, high-heeled pumps, and wig, he easily wins Elmer's love, much to the duck's disgust. Daffy tears off Bugs's wig, exposing the rabbit. "Now's your chance, Hawkeye," Daffy calls to Elmer. "Shoot him! Shoot him!" But Daffy gets the final blast from Elmer's gun.

CREDITS

A Merrie Melodies Cartoon

Directed by Charles M. Jones

Story: Michael Maltese

Animation: Ben Washam, Lloyd Vaughan, Ken Harris

Layouts: Maurice Noble

Backgrounds: Philip DeGuard

Voices: Mel Blanc

Musical direction: Carl W. Stalling

PRONOUN TROUBLE

BUGS: *It's true, Doc, I'm a rabbit alright. Would you like to shoot me now or wait till you get home?*

DAFFY: *Shoot him now! Shoot him now!*

BUGS: *You keep outta this. He doesn't have to shoot you now.*

DAFFY: *He does so have to shoot me now. [To Elmer] I demand that you shoot me now. BANG!*

DAFFY: *Let's run through that again.*

BUGS: *Okay. Would you like to shoot me now or wait till you get home?*

DAFFY: *Shoot him now. Shoot him now.*

BUGS: *You keep outta this. He doesn't have to shoot you now.*

DAFFY: *Ha! That's it! Hold it right there. [To the audience] Pronoun trouble. [To Bugs] It's not "he doesn't have to shoot you now." It's "he doesn't have to shoot me now." Well, I say he does have to shoot me now! [To Elmer] So shoot me now! BANG!*

RABBIT SEASONING

In our stuff—even the talkiest things, like the Bugs Bunny–Daffy Duck stuff—even if you turned the sound off, it was interesting, and you could truly tell what was happening. I never recorded a film until I'd completely laid it out. I'd just make the drawings, and then I'd time it, but I always wrote the dialogue right on the drawings—I didn't write it as a script. I worked out the whole thing visually, and then when I'd finished, I'd go back and I'd type the dialogue off the drawings, so it always related to the drawings. Because if the writer wrote the dialogue and then you recorded it and then you tried to make the drawings fit the dialogue, it was bound to suffer.

—*Chuck Jones*

R*abbit Seasoning* is the second in a series of three cartoons in which Bugs and Daffy, the intended victims of Elmer Fudd's hunting ambitions, stall him with an extended filibustering debate over which one of them is in season at the moment, and flummox him into doing nothing but shooting Daffy point-blank in the head from time to time—and, from the evidence, doing no more damage to the duck than humiliating him by positioning his beak on the wrong side of his head. Noble's autumnal colors are virtually all that distinguish this from *Rabbit Fire*, the first in the series: the same basic situation is explored, some of the same gags reappear, and little transpires to indicate a twist or development on the concept of the previous cartoon. In fact, there's no development whatsoever—just the acknowledgment by Jones and Maltese that this is too good to drop after seven minutes, there's more fun we can have with this. (*Duck! Rabbit, Duck!* is the title of the third cartoon, with little to distinguish that one from the other two, except that it takes place in a foot of snow.) All three pictures are apparently inspired by a single gag from Art Davis's *What Makes Daffy Duck?*, in which Daffy gets both Elmer and a hungry fox off his trail by dressing as a game warden and posting a pair of notices—"Duck Season Over" and "Fox Season Opens."

This is the most famous authentic trilogy in the history of American studio animation, and, assembled together, would constitute the only Bugs Bunny two-reel comedy (an anomaly on the order of the two matching Laurel and Hardy comedies, *Them Thar Hills* and *Tit For Tat*, which were sometimes run together as a featurette).

The dialogue in these cartoons, savored by connoisseurs for years, was an element singled out for praise by *Boxoffice* as soon as the first of the trilogy appeared. Since Carl Stalling wrote the scores, there are now published pieces of music entitled "Rabbit Season," "Duck Season," "Elmer Season," and "Pronoun Trouble."

The levels of irony, role-playing, role-reversal, and slapstick that rebound, highlight, overlap, intensify, and ricochet off each other in all three of these cartoons have been the subject of endless analysis. When Bugs bulldozes Elmer in *Rabbit Seasoning* with a female disguise distinguished by nothing so much as its obviousness, Daffy can take it no longer. He turns to the camera as if to deliver a deathless line, but can summon up nothing more than a cluck of his tired tongue, which emerges, in the 50s understated comedy style of Jack Benny or George Gobel, as a sputter of disgust. It is one of the most finely shaded bits of acting ever to appear in a one-reel cartoon.

With animators like Ken Harris, Ben Washam, and Lloyd Vaughan already on board, the Jones crew was about the only group in the shrinking short-subject business capable of turning out the fine realization of the clever concept inherent in a picture like *Rabbit Seasoning*.

—*Joe Adamson*

The Scarlet Pumpernickel

WARNER BROS., 1950

Its title is a takeoff on the 1934 costume drama *The Scarlet Pimpernel*: It has been called an animated tribute to Michael Curtiz, the famous director of a series of swashbucklers starring Errol Flynn, and its cast of thousands includes a host of familiar Warner Bros. characters. It's an epic—and it stars Daffy Duck.

The cartoon begins with Daffy pleading with "J. L." (Jack L. Warner), "You're killing me! I'm telling you, J. L., you're typecasting me to death. Comedy, always comedy." Daffy wants to prove himself in a serious role and has just the story, written by Daffy Dumas Duck. The hero is the Scarlet Pumpernickel (Daffy, of course, in an Errol Flynn role), a dashing masked highwayman; his lady love, Milady Melissa; his enemy, the Lord High Chamberlain (Porky Pig as Claude Rains). The Chamberlain sets a trap for "that masked stinker" by announcing the betrothal of Melissa to the Grand Duke (Sylvester as Basil Rathbone). Cleverly disguised, the Pumpernickel stops at "King Nostril's Inn" (run by Elmer Fudd) before crashing the wedding and rescuing Melissa. Back at the inn, he is spotted by the Duke, and the daring escapade climaxes in a sword fight that—as the studio boss pleads for the finish—is only the first of a series of dramatic climaxes (including skyrocketing prices of kosher food).

"There were a lot of in-house jokes in that cartoon, mostly in casting," said Chuck Jones. "We put in the Mother Bear from the early Three Bears cartoons, and 'Henery' Hawk appeared as a messenger. It was an epic, so all my characters had to be in it. Everybody appreciated it except Jack Warner, and I don't think he ever realized we were talking about him in the cartoon."

While today the idea of "genre parody" ranks high as a format of choice among cartoon story people, the genre parody of *The Scarlet Pumpernickel* was unusual for 1950, something of an anomaly in its time. Still, Jones's character poses have never been sharper, and Michael Maltese's dialogue and Mel Blanc's line-reading never more extraordinary.

Maltese's keen ear for mangled grandiloquence never lets down, nor does the writer's very knowing, acute sensitivity to the desperate hyperbole of a frazzled, frantic pitchman (e.g. Daffy Duck) as he piled on one voiced-over, cooked-up crescendo after another (dams bursting, volcanos erupting, and cavalries charging—so much sturm and drang) that all boils down to the inspired bathos of overpriced kreplach.

Genre parody notwithstanding, what's funniest about *The Scarlet Pumpernickel* is precisely Daffy's character and the vast chasm that exists between Daffy's inflated perception of himself and highly flawed "little black duck" that he really is.

—*Greg Ford*

31

CREDITS

A Looney Tunes Cartoon

Directed by Charles M. Jones

Story: Michael Maltese

Animation: Phil Monroe,

Ben Washam, Lloyd Vaughan

Layouts: Robert Gribbroek

Backgrounds: Peter Alvarado

Voices: Mel Blanc

Musical direction: Carl W. Stalling

The Cat Came Back

NATIONAL FILM BOARD OF CANADA, 1988

In his house on a hill, Mr. Johnson is interrupted from his tuba practice by a knock at the door, and finds a kitten left in a baby basket on his front step. Johnson brings it inside and entertains it with his eighty-year-old baby rattle—which the kitten promptly destroys. Johnson puts the cat outside and retrieves his "welcome" mat—but in a hilarious streak of bad luck, the cat comes back again and again—and Johnson can't get rid of it no matter what he does. The cat survives Mr. Johnson's attempts to drown him, drop him from a hot air balloon, and tie him to a train track.

In true cartoon tradition, Mr. Johnson ends up as victim each time, and the cat returns to the house to resume his destruction of it. Finally, the crazed Mr. Johnson fills his house with dynamite and lights the fuse. The explosion kills him, but his spirit returns to the house to haunt and taunt the cat. Unfortunately, Johnson's lifeless body crashes back to earth—crushing the kitten and creating nine ghostly cats who chase the terrified Johnson into the afterlife.

When Winnipeg animator Cordell Barker approached the National Film Board of Canada with an idea for a film about an old man and a cat (which he considered to be a perfect conflict), the NFBC asked him to modify his plan and work with them on animating the century-old folk song "The Cat Came Back." Barker spent an astronomical amount of time on the film, working eight hours a day, plus weekends and evenings for more than three years. *The Cat Came Back* premiered at the 8th World Festival of Films in Zagreb, where it won three prestigious awards.

Absolutely everything in this classic tale of revenge works. Every sort of twisted irony and bit of slapstick humor one can think of is incorporated into the gags. The music and color styling are perfect. The timing is so good that you are completely in sync with the cat as he shreds the sofa piece by piece. And the railroad scene is a classic. *The Cat Came Back* stands up to repeated viewings; first you need to see it a few times to catch all the gags. Then you want to see it a few more times because it's so funny. After that you keep watching it, just because.

—*Linda Simensky*

CREDITS

The National Film Board of Canada

Directed by Cordell Barker

Executive producer: Ches Yetman

Producers: Richard Condie, Cordell Barker

Story, animation, and backgrounds: Cordell Barker

Music arrangements: John McCulloch

Sung by: John McCulloch, Ed Ledson, Richard Condie, Cordell Barker

Character voice: Richard Condie

Superman

PARAMOUNT, 1941

he story has become a part of American folklore: Planet Krypton, the "man of steel" who moves faster than a speeding bullet, Clark Kent, Lois Lane, and the *Daily Planet.* In the cartoon, Superman's birth and arrival on Earth are recounted in a series of still paintings, followed by a thrilling new episode, complete with a mad scientist threatening total destruction by a deadly ray, a helpless Lois tied to a chair, and mild-mannered Kent stepping into a handy closet to emerge in mask and cape. Will the city be saved? Will Superman rescue Lois?

In 1940 Paramount secured the screen rights to Superman—the era's most popular hero—and approached the Fleischer studio about producing Superman cartoons. The Fleischers were hesitant: Animation had never been used for realistic adventure stories, and their staff was used to the exaggerated proportions of Popeye and Betty Boop. Paramount allotted almost $100,000 for the first film—four times the budget of an average Popeye short—and work began in the winter of 1940 at the Fleischers' Miami studio. Great care was given to all phases of production, and the characters and story were modeled after Siegel and Shuster's design. Fleischers' artists had previously based their characters on simple circular designs, but for the Superman cartoons they strove for a realistic "pulp magazine" look and devised many animation effects techniques that later became industry standards. Bud Collyer, Superman's radio voice, was the voice for this first cartoon, which was nominated for an Oscar.

The *Superman* series continued with sixteen more adventures which stand out as unique for their period.

CREDITS

Paramount Pictures Presents a Max Fleischer Superman Cartoon

Directed by Dave Fleischer

Story: Seymour Kneitel, Isadore Sparber

Animation: Steve Muffati, Frank Endres

Musical arrangement: Sammy Timburg

SUPER BIRTH

Superman was created by teenagers Jerry Siegel and Joe Shuster, and first appeared in June 1938 on the cover of *Action Comics.* Superman became a sensation, spawning a radio show and newspaper comic strip. He first appeared in live action in 1948. George Reeves played Superman in a 1950s TV series, and Christopher Reeve portrayed him in big-budget films in the 1980s. The comic book character was "officially killed" in 1992. Dean Cain portrays him in a nineties TV version.

33

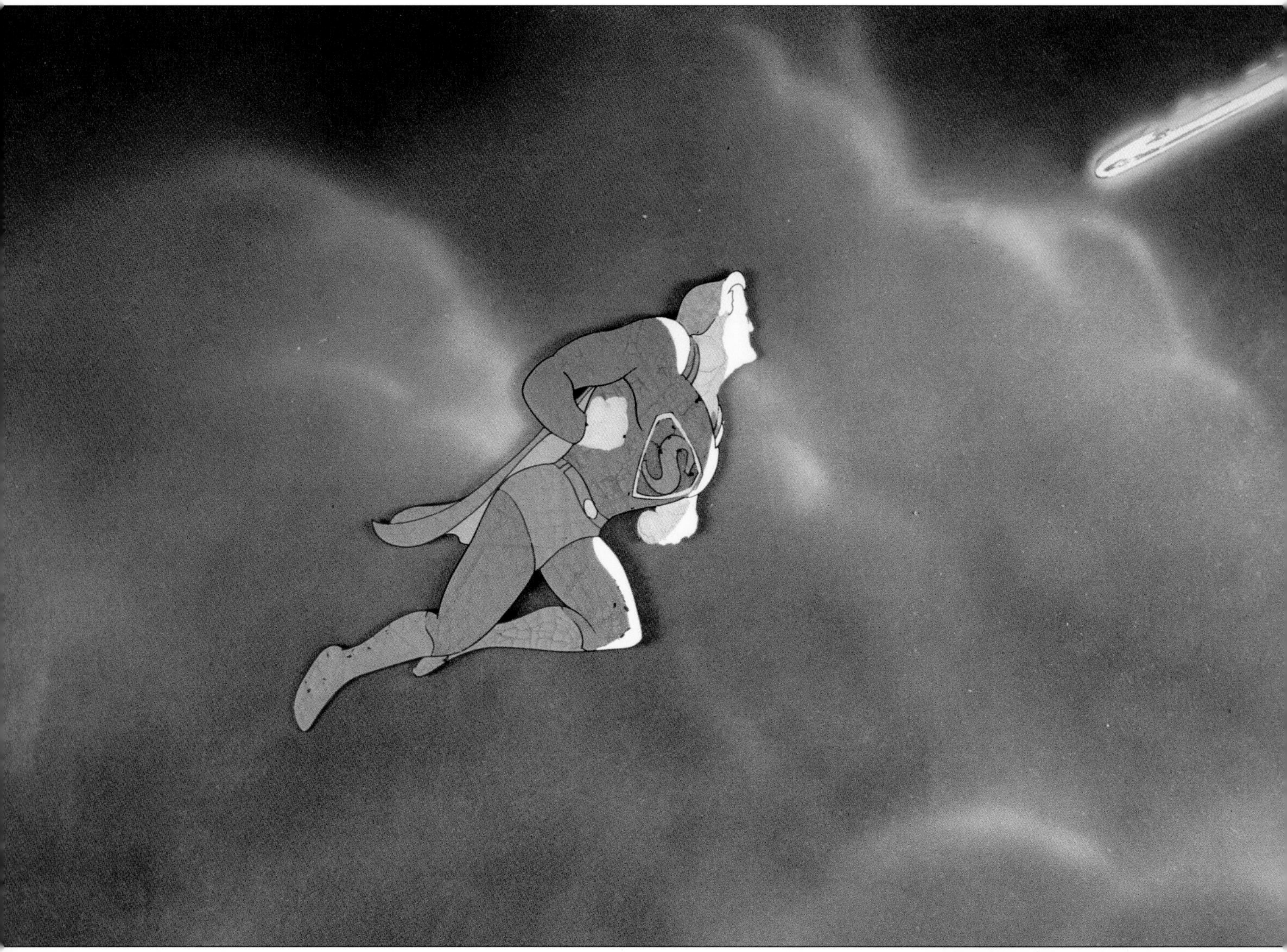

THIS MUST BE A JOB FOR SUPERMAN

Many of the now-famous phrases associated with Superman—"Look up in the sky—it's a bird . . . no, it's a plane . . . no, it's Superman!" and "faster than a speeding bullet"—were first brought to the screen by the Fleischers. Other than those legendary clichés, dialogue was kept to a minimum. With less than ten minutes of screen time, each of the cartoons in the Paramount Superman series packs a feature film's worth of a action and fantastic ideas. The Bulleteers, the Mechanical Monsters, the Magnetic Telescope, and the Arctic Giant are just some of the fantastic perils the Fleischer studio produced in the first series of nine cartoons. The remaining eight, produced by Famous Studios, reflected more realistic World War II themes, such as in Secret Agent and Eleventh Hour.

ANIMATING SUPERMAN

When first asked by Paramount to produce Superman cartoons, Dave Fleischer worried about the cost of animating realistic human action, and in order to dissuade Paramount without summarily rejecting the project, he requested a budget of almost $100,000— almost four times the going rate. But Paramount approved the budget, and the Fleischers used the opportunity to turn out some of the best animation ever drawn. Model sheets were devised by using square shapes and cubes as the basis for the figure drawings. The blocks aided the artists in achieving the proper perspective for their realistic animation. The Fleischers were striving for realism and to that effect employed Max's original invention, the rotoscope, for the simplest scenes, while relying on their best draftsmen to animate more sophisticated movements.

From the very beginning of film, efforts were made to translate comic-strip characters to the silver screen. More often than not, such efforts failed because the two-dimensional world of comic art allows for things not possible in the three-dimensional world of reality. When animation came along, it proved to be a middle ground between the comics and film and made for easier adaptation.

The one adaptation that remained closest to the original was the series of Superman films released by Fleischer studios from 1941 to 1943. By paying more attention to design and color than to achieving the effect of dimensionality, and by crafting tightly-knit plots that could be resolved satisfactorily in minutes, each film came close to reproducing the experience of reading a comic-book story. The Art Deco settings, the flat character designs, and the use of colors to create mood combine to elevate the films to a level of pure artistry seldom found in animation outside *Fantasia* of the year before. Nothing else the Fleischers did quite matched the Superman cartoons for power, charm, and enduring pleasure.

—*Thomas Inge*

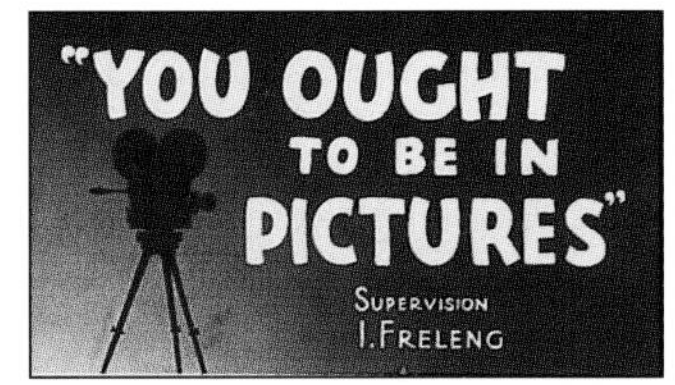
"YOU OUGHT
TO BE IN
PICTURES"
SUPERVISION
I. FRELENG

You Ought to Be in Pictures

WARNER BROS., 1940

The Warner Bros. cartoon staff had access to a 35mm movie camera—they used it to shoot live action for reference and to make a gag film every Christmas. Friz Freleng decided to use the camera, staff, and studio lot to make his first Porky Pig cartoon since the pig's 1935 debut in *I Haven't Got a Hat*. The result—a combination of live action and animation—is a unique cartoon and one of the most popular creations of the Termite Terrace.

During lunchtime at the cartoon studio, pictures of Daffy Duck and Porky Pig come alive. Daffy convinces Porky to quit cartoons and go into feature films. In producer Leon Schlesinger's office Porky asks to have his contract canceled, and Schlesinger gives in, aware that the pig will soon be back. Porky drives to the feature lot (Daffy, Porky, and Porky's car are the only animated parts of the film), but is thrown out by a guard (played by Michael Maltese). Disguised as Oliver Hardy, Porky sneaks onto a stage set but is thrown out by a stage hand. A stampede on the set of a western convinces Porky to get his old job back. Meanwhile, Daffy is performing for Schlesinger—he wants Porky's job. Porky gives Daffy a drubbing and goes back to work—Schlesinger has not torn up his contract. Bandaged Daffy asks for a job "opposite Greta Garbo" and gets hit with a tomato.

In addition to Schlesinger and Maltese, animator Gerry Chiniquy and others appear in small parts (except for Schlesinger's, all their voices were done by Mel Blanc), and the film uses stock footage from Warner Bros. films (*The Great Ziegfield* and *California Mail*) and shots from Christmas gag films.

This film has been credited with inspiring Steven Spielberg's *Who Framed Roger Rabbit?*

CREDITS

A Looney Tunes Cartoon

Directed by I. Freleng

Story: Jack Miller

Animation: Norman Cohen

Musical direction: Carl W. Stalling

You Ought to Be in Pictures is a wonderful, novel film experience in which Porky, Daffy, and a car are animated, and the rest of the visuals are either live-action images or still photographs. Far more ambitious than earlier works that combine live action and animation, the images used take us on a behind-the-scenes tour of both Warner Bros. and Leon Schlesinger studios, providing special appeal to anyone fascinated with the magic of Hollywood; it includes Michael Maltese as a studio guard, and a handshake between Daffy Duck and Leon Schlesinger. These treats make the film fun, but what makes it great is Porky's acting ability, Friz Freleng's ability to direct his star, and Jack Miller's script. Porky is not just another funny animal, but a real actor in this film, displaying a wide range of emotions in a convincing manner.

—*Karl Cohen*

FRIZ FRELENG

Isadore 'Friz' Freleng entered the animation world when he went to work for Hugh Harman at Kansas City Film Ad in the 1920s. Walt and Roy Disney had already left the company to continue their Alice comedies in Hollywood, and shortly called upon Harman and his partner, Rudolf Ising, to join them; Freleng followed in 1927.

Freleng worked on Disney's Oswald the Rabbit series, and later rejoined Harman-Ising in 1930 as head animator for their new series of Looney Tunes for Warner Bros. and producer Leon Schlesinger. Freleng became invaluable to Warner Bros., particularly when Harman and Ising left the studio, taking their star character, Bosko, with them.

Promoted to director in 1933, Freleng concentrated on the color Merrie Melodies, becoming a master of timing and musical synchronized animation. He directed Porky Pig's first cartoon, *I Haven't Got a Hat*, 1935, and created both Yosemite Sam and Sylvester.

You Ought to Be in Pictures parallels Friz Freleng's personal life. In 1937, MGM lured him away from Warner Bros. with a flattering offer. When his MGM contract expired, he realized that he missed the freedom to develop new characters and returned to Warner Bros.—and set about creating his greatest works. Freleng was a major force at Warner Bros. from its first days in 1930 until it closed its doors in 1962. He directed dozens of cartoons featuring Bugs Bunny, Daffy Duck, and Porky Pig, as well as the entire Tweety and Sylvester series, including four Oscar-winning cartoons: *Tweetie Pie* (1947), *Speedy Gonzales* (1955), *Birds Anonymous* (1957), and *Knighty Knight, Bugs* (1958).

After Warner Bros. animation studio closed, Freleng founded his own studio (Depatie-Freleng Enterprises), creating TV series and theatrical shorts, commercials, and the Oscar-winning *Pink Panther*. He returned to Warner Bros. in 1980 to direct TV specials and compilation features.

I made *You Ought to Be in Pictures* because I thought it was novel and I had the freedom to do it. I think Schlesinger let me because showing him as the boss appealed to his ego.

—*Friz Freleng*

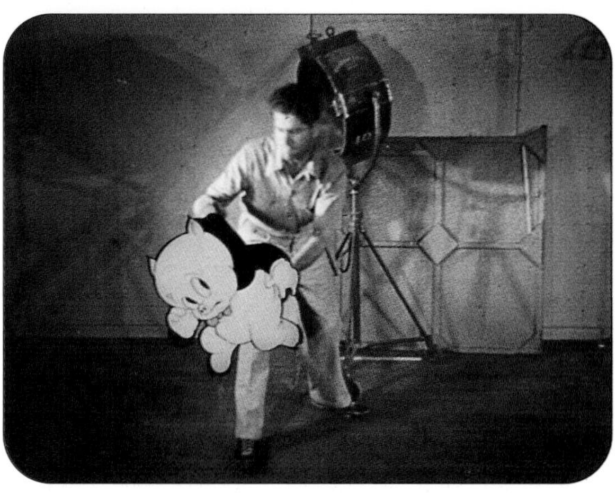

Ali Baba Bunny

WARNER BROS, 1957

CREDITS

A Merrie Melodies Cartoon

Directed by Chuck Jones

Story: Michael Maltese

Animation: Richard Thompson, Ken Harris, Abe Levitow, Ben Washam

Effects animation: Harry Love

Layouts: Maurice Noble

Backgrounds: Philip DeGuard

Film editor: Treg Brown

Voices: Mel Blanc

Musical direction: Carl W. Stalling, Milt Franklyn

Bugs and Daffy—like Hope and Crosby or Laurel and Hardy—are a comedy team. Whether they're rival quarries disputing who'll get blasted by Elmer Fudd in such Chuck Jones cartoons as *Rabbit Fire* and *Rabbit Seasoning*, or show-business rivals in Friz Freleng films like *A Star is Bored* and *Show Biz Bugs*, they create humor just by being together. Their rivalry reaches new heights in *Ali Baba Bunny*, in which their different characters are brought into hilarious sharp focus by the glitter of gold.

The pair believe they're on their way to Pismo Beach ("and all the clams we can eat!"), but a wrong left turn at Albuquerque lands them in ancient Baghdad and a cave full of Arabian treasure. Bugs maintains his ageless cool, but Daffy goes wild. "It's mine! Mine! Mine!" he exults. "I'm rich! I'm wealthy!" But there's a giant ogre of a guard named Hassahn to deal with. Bugs does his best to save his pal's feathers, even pretending to be a genie in a lamp and performing rope tricks, but then Daffy "desecrates the spirit" of a lamp, angering a very real genie. The next scene finds Bugs on the beach, musing about "how that crazy duck ever made out with the genie." One-inch-tall Daffy appears and goes after a pearl that Bugs finds. "It's mine! Mine! Mine! I'm a happy miser!"

Chuck Jones had his own explanation for this cartoon's popularity: "People love Daffy in *Ali Baba Bunny* because they realize they're as greedy as he is. I think Daffy's one of the most attractive characters in all the lexicon. He simply exhibits his greed full face, something we all feel but don't want to admit."

In addition to being perhaps the cleanest delineation of the 1950s Daffy Duck persona, *Ali Baba Bunny* finds Michael Maltese seemingly writing for posterity. Never was the essence of greedy, self-doubting, black-duckness better expressed: "Consequences, schmonsequences, as long as I'm rich;" "I'm socially secure, I'm socially secure;" "Red cap, call me a cab, boy, and be quick about it—I'm a heavy tipper!" When added to the slow-brained hatchet-man Hassahn's "Open, septuagenarian . . . uhh, open, saddle soap," and the immortal "Hassahn CHOP!" the result is a film whose verbal richness forever gives lie to the idea that cartoons need be considered kid stuff.

—*Steve Schneider*

35

"Feed the Kitty"

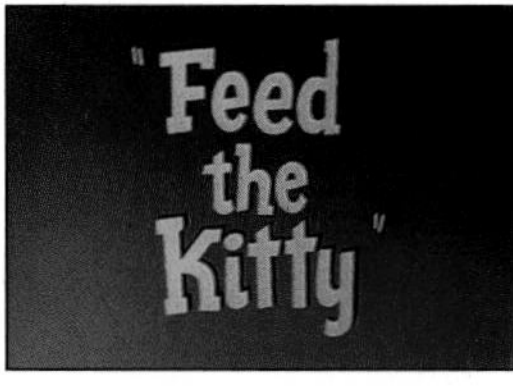

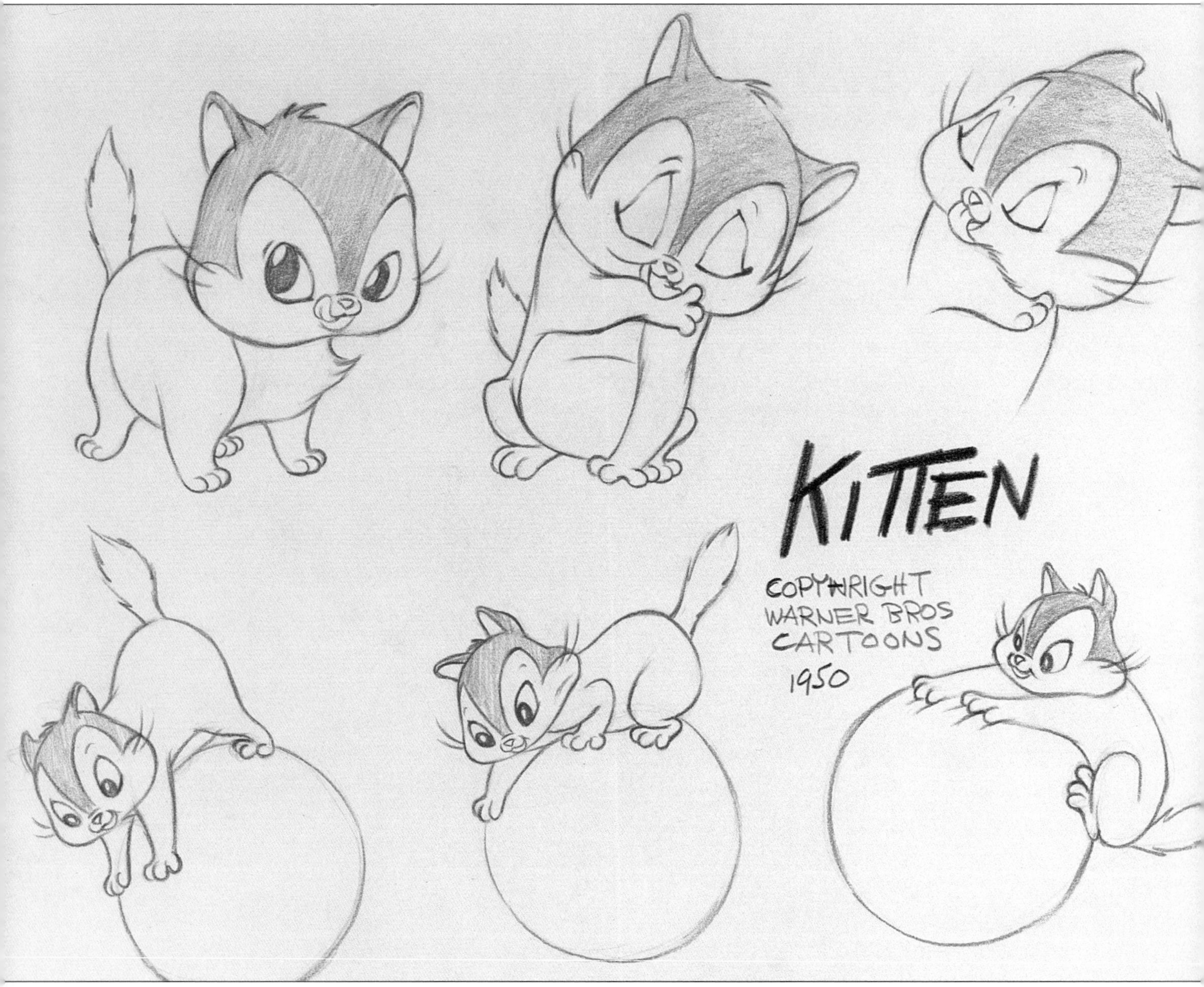

KITTEN
COPYRIGHT WARNER BROS CARTOONS 1950

Feed the Kitty

WARNER BROS., 1952

In the Warner Bros. world of canny—or at least zany—rabbits and ducks, dogs don't always come off well. Chuck Jones made no bones about this: "I feel a lot different about dogs than most people do. I don't feel dogs are particularly trustworthy. I think most dogs are professionals; they play the part you ask them to play." Such sentiments only make *Feed the Kitty* more remarkable. A masterful use of pantomime, posing, and facial expressions, it's one of the studio's funniest cartoons—and also has heart.

Confronted by a kitten, bulldog Marc Anthony assumes his professional stance as a ferocious barking guard dog. The kitten, however, knows no fear and steps through the dog's gaping jaws to climb up onto its back, where it purrs and kneads the dog's fur before settling down for a nap.

Vanquished by all this cuteness, Marc Anthony decides to adopt the kitten. He brings it home, where the lady of the house (seen only from the waist down) warns him not to "bring one more thing into this house." Marc Anthony's efforts to conceal the kitten include pretending it's a wind-up toy and a powder puff. The lady decides to make cookies, the kitten falls into the flour, and the bawling and heartbroken dog watches her cut up the batter with cookie cutters. When the cookies are baked she offers him one—kitten shaped! In a scene of true animated pathos, he places the cookie on his back, just where the kitten once rode. But the kitten escaped the batter, and the cartoon ends happily. "You can keep that dear little kitten if you want to," says the lady of the house—as long as Marc Anthony agrees to take care of his pet.

CREDITS

A Merrie Melodies Cartoon

Directed by Chuck Jones

Story: Michael Maltese

Animation: Robert Gribbroek

Backgrounds: Philip DeGuard

Film editor: Treg Brown

Musical direction: Carl W. Stalling

One of a group of tremendously accomplished cartoons, *Feed the Kitty* contains a hilarious series of grimaces, pouts, strains, shudders, sweats, smirks, smiles, and angelic grins. It's a wonderful illustration of Jones's notion that an animator is "an actor with a pencil," and a convincing display of Jones's use of the emotive power of drawing. Presented with such screen charisma, it's difficult to remember that the entire spectacle reduces to a rippling of graphite on paper.

—*Steve Schneider*

That's All, Folks! The Art of Warner Bros. Animation

Bimbo's Initiation

PARAMOUNT, 1931

When sound films became popular in 1929, Max Fleischer dropped KoKo the Clown, star of his Inkwell Imps series, and began producing Talkartoons, starring a talking dog named Bimbo. Bimbo never achieved a forceful presence, and his appearance changed from cartoon to cartoon at the animator's whim. Betty Boop (also originally a dog) was discovered in *Dizzy Dishes*, a 1930 Bimbo cartoon, and she eventually took over as Fleischer's leading player. *Bimbo's Initiation* was one of the dog's last lead parts.

It's a strange cartoon. Bimbo falls down a manhole—smack into a surreal fraternity of characters with melted candles on their heads and two-by-fours behind their backs. "Wanna be a member?" they ask again and again, and each time Bimbo says no and suffers for it. Bimbo finally meets Betty Boop, who performs an erotic dance and asks him the usual question. Not surprisingly, Bimbo finally says yes.

The cartoon has been the subject of much analysis, particularly for its sexual overtones. "Bimbo's refusal [to become a member] is a refusal to recognize his sexual identity" wrote animation historian Mark Langer in *Film Comment*. "The fraternity members torture Bimbo, but he escapes. Betty Boop calls 'Come in, Big Boy,' and Bimbo responds to the sexual invitation, following Betty down a long vaginal corridor, as huge blades slash down . . . in expression of his castration fears." Whew! Perhaps that's why the Fleischers never developed Bimbo further.

CREDITS

Max Fleischer Presents a Talkartoon

Directed by Dave Fleischer

Bimbo's Initiation is a bad dream, wonderfully portrayed in an unusual cartoon that holds the cartoon format upside down and shakes it heartily. Especially well drawn and neatly painted for a Fleischer cartoon of this period, *Initiation* might as well be a catalog of the occult for all the symbology it employs. In this rare cartoon, many of the background scenes are as animated as the cartoon characters. When Bimbo runs along a moving floor or falls down a chute, a blending of layers takes places that defies the usual two-dimensional cartoon environment. Filled with enough dream imagery to keep an analyst working overtime, *Initiation* captures the distinct personality of the Fleischer style and also provides an emotional response that is the mark of great art.

—*Leslie Cabarga*

37

Bambi
meets
GODZILLA

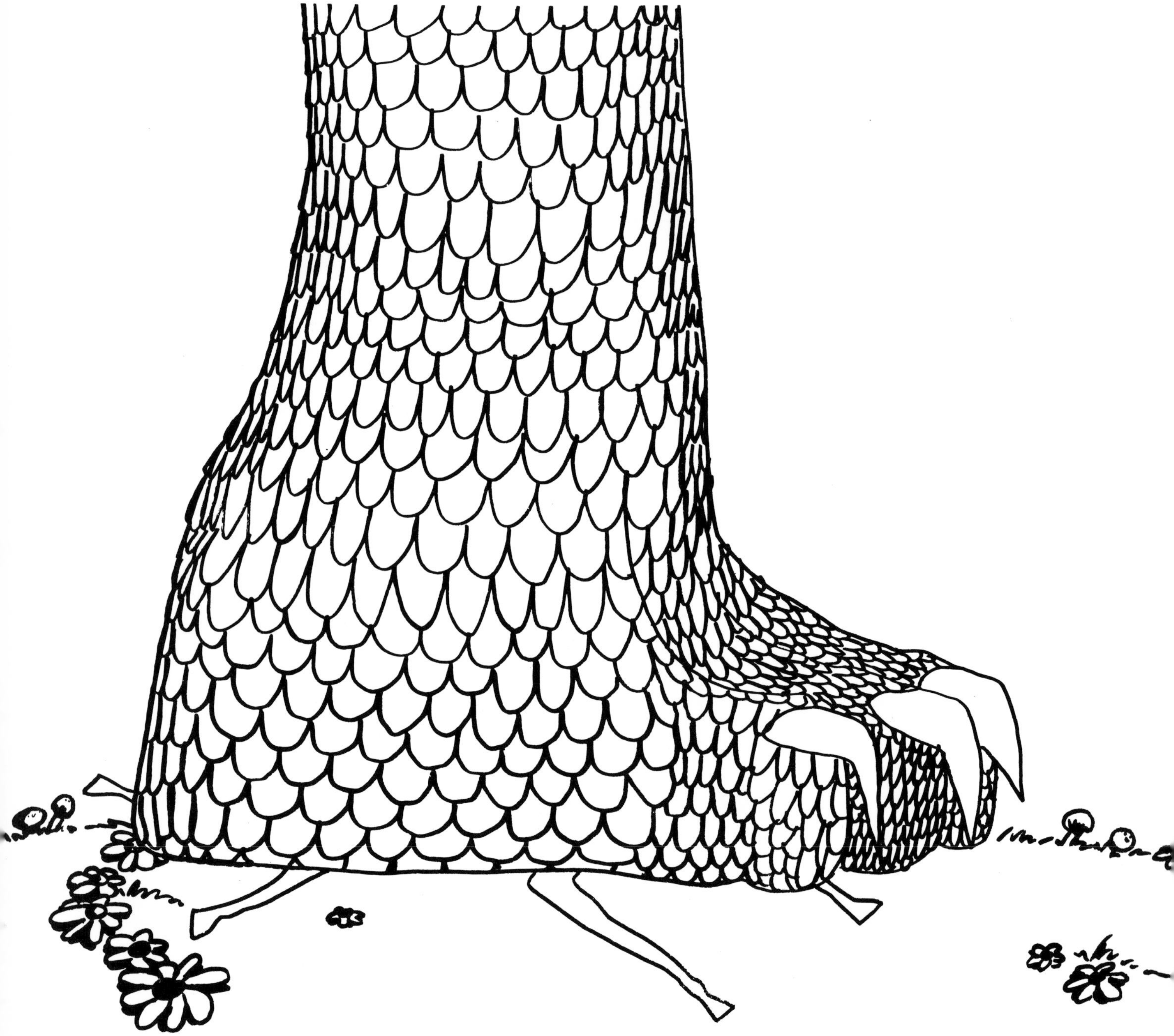

Bambi Meets Godzilla

AN INTERNATIONAL ROCKETSHIP CARTOON, 1969

CREDITS

Distributed by International Rocketship Limited

Written and directed by Marv Newland

Music: Gioacchino Rossini, from the *William Tell Overture*

Although simply drawn in black and white and only one and one-half minutes long, this cartoon has had audiences laughing for more than twenty-five years. The film opens on a line drawing of a young deer looking for food. During an extended opening credits sequence, we are told the film was written and choreographed by Marv Newland, that Bambi's wardrobe was produced by Marv Newland, and that Marv Newland himself was produced by Mr. and Mrs. Newland. At that point Godzilla's foot appears and crushes the harmless fawn. The End. The film delivers what its title promises, and the joke is on us—what more were we expecting?

Marv Newland made *Bambi Meets Godzilla* in a house he was renting from Adriana Caselotti, the voice of Disney's Snow White, while attending the innovative Art Center College of Design in Los Angeles in 1969, studying film. When he failed to get a crucial shot of sunrise for a live action short, he switched gears and made *Bambi Meets Godzilla* in the final two weeks of the semester; it was the first animated film produced at the Art Center. Newland went on to found International Rocketship Limited in Vancouver, B.C., a leading producer of quality animation.

Although essentially a one-note joke, the joke has many repercussions for the cartoon lover—which is why it holds up wonderfully after repeated viewings. The gentle, reassuring music and pronounced lack of action establishes Bambi as an icon rather than a character, not just a cute little deer in the forest, but the archetypal Disney creation with all the emotion baggage that comes with it—family values, children's entertainment, quality, good taste, the middle class world order. Then—serenity interruptus. The quick stomping on the deer by Godzilla—the pacing of the cartoon up to and including the end credits is masterful—is funny on several levels. One is that the title of the cartoon did not tip us off to the nature of its punchline, as it should have if the viewer had been thinking more carefully. After growing up on movies like *Abbott and Costello Meet Frankenstein*, the title formation itself suggests nothing more alarming than pratfalls or double takes, certainly not any actual carnage. The title has lulled us into a false sense of security and removed us from any concept of reality—the reality being that when a fawn and a monster meet, the monster wins, and quickly. Another level of the humor is that Godzilla, representative of jerky, stop-motion animation and low-class, sci-fi B movies, has just run roughshod over all that tasteful Disney stuff. On a third level, *Bambi Meets Godzilla* is a warning, both funny and profound, showing just where irreverence was heading in the area of pop culture and independent cartooning. Killing off Bambi carries the self-conscious, half-guilty joy of uttering your first curse word; now all the rules are broken, and anything is possible.

—*Jami Bernard*

"LITTLE RED RIDING RABBIT"
a MERRIE MELODIE
CARTOON
in
TECHNICOLOR
STARRING
BUGS BUNNY
A
LEON SCHLESINGER PRODUCTION
Warner Bros.

Little Red Riding Rabbit

WARNER BROS., 1941

Making fun of Mother Goose and the Brothers Grimm was standard fare at Warner Bros. in the 1940s. Bugs Bunny added to any fairy tale was a surefire hit, so during the war years the famous rabbit shared the screen with the Three Bears, Jack and his beanstalk, even Hiawatha. In this, one of Bugs's most memorable cartoons, he takes on Little Red Riding Hood and the Wolf.

These were the 1940s, so Red Riding Hood is a bobby-soxer and first appears singing "The Five O'Clock Whistle" (made popular by Glenn Miller in the 1940s). The obnoxious teenage Red is taking Bugs to Grandma's house; Granny herself is working the swing shift at Lockheed. The Wolf is in Granny's bed, and when Red arrives and screams "Hey, Grandma! I brought a little bunny rabbit for you—TA HAVE," the Wolf goes for Bugs. Red makes the usual comments about big nose and ears, and Bugs takes care of the Wolf. He imitates a stool pigeon, whistling and pointing to various rabbit hiding places (he's actually in one of them) and distracting the Wolf by making him sing "Put on Your Old Grey Bonnet." But it's Red who is truly annoying, and in the end Bugs locates her to where she'll be less bothersome and shares a carrot with the Wolf.

Little Red Riding Rabbit is in some ways the quintessential Warner Bros. cartoon. It's got everything we've come to expect in a Bugs Bunny classic: a wolf, stair and door gags, fairy-tale spoofs, a song-and-dance gag, and, of course, all the Warner Bros. cartoon sound effects. It's even got a "Silly, Isn't He?" sign. I tend to think about Warner Bros. cartoons in terms of their quotability—how many lines you can remember and repeat, and how many people you know who can quote from the cartoon, or recognize what you are quoting from it. *Little Red Riding Rabbit* has a high degree of quotability. All fans know the phrases "ta have" and "I'll do it, but I'll probably hate myself in the morning." I've found I can go anywhere and sing, "The five o'clock whistle is on the blink" and find someone will finish it with Red's chorus of "da-da-da-da-da-da."

—*Linda Simensky*

CREDITS

A Merrie Melodies Cartoon

Directed by I. Freleng

Story: Michael Maltese

Animation: Manuel Perez

Voices: Mel Blanc

Musical direction: Carl W. Stalling

Peace on Earth

MGM, 1939

Peace on Earth is unusual by any standard: a serious anti-war parable told in cartoon form through the eyes of a family of cute, fuzzy squirrels. It was hailed for its unique antiwar message and nominated for an Academy Award and a Nobel Peace Prize. Like most antiwar messages, it seems sadly dated and tinged with a certain futility. WWII was into its fourth month when this was released.

The story takes place at Christmas near a ruined church overlooking an old battlefield. A trio of squirrels sing "Hark! The Herald Angels Sing." Gran'pa squirrel's grandchildren ask him the meaning of "Peace on earth, good will to men," for they have never seen a man. Gran'pa tells them the story of huge monsters with flashing eyes and snouts (gas masks) carrying guns tipped with knives who argued and fought continuously until only two men were left, and they destroyed each other. The forest creatures build Peaceville from the discarded implements of war. The film ends with the words "Peace on Earth" superimposed on a bright sunrise.

Peace on Earth was produced by Hugh Harman, a former Disney collaborator who strove for a cinematic approach to animation. "We shouldn't have made it as a one-reeler, we should have made it about three to five reels," said Harman in a 1973 interview. "They tried to stop me from making it—it was too serious." But Harman believed in animation's potential beyond comedy and wanted his films to make audiences cry—and think.

The technique is arresting for it combines realism and fantasy in a way which throws overboard all traditions of cartoon craft. Scenes of marching soldiers, rumbling tanks, bombing airplanes, ruined cathedrals, and no-man's-land give the soft impression of aquatints or photogravures. The outlines of the cartoon characters also blend into the lovely backgrounds of the fantasy, and there is an easy flow of motion which emphasizes naturalness. Sound technique is borrowed from the realism of feature films, and with the exquisite musical score, creates a definitely emotional mood.

—*Parents magazine*

CREDITS

An MGM Cartoon

Produced by Hugh Harman

Story: Jack Cosgriff, Hugh Harman, Charles McGurl

Animation: Carl Urbano, Arnold Gillespie, Jerry Brewer, Irv Spence

Voices: Mel Blanc, Bernice Hansen, Sara Berner

40

VEGETARIANS

MEAT EATERS

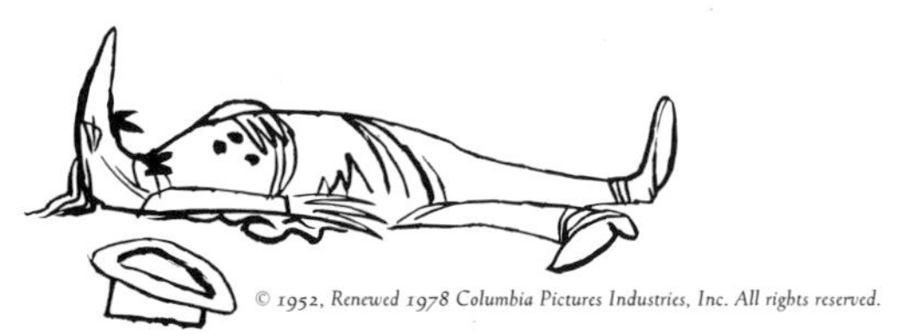

© 1952, Renewed 1978 Columbia Pictures Industries, Inc. All rights reserved.

Rooty Toot Toot

UPA, 1952

CREDITS

Columbia Pictures presents a

Jolly Frolics Cartoon

Directed by John Hubley

Executive producer: Stephen Bosustow

Lyrics: Alan Arch

Music: Phil Moore

Vocals: Annette Warren

Choreography: Olga Lunick

Written by: John Hubley, Bill Scott

Animation: Art Babbit, Pat Matthews, Tom McDonald, Grim Natwick

Color and design: Paul Julian

Production manager: Herb Klynn

Technical supervision: Sherm Glas

"Something completely new:" That's what reviewers thought of *Rooty Toot Toot* when it was first released, and the cause of their excitement is clear. UPA's creations caused sensations and expanded the boundaries of animation, in this case combining ballet, music, and animation to tell the tragic story of Frankie and Johnny. Bill Scott first suggested the cartoon; director John Hubley ran with it, hiring ballerina Olga Lunick to choreograph, animation dance specialist Art Babbit for key scenes, and Phil Moore (the first black musician to compose for the Hollywood studios) to arrange the music. The cartoon is a musical in which all the lines are sung, and its scene is a courtroom, where Frankie stands accused of shooting her man, Johnny, and is defended by white-suited Honest John. The bartender and singer Nellie Bly (who admits she was with Johnny, but only to rehearse) testify that Frankie "shot her man, rooty toot toot, right in the snoot." Honest John then addresses the jury, explaining the "true story": that a wildly ricocheting bullet shot by the jilted Johnny at Frankie killed the shooter instead. Honest John is so convinced of Frankie's innocence that he vows to marry her—but when Frankie sees Nellie dancing with Honest John, she grabs "Exhibit A"—the murder weapon—and shoots him rooty toot toot.

Twenty-five or thirty years ago we remembered seeing our first Disney picture. It was such a departure from the old junk that had been unloaded on the screen for years that his new technique became a sensation. We had the same feeling the other night . . . as a result of this *Rooty Toot Toot*. It's a gem, something completely new, wonderfully entertaining, with a beautiful background handling that brought applause from the big theater audience.

—*W. R. Wilkerson,*
The Hollywood Reporter, 1952

The Cat Concerto

MGM, 1947

MGM searched for a winning cartoon star throughout the 1930s. Disney had Donald Duck, Fleischer had Popeye, and Warner Bros. had Porky Pig, but MGM stood empty-handed. Hugh Harman and Rudolph Ising did their best with a series of beautiful Happy Harmonies, but their lethargic Barney Bear went nowhere. In 1937, MGM's cartoon division tried with the Captain and the Kids cartoons, but these were poorly received.

Thus, when animator William Hanna and storyman Joseph Barbera were teamed in 1939 to direct a cat-and-mouse cartoon, *Puss Gets the Boot*, nothing much was expected. When the film received critical and popular acclaim—and an Academy Award nomination—the pair was asked to continue their efforts. They did so for the next fifteen years, and Tom and Jerry became MGM's cartoon stars.

The Cat Concerto, one of the best of the Tom and Jerry series, begins with Tom Cat walking onstage, sitting at a piano, and beginning the *Hungarian Rhapsody No. 2*. His playing awakens Jerry Mouse, asleep within the instrument. Jerry climbs out of the piano, sees Tom at the keyboard, and begins "conducting" him, setting off a battle of wits between the pair. Their chase and struggle take place both inside and outside the piano, all the while Jerry continuing his performance, at one point forced to do so with his feet.

The Cat Concerto is the first cartoon in which Tom is treated as "human." Dressed in a tuxedo, he performs at the piano for—the viewer assumes—a human audience. Tom's piano playing is remarkably realistic, modeled on performances of musician Scott Bradley. *The Cat Concerto* won an Academy Award for Best Animated Short Subject.

CREDITS

An MGM Tom and Jerry Cartoon

Directed by William Hanna and Joseph Barbera

Producer: Fred Quimby

Animation: Kenneth Muse, Ed Barge, Irven Spence

Backgrounds: Bob Gentle

Editing: Fred McAlpin

Photography: Jack Stevens

Music: Scott Bradley

42

HANNA–BARBERA

Born in Melrose, New Mexico, in 1911, William Hanna studied journalism and engineering in college. He changed course when he entered the animation industry as a cel washer and office assistant at Harman and Ising's studio in 1931. He worked his way up to director on MGM's The Captain and the Kids cartoons in 1937.

Joseph Barbera, born in New York City in 1905, studied accounting and after graduation went to work for the Irving Trust Company. Barbera, with his knack for drawing, contributed cartoons to various magazines until he finally decided to quit banking and become a cartoonist full time. After beginning his animation career at New York's Van Buren studio, and later joining Terrytoons, Barbera moved to the West coast in 1937 and joined MGM as a storyman.

"I started there the same day Joe did," recalls Hanna. "I think we gravitated together." Barbera also recalls the now-historic pairing. "Within the first two years we finally ended up in the same room. I suggested 'Why don't we do a picture on our own?'; [producer Fred] Quimby was so desperate he didn't stop us."

Quimby was content to let each MGM cartoon have its own story and characters, unlike every other studio, where star characters were being developed. Quimby once said, "I don't want to put all our eggs in one basket," in reference to the appealing cat and mouse characters Hanna and Barbera came up with in their first film. But when theater owners demanded more Tom and Jerry cartoons, within a year Hanna and Barbera were assigned to do nothing else for the next sixteen years. The series won seven Academy Awards for MGM, a remarkable achievement denoting the consistent level of high quality.

The MGM Tom and Jerry cartoons, however, are only one part of an amazing career. When MGM closed its cartoon department in 1957, Hanna and Barbera were suddenly thrust into a world that no longer required their unique talents. They quickly created a low-budget pilot for television, "Ruff and Reddy," and sold it to Columbia Pictures (Screen Gems). They went from lavish $45,000 budgets to $3,000 for five minutes of animation; from pantomime comedy to dialogue-heavy pictures; from complex full animation to limited movements and sparse settings.

But they tapped a medium hungry for their kind of entertainment. "Ruff and Reddy" was followed by Huckleberry Hound, Yogi Bear, Quick Draw McGraw, the Flintstones, the Jetsons, and Jonny Quest. Hanna-Barbera became the brand name for animation in the TV generation. After many years of "putting all their eggs in one basket," this team unleashed more cartoon star characters and made more diverse animation than any other American studio.

Of all the Hollywood cartoon series, the Tom and Jerry cycle got the most out of the least, wringing over one hundred generally excellent episodes out of the minute, three-word plot description: Cat chases mouse. While the formula itself remained the same, different aspects of the equation were occasionally altered to distinguish the individual one-reelers from each other, which usually entailed the setting or the introduction of a character. In *The Cat Concerto*, the extra element is the music (Liszt's *Hungarian Rhapsody No. 2*), which functions as the dominating element of both the background setting and the foreground action. The two protagonists revel in the new opportunities for comic violence found in the mechanisms of the music-making process—parodying not only the hoity-toity manner of the concert virtuoso but the hammers and strings of the piano itself.

—*Will Friedwald*

One of the classic screwball cartoons of the 1940s, *The Barber of Seville* was James Culhane's first Woody Woodpecker cartoon as new director of the Walter Lantz studio. Culhane had read *Film Technique*, a book by Russian director V. I. Pudovkin, and applied the theories to this cartoon, adding scenes and speeding up the pace with rapid cutting.

As the cartoon begins, Woody Woodpecker admires the hairstyles displayed in the window of the Seville Barber Shop (Tony Figaro, proprietor) and decides to be patriotic and get a Victory Haircut. ("How can I lose with a victory?") Finding a note reading "Gone to take my physical. Back soon," Woody realizes Tony is out for the duration and fools around in front of the mirror. A Native American mistakes Woody for the barber; Woody puts hot towels over his customer's headdress, overheating him so much that bread toasts in his mouth and the headdress shrinks, then uses the springlike barber chair to catapult his customer out of the shop and onto the front of a cigar store.

Next, a construction worker asks for "the whole works." Woody removes his hard hat with a blowtorch and begins singing "Largo el Factorum" from *The Barber of Seville* as he lathers all exposed parts, including the worker's shoes. Swinging the razor while singing a high-speed version of "Figaro," Woody raises the chair and smashes his customer's head against the ceiling. He completes the hair-raising haircut in record time. The woodpecker heckles his client outside, and the irate customer throws him through the window back into the shop. Woody gets bopped with a supply of shaving mugs and ends up stuck inside the revolving barber pole.

Dash is what Woody did, it's what he had, it's what he was—a hyphen between the audience and the screen, at first a Technicolor shock wave, here a Technicolor synapse between shadow and substance, between ourselves and our more outrageous fantasies. His impossible actions are still a cartoonist's convenience, but in Culhane's hands Woody destroys himself on one level only to re-create himself on another. We can still ask the logical questions, but rather than just evade them, Woody in *The Barber of Seville* is transcending them, making himself an understandable personality, if never quite an explicable one, and one of the greatest cartoon characters of Hollywood animation's golden age, even if he was all cartoon and no character.

—Joe Adamson

43

The Barber of Seville

WALTER LANTZ, 1944

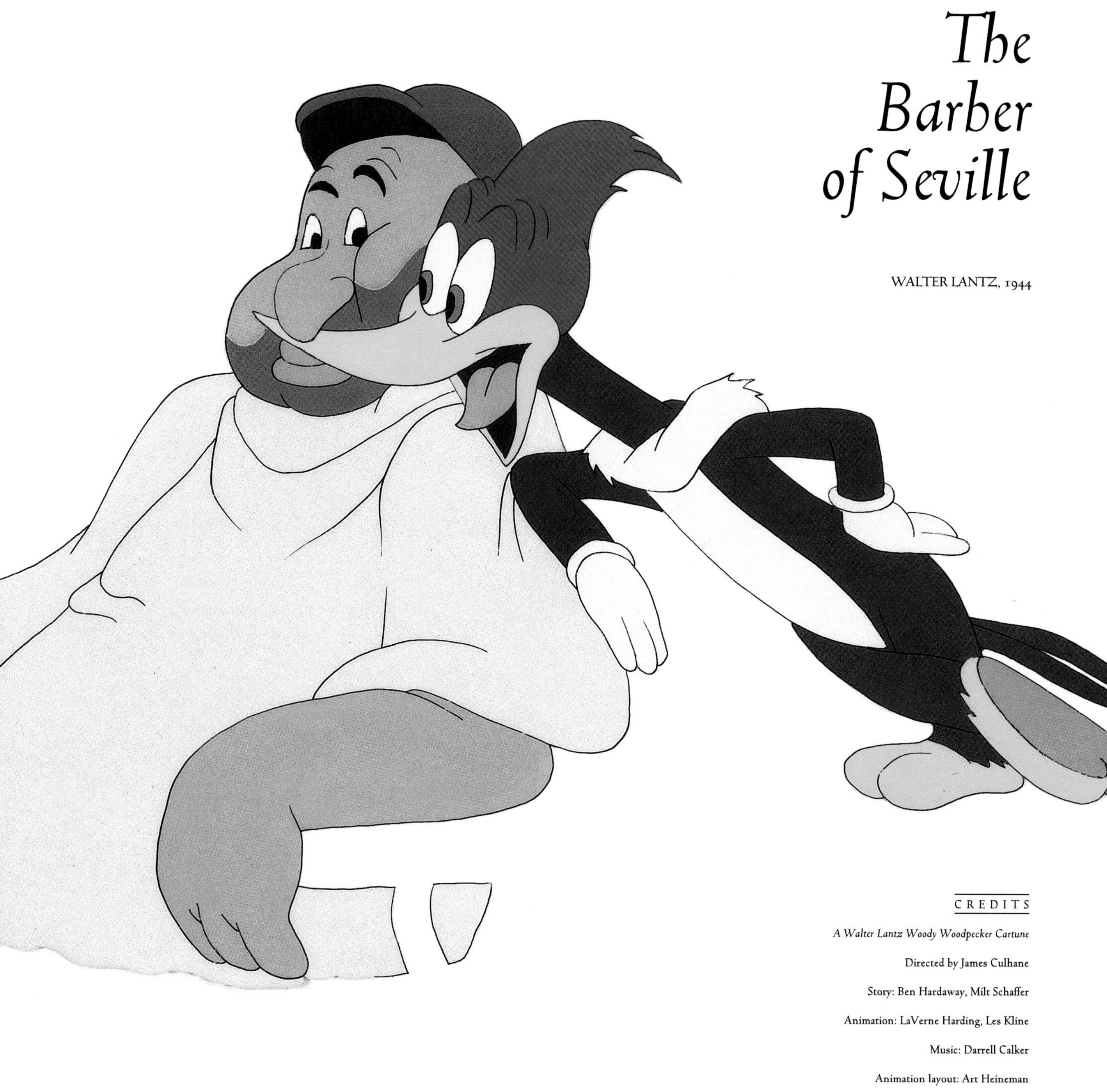

CREDITS

A Walter Lantz Woody Woodpecker Cartune

Directed by James Culhane

Story: Ben Hardaway, Milt Schaffer

Animation: LaVerne Harding, Les Kline

Music: Darrell Calker

Animation layout: Art Heineman

Backgrounds: Philip DeGuard

Frederic Back, born in Saarbrücken, Germany, in 1924, has lived in Montreal, Canada, since 1948. A man of many talents, he worked on several educational television series for Radio-Canada during the 1950s and 1960s and created stained-glass artwork for the Place-des-arts subway station in Montreal in 1967. In 1968 he joined the CBC French Network's animation section. His first animated film, a collaboration with Graeme Ross, was *Abracadabra* (1970), which uses cut-outs to tell the story of a little girl and her friends who rescue the sun from an evil magician. His other films include *Illusion?* (1975); *All Nothing* (1979), his first film using the technique of colored pencil on frosted acetate; and *Crac!* (1981), an Academy Award-winning film about a century of change told from the point of view of the family rocking chair. *The Man Who Planted Trees* won Back his second Academy Award.

The Man Who Planted Trees

SOCIETE RADIO-CANADA, 1987

CREDITS

A Societe Radio-Canada Production

Directed and produced by Frederic Back

Executive producer: Hubert Tison

Story: Jean Giono

Scenario and animation: Frederick Back

Assistant: Lina Gagnon

Music: Normand Roger

Narrator: Phillippe Noiret (French version)

Narrator: Christopher Plummer (English version)

When filmmaker Frederic Back first encountered the story of Elzeard Bouffier in a magazine in the early 1970s, he knew he had much to learn before undertaking a film about him. When he felt prepared, he devoted five years to the project, and the result, *The Man Who Planted Trees*, is a testament to the indomitable spirits of both men. It is also a rare work, for its style—a flowing wash of pencil sketches with "real" sounds and a narrator—seems eminently suitable to its subject.

The story begins with a young man hiking through barren and windy terrain in the French Alps. He encounters a shepherd who offers him water, a meal, and lodging for the night. That night, he observes the shepherd counting acorns. He stops when he has one hundred. Intrigued, the young man follows the shepherd the next day and watches as he plants the acorns. This was Elzeard Bouffier, and when the young man met him he was fifty-five and had been planting acorns for three years. "It was his opinion that the land was dying for lack of trees, and he had resolved to remedy the state of affairs." He planted and nurtured a forest of thousands of oak trees as well as beech.

Years later, after WWI, the man returns to the site. The first plantings are now ten years old and impressive. His fascination with the man leads him to return time and again, and he sees the windswept, forsaken landscape transformed into green fields, thriving villages, and prosperous farmland, the result of Bouffier's forest. He observes that "Men could be as effective as God in tasks other than destruction." In 1935 Bouffier's "natural forest" was placed under government protection. Bouffier died in 1947 at the age of eighty-nine. As the narrator states, "A man's destiny can be truly wonderful."

The Man Who Planted Trees represents the fusion of art and belief into a seamless masterpiece. The cartoon opens with an image of a lonely traveler wandering in a world of grays and browns; the desolate earth can support only rudimentary forms of life. But as Bouffier works his ecological miracle, the animation, music, and narration blossom with the land. By the end of the film, the screen is filled with the vibrant colors of an impressionist canvas. *The Man Who Planted Trees* represents the culmination of Back's righteous posturing that spoils many "message" films. Understated and imbued with profound dignity, *The Man Who Planted Trees* shines as an example of the art of animation in the truest sense of the term.

—*Charles Solomon*

Book Revue

WARNER BROS., 1946

Book and magazine covers came to life so often during the 1930s that the device is considered a cartoon genre—which this masterpiece both mocks and thoroughly outdoes. Modern audiences may not understand all the book references and celebrity caricatures, but this cartoon remains a marvel of comic timing and funny animation.

In a bookstore at midnight, a *Young Man with a Horn* (Harry James) comes alive to perform a trumpet solo; *The Whistler* and *The Sea Wolf* leer at *Cherokee Strip*; *The Complete Works of Shakespeare* pops a spring; *Henry the Eighth* runs home to *The Aldrich Family*; *The Voice in the Wilderness* (Frank Sinatra) drives the *Little Women* crazy; also falling for him are *Freckles*, *The Girls' Dormitory*, *Lady in the Dark*, *Whistler's Mother*, and *Mother Goose*. *Brass* (Tommy Dorsey), *Drums Along the Mohawk* (Gene Krupa), *The Pie-Eyed Piper* (Benny Goodman), and the *Arkansas Traveler* have a jam session. Their music bothers Daffy Duck, who steps off the cover of *The Looney Tunes and Merrie Melodies Comics* to complain. He gets a zoot suit and wig out of the *Saratoga Trunk*, stands in front of *Danny Boy*, and imitates Danny Kaye singing "Saratoga in the Morning" with a Russian accent. He then gets into a lively replay of *Little Red Riding Hood*, is chased on pogo sticks in *Hopalong Cassidy* to *Uncle Tom's Cabin*, and finally *The Petrified Forest*. The *Police Gazette* calls *The Long Arm of the Law* to bring the wolf before *The Judge*. Sentenced to *Life*, the wolf manages to *Escape*, but he trips on Jimmy Durante's *So Big* nose and slides along *Skid Row* right into Dante's *Inferno*. The book characters dance a celebratory jitterbug, to which the wolf responds, "Stop that dancing up there, you sillies."

TWO TOP TALENTS

Rod Scribner's animated reaction of Daffy to the Big Bad Wolf—turning into a giant eyeball for six frames—is one of the classic moments in cartoon history. Mel Blanc deserved an award for his performance of Daffy frantically warning Little Red Riding Hood of the Wolf. Warren Foster wrote the Danny Kaye-esque skat song sung in that scene. It is worth noting that Danny Kaye later recorded one of Foster's original songs, the hit tune "I Tawt I Taw A Puddy-Tat" (cowritten by Alan Foster and Billy May) for a children's album.

CREDITS

A Looney Tunes Cartoon

Directed by Robert Clampett

Story: Warren Foster

Animation: Robert McKimson, Rod Scribner, Manny Gould, C. Melendez

Layouts and backgrounds: Thomas McKimson, Cornett Wood

Voices: Mel Blanc

Musical direction: Carl W. Stalling

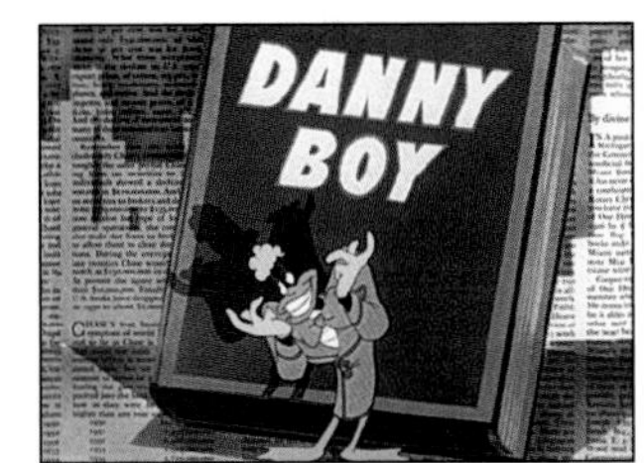
DANNY
BOY

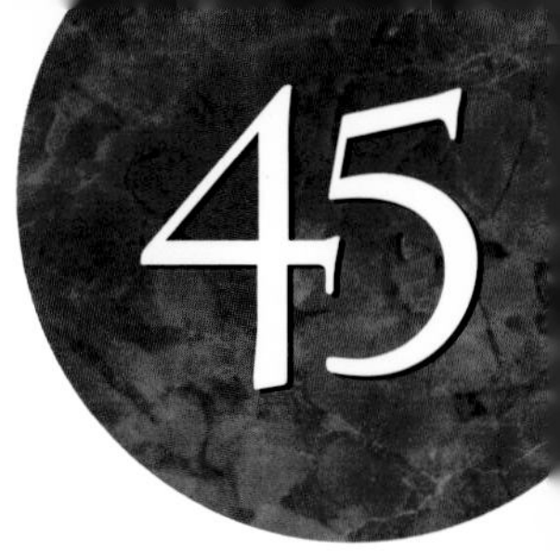
45

MERRIE MELODIES
LOONEY TUNES
COMICS

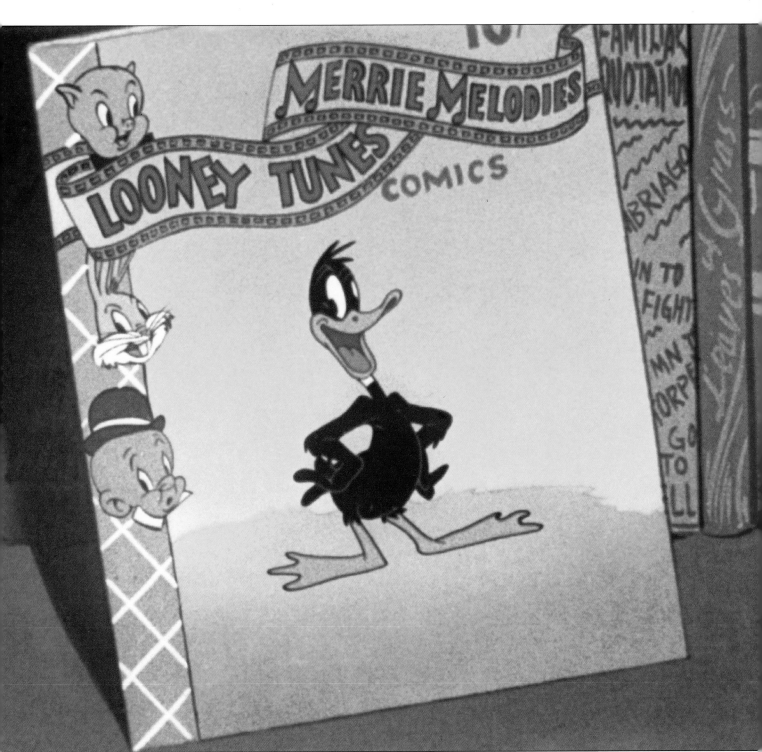

The apotheosis of the early Warner Bros. cartoons: Warner's quintessential 1930s story line—book covers coming to life—the technical brilliance and explosive exuberance that defined the studio in the 1940s, supplanted by a performance by Daffy Duck that is, well, one for the books. Director Bob Clampett brings us astonishment after astonishment in this breathless compendium of 1940s popular culture, appropriating and transforming fragments of America's imaginative landscape with a verve and deftness that remain breathtaking—despite the fact that this cartoon was completed nearly 50 years ago and that its cascading cross-cultural references necessarily pack less punch than they did at the time of the film's release. Filled with spectacularly florid, even baroque, animation (although the production seems to have run out of money, or something, for the concluding dance), the film all but bursts at the seams; yet thanks to Clamplett's remarkably disciplined use of excess, the cartoon's anarchic energy feels anchored, earned, and utterly credible. From this comes its power to engage us deeply.

And there is more: Clampett's great gift for conjuring phantasmagorias has been widely admired, but *Book Revue* also shows the director's virtuoso ability to evoke character. When Daffy Duck emerges from his *Looney Tunes* comic book, the cartoon is immediately taken to another level: The duck virtually seizes the screen, and instantly becomes the film's center of gravity; we feel his presence as something far stronger than even all the churning activity that surrounds him. In a world of frenetically moving graphics, Daffy is the graphic that moves us.

When all this is melded to the cartoon's immense humor, stunning staging, gloriously cartoony manipulation of the film's medium, and almost savage recklessness, the result is a summation of what the Golden Age of Animation has to offer us. If any one animated short can be considered a work of genius, *Book Revue* is it.

—*Steve Schneider*

BOB CLAMPETT

Bob Clampett (1913–1984) was one of the pioneers in American animation. While still in his teens, he helped design the first Mickey Mouse doll; shortly thereafter, he joined the Harman–Ising studios and animated scenes for the very first Merrie Melodies cartoon, *Lady, Play Your Mandolin*. In 1935, Clampett was assigned animator and key gagman to director Tex Avery and his team at "Termite Terrace." Avery and Clampett led the studio in a new direction, displaying a wild, irreverent humor that became known as the Warner style. Clampett was promoted to director in 1937, and for the next nine years directed some of the funniest, wildest, and most memorable cartoons in animation history (five of them appear in this book: *Porky in Wackyland*, *The Great Piggy Bank Robbery*, *Coal Black and de Sebben Dwarfs*, *Book Revue*, and *Corny Concerto*).

Clampett was also instrumental in the creation and development of Porky Pig, Daffy Duck, and Bugs Bunny. He introduced Tweety Bird, patterned on his own nude baby picture. He left Warner in 1946, opened his own studio, and created the popular Beany and Cecil.

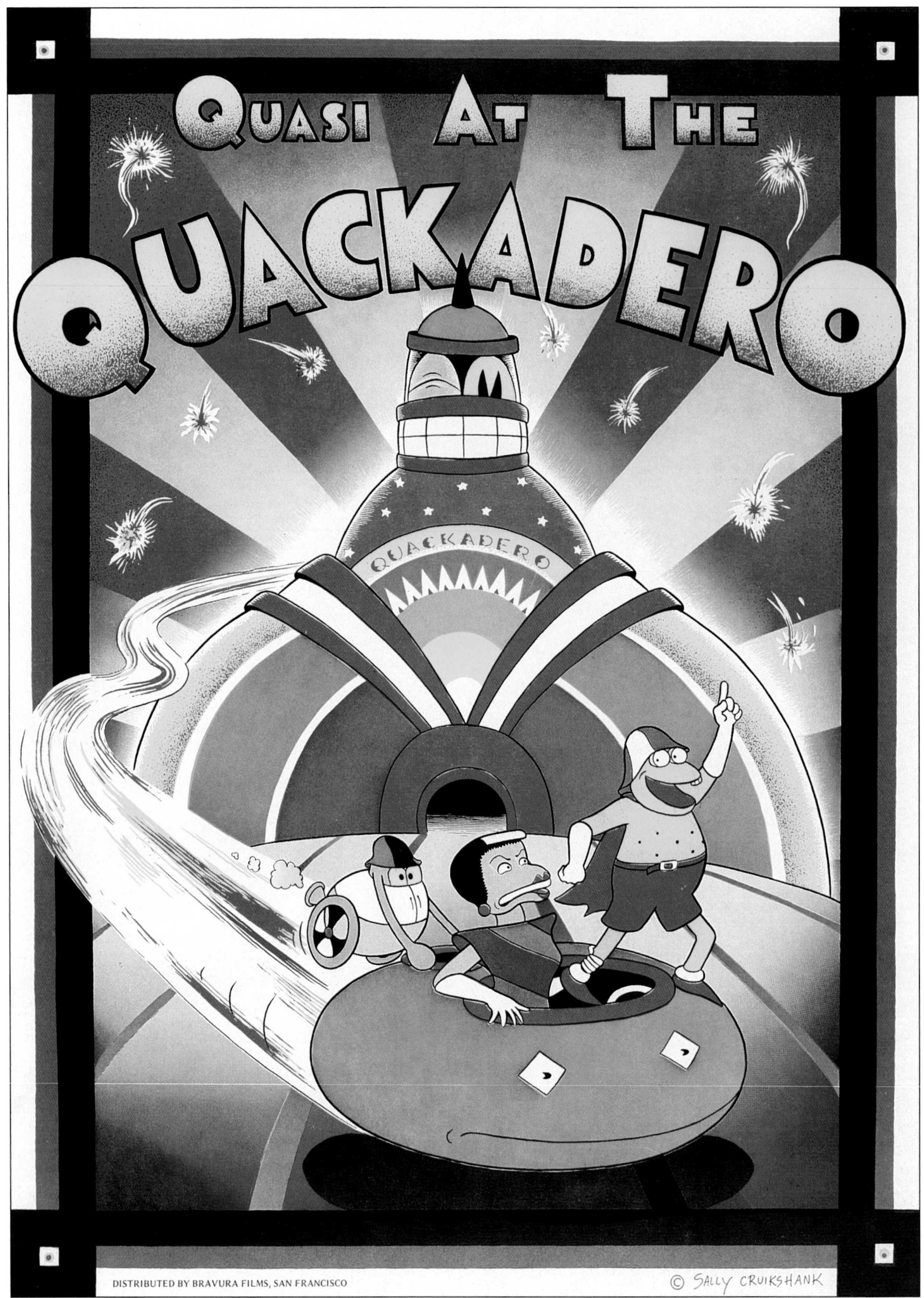
QUASI AT THE
QUACKADERO
QUACKADERO
DISTRIBUTED BY BRAVURA FILMS, SAN FRANCISCO
© SALLY CRUIKSHANK

Quasi at the Quackadero

CRUIKSHANK, 1975

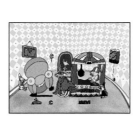

I love to look at pictures of people working," remarks Quasi, lying in bed, eating chocolate cake, and watching TV. Anita arrives with her wheeled friend Rollo to remind him of their trip to the Quackadero, a psychedelic amusement park whose attractions include the "Hall of Time Mirrors—See yourself at every age," where Quasi, Anita, and Rollo see themselves as youngsters and as skeletons; "Roll Back Time," a crank machine that turns skyscrapers into grassy hills; "Think-O-Blink," which paints pictures of your thoughts (Quasi's are shocking); and "See Last Night's Dream Today," which reveals an animated stream of consciousness. After lunch at Porky's Diner they visit "9 Lives 2 Live," where Quasi is rooked into seeing his former lives. Finally they visit the "Time Holes," which offer peeks at the past. Here Anita and Rollo rid themselves of Quasi: She drops a chocolate cake over a railing, and with a helpful push from rolling Rollo, Quasi tumbles back in time. Two guards later notice a new addition to the prehistoric Time Hole: Quasi being chased by a reptile.

Sally Cruikshank began making cartoons while in college and joined San Francisco's Snazelle Films in 1972. She wrote, designed, directed, and animated *Quasi at the Quackadero* on her own, without the help of a large, experienced studio. Its style is a mixture of funky 1930s Van Beuren cartoons and 1960s R. Crumb comics with a dash of Sam Flax, and with its rolling, folding perspective and soundtrack of sighs, it enthralls some viewers and leaves others cold—the traits of a true "cult classic."

Anything can happen in Sally Cruikshank's Quackadero. Like Bob Clampett's *Porky in Wackyland*, her film is full of strange creatures: A house talks, a clock has arms and legs that move, objects bound back and forth in time—and all to a fine soundtrack. As J. Hoberman put it, "Sally Cruikshank has all but single-handedly resurrected the Depression-era 'funny animal' cartoon—as authentic an American idiom as jug band music or situation comedy—and made it totally her own."

—*Karl Cohen*

CREDITS

A Cartoon by Sally Cruikshank

Directed by Sally Cruikshank

Music: Bob Armstrong, Al Dodge

Ink and paint: Katheryn Lenthan

Special art assistant: Kim Deitch

Sound engineer: Steve Halbert

Special thanks to: E. E. Gregg Snazelle, Rose S. Cruikshank, Diana Pellegrini

INDEPENDENT ANIMATION

A handful of the fifty cartoons in this volume, such as *Quasi at the Quackadero* and *Bambi Meets Godzilla*, are representative of the work of independent animators. While the traditional Hollywood studios are factories of popular animation, independent filmmakers have the unique opportunity to experiment and enjoy a freedom in style, concepts, and techniques that often influence the artform and expand its potential.

Solo artists have been making their films independently since animation began (in fact, Winsor McCay could be considered the father of independent animation). Usually working alone, sometimes taking years to produce a short film, the works of independent animators are celebrated in touring animation festivals such as in Annecy, France, and Ottawa, Canada. Lotte Reiniger, Oskar Fischinger, Norman McLaren, John and Faith Hubley, George Griffin, Carolyn Leaf, and Bill Plympton are just a few of the animators whose independent works have influenced the entire field.

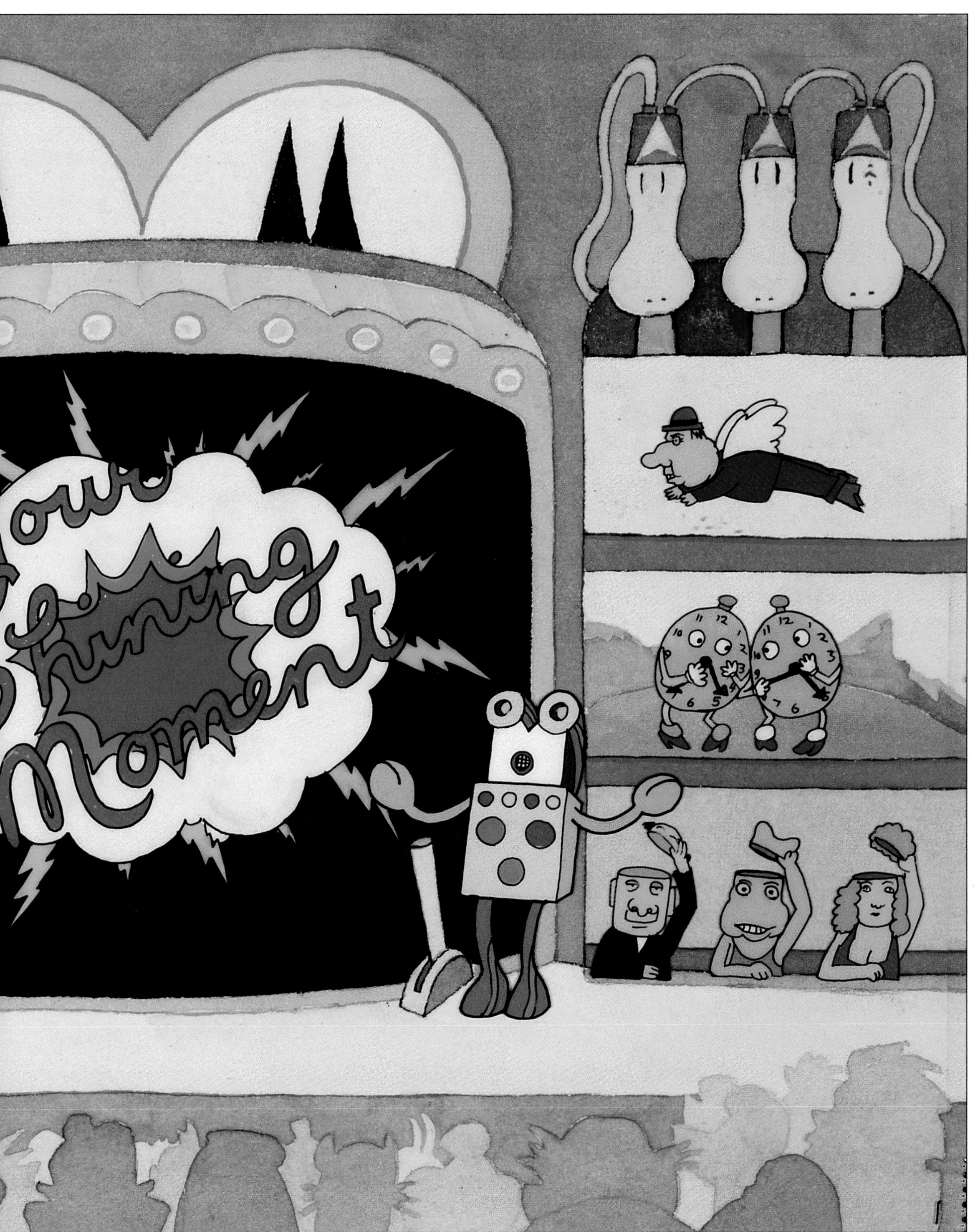
our
hining
Moment

Corny Concerto

MERRIE MELODIES, 1943

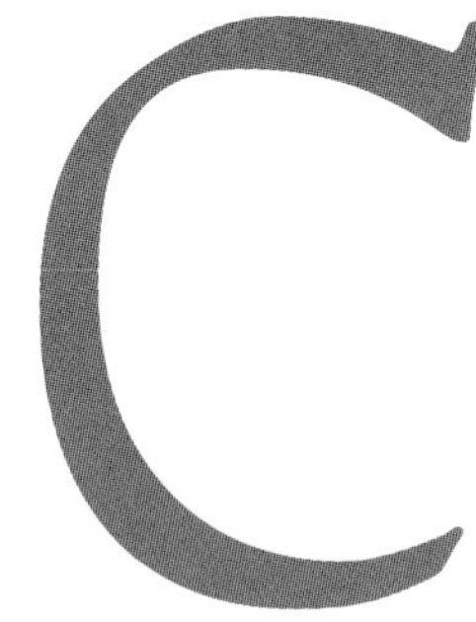

Corny-Gee Hall," with Elmer Fudd as master of ceremonies, is the setting for an affectionate but scathing send-up of Disney's *Fantasia*.

Elmer first introduces a "A Tale of the Vienna Woods," praising the "whispering whythym of the woodwinds, as it wolls awound and awound . . . and it comes out here!" The tale in the wood concerns Porky and his dog (a pointer) out hunting rabbit. They encounter Bugs, who reminds the dog, "It ain't polite to point." Porky chases Bugs, but an angry squirrel gets his gun and shoots them. The pig, dog, and rabbit all fall to the ground, Bugs pretending to be shot. Bugs eventually ties up Porky and his dog and pirouettes into the horizon.

The next piece is the "Blue Danube," which recounts the tale of an ugly duckling who tries to join a family of swans. A vulture kidnaps the swans but reject the duck as 4-F. The black duck uses "cartoon license" to rescue the family and does away with the vulture.

Corny Concerto is a classic unto itself, but Bob Clampett wasn't completely satisfied with it. "It was a considerable departure, an experiment, for me to animate Bugs Bunny, Porky Pig, and our characters in synchronization with such classical compositions. Imagine mixing 'Eh, what's up, Doc?' with Strauss. But when I first saw the rough cut with the music track I knew I could have made it beautiful, almost perfect, by making some minor adjustments in the timing . . . "

CREDITS

A Merrie Melodies Cartoon

Directed by Robert Clampett

Story: Frank Tashlin

Animation: Robert McKimson

Musical direction: Carl W. Stalling

Other directors imitated or made fun of the Disney cartoons; only Bob Clampett paid them homage, acknowledging a debt even as he asserted his own identity. *Corny Concerto* makes a deep and genuinely respectful bow to *Fantasia*—but with a sly grin on its face.

—*Mike Barrier*

47

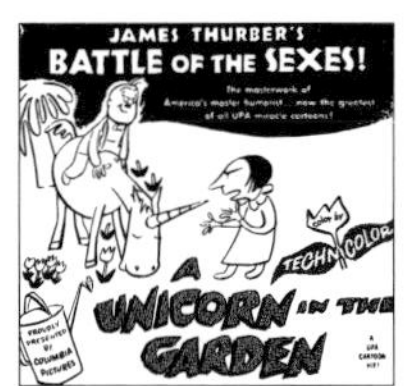

JAMES THURBER'S
BATTLE OF THE SEXES!
TECHNICOLOR
A UNICORN IN THE GARDEN
PROUDLY PRESENTED BY COLUMBIA PICTURES

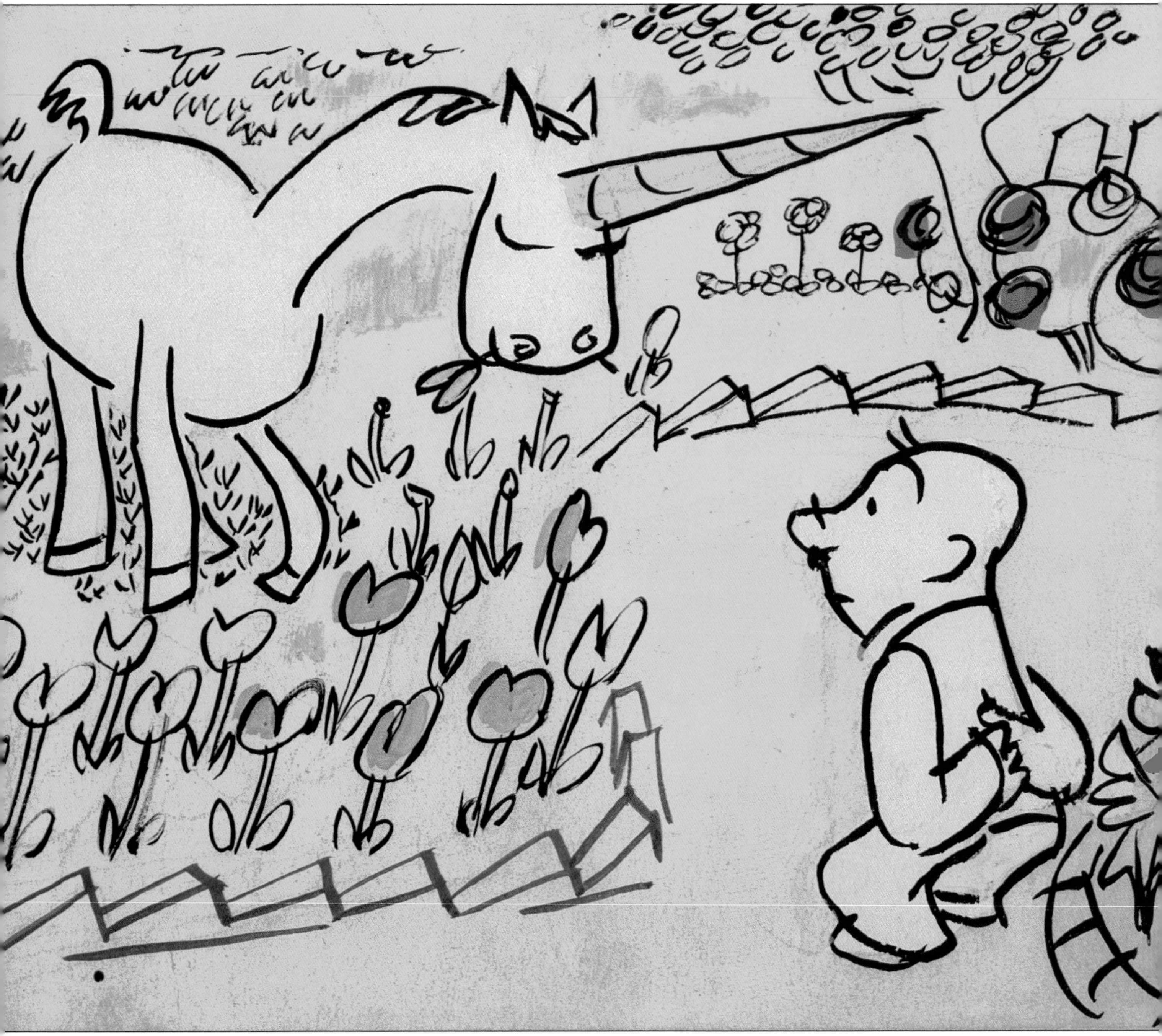

48

A Unicorn in the Garden

UPA, 1953

To audiences accustomed to Donald Duck or Bugs Bunny as the stars of animated shorts, it must have been startling to see the characters of James Thurber coming to life. Since that time, the idea of adapting illustrators' work has become a familiar one, but when UPA tried it, it was revolutionary. The studio's second challenge was to retain the spirit and tone of Thurber's work. That they succeeded is now a fact of animation history, and one of the many feathers in their collective cap.

—*Leonard Maltin*

A *Unicorn in the Garden*, an adaptation of humorist James Thurber's short story, begins, "Once upon a sunny morning" with a hen-pecked husband eating breakfast. Spotting a unicorn eating roses in his backyard, he rushes to tell his sleeping wife the news. She dismisses him curtly with "A unicorn is a mythical beast."

The man goes into the garden for a closer look at the cute and affectionate beast. He feeds it a lily and then awakens his wife again to tell her, but she rudely replies, "You are a booby, and I am going to have you put in the booby hatch!"

The man returns to the garden but finds the unicorn gone. Meanwhile, his wife calls the police and a psychiatrist, and suggests a straitjacket be called for. When they arrive she announces, "My husband saw a unicorn this morning." The doctor and police exchange glances and put the straitjacket on her. As they take her away, the doctor asks the husband if he told his wife about seeing a unicorn. He replies, "Of course not. A unicorn is a mythical beast."

The films ends with a moral: "Don't count your boobies until they're hatched." Stephen Bosustow had long wanted to produce a feature film based on Thurber's work, but when funding for such an erudite project proved difficult he asked director William Hurtz to adapt a Thurber subject as a short. Hurtz chose "A Unicorn in the Garden" because it featured human characters, and UPA was trying to avoid the animal subjects traditional to Hollywood cartoons.

The film continued UPA's critically acclaimed series, but Bosustow was reportedly disappointed. He refused to enter it for Academy Award consideration and reluctantly changed his feature-film plans for a more commercial vehicle for Mr. Magoo.

To animate Thurber's crude line-drawing style faithfully, William Hurtz "studied every drawing he ever did. Using color bothered me at first, but I thought if he ever got around to it he probably would do it this way—as long as it was strongly linear."

CREDITS

A Columbia Pictures Cartoon

Directed by William T. Hurtz

Story: James Thurber

Design: Robert Dranko

Animation: Phil Monroe, Rudy Larriva, Tom McDonald

Backgrounds: Robert Dranko

Music: David Raskin

Production manager: Herbert Klynn

The Dover Boys

WARNER BROS., 1942

The full on-screen title of this cartoon is *The Dover Boys at Pimento University; or The Rivals of Roquefort Hall*. It is a parody of the 1890s dime-store novel melodramas, which was nothing new in cartoons, but it's also the film with which Chuck Jones began taking artistic risks and which stands as a watershed in animation history. Until this film, Hollywood animators—including Jones—tried to achieve realism with their characters. *The Dover Boys* was devised with stylized settings and intentionally unrealistic movements.

The story takes place at Pimento University, also known as Pimento U., or simply "Good Old P. U." The most popular students are the Dover Boys—a spoof of the Rover Boys dime-store novels—Tom, Dick, and Larry, exaggerated human caricatures who play hide and seek with Dainty Dora Standpipe, who rolls along the screen as if on wheels. The bullying cad Dan Backslide kidnaps her and takes her to his mountain cabin hideout. True to form, the Dover Boys rescue her, but she prefers the company of an oddly-dressed oldtimer who keeps popping up unexpectedly.

Chuck Jones claims that he almost got fired from Warner Bros. for this cartoon. "They hated it, and if they hadn't been block-booking theaters, they would have withheld it and thrown me out." But the new style caught on, and after *The Dover Boys*, Warner cartoons—and those of the other studios—became faster and funnier.

The *Dover Boys* is a major milestone, the first cartoon to contain such sly, intelligent humor combined with highly stylized human characters and equally stylized movements. (For the most part, this style was not explored further for several years, until the advent of UPA in 1948, and the series of Ward Kimball cartoons at Disney in 1953.) Even a half-century later, *The Dover Boys* stands as one of the most elegant examples of the principle that the less literal the character design, the more innovative the animation can be without losing believability.

—*Milt Gray*

These scenes from *The Dover Boys* are three actual successive frames from the film, demonstrating the innovative use of limited animation throughout the picture. Characters pop from pose to pose with a frame of "smear" animation between them.

CREDITS

A Merrie Melodies Cartoon

Directed by Charles M. Jones

Story: Ted Pierce

Animation: Robert Cannon

Musical direction: Carl W. Stalling

49

SNOOKER
101

I'LL HAVE TO SACRIFICE MY ART AND GO IN THE MOVIES,

Felix in Hollywood

M. J. WINKLER, 1923

CREDITS

M. J. Winkler Presents a Pat Sullivan Comic

Animation: Otto Messmer

The earliest ancestors of today's cartoon characters moved across a silent screen; most became extinct before the advent of sound. The lineage of such sapient creatures as Mickey Mouse and Bugs Bunny leads to a cat named Felix—the first cartoon star to originate within the medium itself. Most of his contemporaries were either based on popular comic strips (Krazy Kat, Mutt and Jeff) or were designed with little individuality (KoKo the Clown, Farmer Alfalfa). Felix was different: A thinker, he solved problems with solutions appropriate to his environment—the animated world ruled by lunacy. Within a few years of his appearance (1919), Felix was as popular as Charlie Chaplin and Buster Keaton.

Felix reached the apex of his popularity in 1923, the year of *Felix in Hollywood* (he played the pet of an out-of-work actor). The actor sends him out to find money for a trip to Hollywood. Felix discovers a bankrupt shoe store, sells out the shop, and hands his owner $500. In Hollywood, Felix ditches the actor to pursue his own career at Static Studio, where he asks the boss (a caricature of censor Will Hays) for a job and demonstrates his acting, emoting joy and sorrow. Felix hears a cry for help and finds Douglas Fairbanks being attacked by giant mosquitoes. Swiping a gun from William S. Hart, Felix shoots two of them, and his duel with the third delights Cecil B. DeMille, who signs him to a contract.

Felix was the first cartoon character licensed for use on merchandise, including dolls, baby oil, and even his own brand of cigars. More than seventy years later, he's still one of America's best-known cats.

Feisty Felix barges into a Hollywood studio and mingles with caricatures of the gods and goddesses of the human screen. In a particularly memorable encounter— after the cat performs an astonishingly accurate impression of Charlie Chaplin's walk—Felix is accused by the Little Tramp himself of "stealing my stuff!" This brief sequence was an in-joke inserted by Otto Messmer, Felix's creator and chief animator, who, in 1916, studied Chaplin's pantomime and facial expressions for an animated series of Chaplin films produced by Pat Sullivan. This thorough research influenced the personality and movements of Felix the Cat when he first appeared in 1919.

—John Canemaker

Soon the whole town was gummed up.

Other Great Cartoons

There are, of course, many more than fifty great cartoons. Although our balloting process resulted in a remarkably well-rounded and diverse list, there were some surprising omissions. Toward the end of the list, the point spread was minute; in some cases, only one or two votes separated cartoons that made the top-fifty list from those that didn't. In another time, in another place, these cartoons may have been included. Following are all cartoons that received a substantial number of votes from our panel. Each is a classic.

Note: The fifty greatest cartoons, with the exception of *Gertie the Dinosaur*, are all cel-animated. Some of the silent and independently produced cartoons that appear on the following list are paper-animated. This list does not include computer-animated or puppet-animated films.

Winsor McCay
Little Nemo (1911)

Disney Studios
Education for Death
(Clyde Geronimi/Special/ 1943)

Ferdinand the Bull
(Dick Rickard/Special/ 1938); Academy Award winner

Flowers and Trees
(Burt Gillett/Silly Symphonies/ 1932); first color Silly Symphony; Academy Award winner

Lonesome Ghosts
(Burt Gillett/A Mickey Mouse Cartoon/1937); Mickey Mouse, Donald Duck, Goofy

Mickey's Service Station
(Ben Sharpstein/A Mickey Mouse Cartoon/1935); Mickey Mouse, Donald Duck, Goofy

Mickey's Trailer
(Ben Sharpstein/A Mickey Mouse Cartoon/1938); Mickey Mouse, Donald Duck, Goofy

Mother Goose Goes Hollywood
(Wilfred Jackson/Silly Symphonies/1938)

Moving Day
(Ben Sharpstein/A Mickey Mouse Cartoon/1938); Mickey Mouse, Donald Duck, Goofy

Music Land
(Wilfred Jackson/Silly Symphony/1935)

Plane Crazy
(Walt Disney/1928); Mickey Mouse's first appearance; silent film

The Pointer
(Clyde Geronimi/A Mickey Mouse Cartoon/1939)

Thru the Mirror
(David Hand/A Mickey Mouse Cartoon/1936)

Who Killed Cock Robin (David Hand/Silly Symphony/1935)

Fleischer Studio
Koko's Earth Control
(Inkwell Imps/1928)

Mechanical Monsters
(1941); Superman

The Old Man of the Mountain
(1933); Betty Boop, with Cab Calloway

Poor Cinderella
(Color Classic/1934); Betty Boop; first short in color

Popeye the Sailor Meets Ali Baba's Forty Thieves
(Popeye Special/1937)

Ub Iwerks Studio
Balloonland (aka *The Pincushion Man*) (1935)

Walter Lantz Studios
Woody Woodpecker
(aka *The Cracked Nut*) (Walter Lantz/1941); First Woody Woodpecker cartoon

Van Beuren Studios
The Sunshine Makers
(Burt Gillett, Ted Eshbaugh/ Rainbow Parade/1935)

Warner Bros. Studios
Baseball Bugs
(I. Freleng/Looney Tunes/ 1946); Bugs Bunny

The Big Snooze
(Robert Clampett/Looney Tunes/ 1946); Bugs Bunny, Elmer Fudd

Bugs Bunny Gets the Boid (Robert Clampett/Merrie Melodies/1942)

Bugs Bunny and the Three Bears
(Charles M. Jones/Merrie Melodies/1948)

Fast and Furry-ous
(Charles M. Jones/Looney Tunes/ 1949); Road Runner and Wile E. Coyote

Gorilla My Dreams
(Robert McKimson/Looney Tunes/1948); Bugs Bunny

Hair-Raising Hare
(Charles M. Jones/Looney Tunes/1946); Bugs Bunny

I Love to Singa
(Tex Avery/Merrie Melodies/1936)

Kitty Kornered
(Robert Clampett/Looney Tunes/ 1946); Porky Pig, Sylvester

The Old Grey Hare
(Robert Clampett/Merrie Melodies/1944); Bugs Bunny, Elmer Fudd

Rhapsody in Rivets
(I. Freleng/Merrie Melodies/1941)

Rhapsody Rabbit
(I. Freleng/Merrie Melodies/1947); Bugs Bunny

Rabbit Hood
(Charles M. Jones/Merrie Melodies/1950) Bugs Bunny

Scaredy Cat
(Charles M. Jones/Merrie Melodies/ 1948); Porky Pig, Sylvester

A Tale of Two Kitties
(Robert Clampett/Merrie Melodies/1942);Tweety

Tweetie Pie
(I. Freleng/Merrie Melodies/1947); Tweety, Sylvester

A Wild Hare
(Fred Avery/Merrie Melodies/ 1940); Bugs Bunny, Elmer Fudd

MGM Studios
The Blitz Wolf
(Tex Avery/1942)

Mouse Cleaning
(Hanna-Barbera/1948); Tom and Jerry

Screwball Squirrel
(Tex Avery/1944)

Señor Droopy
(Tex Avery/1949); Droopy

Swing Shift Cinderella
(Tex Avery/1945)

UPA
When MaGoo Flew
(Pete Burness/1955); Mr. Magoo

Terrytoons
Flebus
(Ernest Pintoff/1957)

Independents
Allegretto
(Oskar Fischinger/1981)

The Box
(Murakami-Wolf Films/ 1967)

Crac
(Frederic Back/1981)

The Crunch Bird
(Maxell-Petok-Petrovich Productions/1971)

Ersatz
(Zagreb Studios/1961)

Frank Film
(Frank Mouris/1973)

The Furies
(Sarah Petty/1976)

Lupo the Butcher
(Danny Antennucci/1987)

Moonbird
(The Hubley Studios/1959)

The Street
(Carolyn Leaf/1976)

Your Face
(Bill Plympton/1987)

ILLUSTRATIONS AND CONTRIBUTOR CREDITS

What's Opera, Doc?, Page 30: production cel with re-created background. Page 31: layout sketches by Chuck Jones. Pages 32–33: concept painting by Maurice Noble. Page 34: background with cel and overlay. Page 35, top: color chart; bottom: concept paintings by Maurice Noble.

Duck Amuck, Page 36: re-created cel and background. Page 38, center: layout drawing by Chuck Jones.

The Band Concert, Pages 40–41: production cels and backgrounds. Page 42: production cel and background. Page 43: animation drawing by Les Clark.

Duck Dodgers in the 24 1/2th Century, Page 44: production cels. Page 45: production cel with background from another film. Page 46: production cel. Page 47: layout drawing.

One Froggy Evening, Page 48: background. Pages 49–51: sketches by Chuck Jones.

Gertie the Dinosaur, Page 52: production art. Page 53: lithographed publicity poster. Pages 54–55: production art.

Red Hot Riding Hood, Page 56: cel and background. Page 59: production cel.

Porky in Wackyland, Page 60: storyboard sketches. Page 61: storyboard sketch; limited edition cel and background. Page 62, top: storyboard sketch; bottom: production background. Page 63: storyboard sketch.

Gerald McBoing Boing, Page 64: color key by Herb Klynn and Jules Engel. Page 65: production cel. Pages 66–67: color key by Herb Klynn and Jules Engel; record jacket.

King-Size Canary, Page 69: re-created cel; model sheet.

Three Little Pigs, Page 72, top: model sheet drawings; bottom: poster. Page 73: animation drawings.

Rabbit of Seville, Pages 74–75: limited edition cels and backgrounds. Page 76: background. Page 77: cel.

Steamboat Willie, Page 78, top: poster; bottom: animation drawing by Les Clark. Page 79: animation drawing by Les Clark.

The Old Mill, Page 80: model sheet; Walt Disney and Mrs. Ugo D'Orsi study a reference model of the mill. Page 81: storybook illustration.

The Great Piggy Bank Robbery, Page 82: animation drawing. Page 83: limited edition cel and background. Page 84: limited edition cel and background.

Popeye the Sailor Meets Sindbad the Sailor, Page 86: poster. Pages 88–89: production cel and background.

The Skeleton Dance, Page 90: animation drawing.

Snow White, Pages 96–97: calendar illustration.

Minnie the Moocher, Page 98: original art by Leslie Cabarga, created for this volume. Page 101: animation drawing.

Coal Black and de Sebben Dwarfs, Page 102: cel and background. Page 103: storyboard illustrations. Page 104: model sheet. Page 105: storyboard illustration.

Der Fuehrer's Face, Page 106: sheet music illustration. The title song of *Der Fuehrer's Face* was recorded by Spike Jones in 1942 and became a huge hit, selling more than 1.5 million copies.

Little Rural Riding Hood, Page 110: animation drawings. Page 111: animation drawings.

The Tell-Tale Heart, Page 112: production art. Page 114: Steven Busustow and Ted Parmalee. Page 115: production art

The Big Snit, Pages 116–119: production cels and backgrounds.

Brave Little Tailor, Page 120: poster; production cel and background. Page 121: publicity art. Page 122: publicity art. Page 123: cel and background.

Clock Cleaners, Page 124: poster; animation drawing. Page 125: production cel.

Northwest Hounded Police, Page 126: animation drawings.

Toot, Whistle, Plunk and Boom, Page 130: production cel. Page 131: production cel and background.

Rabbit Seasoning, Pages 132–33: production cels.

The Scarlet Pumpernickel, Page 137: re-created cel.

The Cat Came Back, Page 138–39: production cels and backgrounds.

Superman, Page 141: production cel and background. Page 142: production cel and background. Page 143: model sheet; production cels and backgrounds.

You Ought to Be in Pictures, Page 144: still photograph.

Ali Baba Bunny, Page 148: sketch by Chuck Jones. Page 149, top: sketch by Chuck Jones; bottom: limited edition cel and background.

Feed the Kitty, Page 150: model sheet.

Bimbo's Initiation, Page 153: original painting by Leslie Cabarga, created for this volume.

Bambi Meets Godzilla, Page 154: production art. Page 155: production art.

Little Red Riding Rabbit, Page 156, top: production cel; bottom: production cel and background. Page 157, top: production cel. Bottom: animation drawing.

Rooty Toot Toot, Page 160: production cel and background. Page 161: concept sketch.

The Cat Concerto, Page 162: animation drawings. Page 163: background painting from *The Cat Concerto*, with cel from another Tom and Jerry cartoon. Page 164: animation drawings.

The Barber of Seville, Pages 166–67: production cels.

The Man Who Planted Trees, Pages 168–69: production cels and backgrounds.

Book Revue, Page 172: model sheet.

Quasi at the Quackadero, Pages 174-177: production cels and backgrounds.

Corny Concerto, Page 178: production cel. Page 179: animation drawings.

A Unicorn in the Garden, Page 180: concept painting.

How to Find the 50 Greatest Cartoons

Most of the fifty greatest cartoons can be seen on broadcast television, cable television, or home video tapes and laser discs.

What's Opera, Doc?
TV: "Bugs Bunny and Tweety" on ABC. Tape: *The Bugs Bunny Road Runner Movie.* Laser disc: *Looney Tunes Curtain Calls.*

Duck Amuck
TV: "Bugs Bunny and Tweety" on ABC. Tape: *The Bugs Bunny Road Runner Movie.* Laser disc: *Duck Victory.*

The Band Concert
Not currently available on tape. Shown often on The Disney Channel.

Duck Dodgers in the 24½th Century
TV: "Bugs Bunny and Tweety" on ABC. Laser disc: *Duck Victory.*

One Froggy Evening
TV: "Bugs Bunny and Tweety" on ABC. Tape: *Bugs Bunny's 3rd Movie: 1001 Rabbit Tales.* Laser disc: *Looney Tunes Curtain Calls.*

Gertie the Dinosaur
Tape and laser disc: *Winsor McCay: Animation Legend.*

Red Hot Riding Hood
TV: Shown on various cartoon blocks on Turner's TNT and The Cartoon Network. Tape: *Tex Avery's Screwball Classics Vol. 2.* Laser disc: *The Compleat Tex Avery.*

Porky in Wackyland
TV: "Looney Tunes" on Nickelodeon; Laser disc: *Porky Pig: Ham on Wry.*

Gerald McBoing Boing
TV: "Weinerville" or "Cartoon Kab-looey" on Nickelodeon. Tape: *Columbia Cartoon Classics Vol. 3.*

King-Size Canary
TV: Shown on various cartoon blocks on Turner's TNT and The Cartoon Network. Tape: *Tex Avery's Screwball Classics Vol. 2.* Laser disc: *The Compleat Tex Avery.*

Three Little Pigs
Not currently available on tape. Shown often on The Disney Channel.

Rabbit of Seville
TV: "Looney Tunes" on Nickelodeon. Laser disc: *Looney Tunes Curtain Call.*

Steamboat Willi,
TV: "Mickey's Mouse Tracks" on The Disney Channel. Laser disc: *Mickey Mouse: The Black and White Years.*

The Old Mill
Shown occasionally on The Disney Channel.

Bad Luck Blackie
TV: Shown on various cartoon blocks on Turner's TNT and The Cartoon Network. Tape: *Tex Avery's Screwball Classics Vol. 2.* Laser disc: *The Compleat Tex Avery.*

The Great Piggy Bank Robbery
TV: Shown on various cartoon blocks on Turner's TNT and The Cartoon Network. Tape: *Daffy.* Laser disc: *The Golden Age of Looney Tunes, Vol. 1.*

Popeye the Sailor Meets Sindbad the Sailor
TV: Shown on various cartoon blocks on Turner's TNT and The Cartoon Network. Tape: *Popeye Cartoons Featuring Goonland.* Laser disc: *Popeye Two Reelers.*

The Skeleton Dance
Shown occasionally on The Disney Channel.

Snow White,
Shown occasionally on American Movie Classics. Tape and laser disc: *Betty Boop's Special Collector's Edition, Vol. 1.*

Minnie the Moocher
Shown occasionally on American Movie Classics. Tape and laser disc: *Betty Boop's Special Collector's Edition, Vol. 2.*

Coal Black and de Sebben Dwarfs
Not currently available on tape or television.

Der Fuerher's Face
Not currently available on tape or television.

Little Rural Riding Hood
TV: Shown on various cartoon blocks on Turner's TNT and The Cartoon Network. Tape: *MGM Cartoon Magic.* Laser disc: *The Compleat Tex Avery.*

The Tell-Tale Heart
Tape: *Columbia Cartoon Classics, Vol. 9: UPA Classics*

The Big Snit
Tape: *Incredible Manitoba Animation.* Laser disc: *The National Film Board of Canada's Animation Festival.*

Brave Little Tailor
TV: "Mickey's Mouse Tracks" on The Disney Channel. Tape: *Disney's Cartoon Classics, Vol. 6: Mickey and Minnie.*

Clock Cleaners
TV: "Mickey's Mouse Tracks" on The Disney Channel. Tape: *Disney's Cartoon Classics Special Edition: Fun on the Job.*

Northwest Hounded Police
TV: Shown on various cartoon blocks on Turner's TNT and The Cartoon Network. Tape: *Tex Avery's Screwball Classics, Vol. 2.* Laser disc: *The Compleat Tex Avery.*

Toot, Whistle, Plunk and Boom
Not currently available on tape or television.

Rabbit Seasoning
TV: "Looney Tunes" on Nickelodeon. Laser disc: *Bugs Bunny: Winner by a Hare.*

The Scarlet Pumpernickel
TV: "Merrie Melodies" on Fox. Laser disc: *Looney Tunes Curtain Calls.*

The Cat Came Back
Tape: *Incredible Manitoba Animation.* Laser disc: *The National Film Board of Canada's Animation Festival.*

Superman
Tape: *Superman Cartoons, Vol. 1.* Laser disc: *The Superman Cartoons of Max & Dave Fleischer.*

You Ought to Be in Pictures
TV: "Looney Tunes" on Nickelodeon. Laser disc: *Porky Pig: Ham on Wry.*

Ali Baba Bunny
TV: "Merrie Melodies" on Fox. Tape: *The Bugs Bunny/Road Runner Movie*. Laser disc: *Duck Victory*.

Feed the Kitty
TV: "Bugs Bunny and Tweety" on ABC. Laser disc: *Looney Tunes Assorted Nuts*.

Bimbo's Initiation
Shown occasionally on American Movie Classics. Tape and laser disc: *Betty Boop's Special Collector's Edition, Vol. 1*.

Bambi Meets Godzilla
Tape and laser disc: *The Rocketship Reel*.

Little Red Riding Rabbit
TV: Shown on various cartoon blocks on Turner's TNT and The Cartoon Network. Tape: *The Golden Age of Looney Tunes, Tape 6: Friz Freleng*. Laser disc: *The Golden Age of Looney Tunes, Vol. 1*.

Peace on Earth
TV: Shown on various cartoon blocks on Turner's TNT and The Cartoon Network. Tape: *MGM Cartoon Christmas*. Laser disc: *MGM Cartoon Classics, Vol. 1: Happy Harmonies*.

Rooty Toot Toot
Tape: *Columbia Cartoon Classics, Vol. 9: UPA Classics*.

The Cat Concerto
TV: Shown on various cartoon blocks on Turner's TNT and The Cartoon Network. Tape: *Tom and Jerry's 50th Birthday Classics, Vol. 2*. Laser disc: *The Art of Tom and Jerry, Vol 1*.

The Barber of Seville
Not currently available on tape or television.

The Man Who Planted Trees
Sold on videotape exclusively by Direct Cinema, 1-800-242-6000.

Book Revue
TV: Shown on various cartoon blocks on Turner's TNT and The Cartoon Network. Tape: *Golden Age of Looney Tunes, Tape 8: 1940s Zanies*. Laser disc: *Golden Age of Looney Tunes, Vol. 1*.

Quasi at the Quackadero
Not currently available on tape or television.

Corny Concerto
TV: Shown on various cartoon blocks on Turner's TNT and The Cartoon Network. Tape: *Bugs Bunny Superstar*. Laser disc: *Golden Age of Looney Tunes, Vol. 1*.

A Unicorn in the Garden
Tape: *Columbia Cartoon Classics, Vol. 6*.

The Dover Boys
TV: Shown on various cartoon blocks on Turner's TNT and The Cartoon Network. Tape: *Golden Age of Looney Tunes, Tape 5: Chuck Jones*. Laser disc: *The Golden Age of Looney Tunes, Vol. 1*.

Felix in Hollywood
Tape and laser disc: *Felix!*

Note: Tapes and laser discs can be ordered from: Whole Toon Access, P.O. Box 1910, Seattle, Washington 98111-1910.

ANIMATION ART SOURCES

A growing number of galleries, mail order firms, and auction houses deal in original production art and limited editions. Here are some of the ones that gave us information or lent us artwork for this volume:

Animazing Gallery
549 Warburton Avenue
Hastings on Hudson, NY 10706
914-478-7278

C & A Animation Galleries
77 Middle Neck Road
Great Neck, NY 11021
1-800-541-AART

Cel-ebration
P.O. Box 123
Little Silver, NJ 07739
908-842-8489

Cohen Books and Collectibles
P.O. Box 810310
Boca Raton, FL 33481
407-487-7888

The Cricket Gallery
3108 Roswell Road
Atlanta, GA 30305
1-800-BUY-CELS

Filmart Galleries
P.O. Box 128
Old Bethpage, NY 11804
516-935-8493

The Howard Lowery Gallery
3818 West Magnolia Blvd.
Burbank, CA 91505
818-972-9080

Name That Toon
8483 Melrose Avenue
West Hollywood, CA 90038
213-653-5633

Pixillation: The Animation Source
387 Danbury Road
Wilton, CT 06867
203-762-8507

Silver Stone Gallery
2005 Palo Verde Avenue
Long Beach, CA 90815
310-598-7600

Stay Tuned Gallery
The Arcade
272 East Deerpath
Lake Forest, IL 60045
708-234-3231

World's Greatest Posters
Castle Rock, WA 98611

ASIFA

The Association Internationale du Film D'Animation is an organization devoted to the field of classic and current animation. They hold frequent screenings of animated films. For information about the ASIFA chapter nearest you, contact:

ASIFA East
c/o Linda Simensky
470 West 24th Street, #15A
New York, NY 10011

ASIFA Hollywood
725 S. Victory Boulevard
Burbank, CA 91502

ASIFA Midwest
Animation Plus Gallery
790 N. Milwaukee Avenue
Chicago, IL 60622

ASIFA Portland
4380 SW86th Avenue
Portland, OR 97225

ASIFA San Francisco
478 Frederick Street
San Francisco, CA 94117

ASIFA Washington
P.O. Box 53101
Washington, D.C. 20009

Index

Adamson, Joe, 51, 57, 59, 111, 135, 166
Adventures of Pow-Wow, The, 20
Aesop's Film Fables, 13
Ali Baba Bunny, 148–49
Allegretto, 186
Allen, Robert, 129
American Tale, An, 21
Anchors Aweigh, 16
Anderson, Alex, 19, 25
"Animaniacs", 21
Antennucci, Danny, 187
"Astro Boy", 19, 20
Avery, Tex, 15, 16, 38, 46–47, 57, 59, 62, 68, 70–71, 77, 83, 111,127, 129, 173, 186

Babbit, Art, 18, 22–24, 29, 114
Back, Frederic, 168, 169, 187
Backus, Jim, 24
Bad Luck Blackie, 29, 82–83
Bakshi, Ralph, 20–21
Balloonland, 186
Bambi, 16
Bambi Meets Godzilla, 154–55, 176
Band Concert, The, 28, 40–43
Barber of Seville, The, 166–167
Barbera, Joseph, 16, 18, 20, 24–25, 129, 162, 164
Barker, Cordell, 139
Barnacle Bill, 14
Barre, Raoul, 15
Barrier, Michael, 103, 178
Baseball Bugs, 186
"Batman: The Animated Series", 47
Beaky Buzzard, 16
Beale, Eddie, 103
"Beany and Cecil", 19–20, 22
Beauty and the Beast, 21
Beiman, Nancy, 83
Benedict, Ed, 20
Bernard, Jami, 50, 155
Betty Boop, 14, 22–23, 94, 97, 99–100, 152, 186
Big Snit, The, 29, 116–19
Bimbo, 23, 94, 99–100, 152
Bimbo's Initiation, 29, 152–53
Birds Anonymous, 146
Birth of a Nation, 105
Black Fury, 63
Blackton, J. Stuart, 10, 12, 52
Blair, Preston, 57, 59
Blanc, Mel, 15, 18, 24, 38, 46, 47, 77, 136, 145, 170
Blitz Wolf, The, 59, 187
Bluth, Don, 20
Bluto, 89
"Boing Boing Show, The", 19–20
Book Revue, 29, 170–73
Bosko, 14, 47, 146,
Bosustow, Stephen, 19, 67, 114, 181
Bouffier Elzeard, 169
Box, The, 187
"Bozo the Clown", 20
Bradley, Scott, 162
Brave Little Tailor, 28, 120–123
Bray, J. R., 12, 13, 14, 15
Bryant, Arthur Q., 16, 77
Buckey and Pepito, 20
Bugs Bunny, 13, 16–18, 21–22, 24, 29, 31, 34, 35, 37–38, 44, 55, 74, 76–77, 128 133–135, 146, 148, 157, 173, 178, 181, 185, 186
Bugs Bunny and the Three Bears, 186
Bugs Bunny/Road Runner Movie, The, 20
Bugs Bunny Gets the Boid, 187
"Bugs Bunny Show, The", 20
"Bullwinkle Show, The", 20
Burness, Pete, 24, 114

Cabarga, Leslie, 94, 99, 152
Calloway, Cab, 94, 99–100, 186
"Calvin and the Colonel", 20
Cambria Studio, 20
Canemaker, John, 52, 55, 118, 130, 185
Cannon, Robert, 114
Cannon, Johnny, 19, 78
Captain Pete, 79
"Captain Kangaroo Show, The", 20
Caselotti, Adriana, 155
Casper 14, 17, 18
Cat Came Back, The, 138–39
Cat Concerto, The, 162–5
Champion, Ken, 18
Chaplin, Charles, 28, 50, 185
"Charlie Brown Christmas, A", 19, 21
Charlie Dog, 22
Chiniquy, Gerry, 145
Churchill, Frank, 73
Clampett, Bob, 15–16, 18–20, 22–24, 47, 60, 62–3, 70, 84, 86–7, 103, 172–3, 175, 178, 187
Clampett, Bob, Jr., 62
Clark Kent, 140
Clark, Les, 43, 78, 107
Clock Cleaners, 28, 124–25
"Clutch Cargo", 20
Coal Black and de Sebben Dwarfs, 28, 102–05, 173
Cohen, Karl 118, 145, 175
Cohl, Emil, 12, 52
Collyer, Bud, 140
Colonel Heeza Liar, 12
"Colonel Bleep", 20
Columbia Pictures, 14, 16, 17, 65, 97, 113–14, 160, 164, 181
Colvig, Pinto, 73, 108
Condie, Richard, 118–19
Corny Concerto, 29, 173, 178–79
Costello, Billy "Red Pepper Sam", 91
"Courageous Cat and Minute Mouse", 20
Crac, 168, 186
Crandall, Roland (Doc), 94
Crippen, Fred, 20
Cruikshank, Sally, 175
Crunch Bird, The, 187
"Crusader Rabbit", 17, 19, 101
Culhane, James (Shamus), 19, 22, 78, 166
Culhane, John, 107

Daffy Doc, The, 38
Daffy Duck, 15, 18, 22, 24, 29, 34, 36–38, 44, 46–47, 63, 84, 86–87, 128, 133–36, 145–46, 148, 170, 172–73
Daffy Doodles, 17
Dalton, Carl, 24, 77
Dandridge, Vivian, 103
Dandridge, Ruby, 103
Davis, Art, 135
Depatie-Freleng Enterprises, 19, 25, 146
"Deputy Dawg", 20
Der Fuehrer's Face, 29, 105–07
Dick Tracy, 20, 84, 87
Dietch, Gene, 20
Disney Studios, 14–17, 31, 34, 38, 40–43, 47, 55, 59, 65, 70, 72, 80–81, 83, 92 94, 97, 100–101, 103, 105, 107, 121–22, 124–25, 130, 155, 158, 161–62, 178, 182, 186
Disney, Walt, 13, 16, 18–19, 21, 23, 40, 43, 78–79, 114, 122, 146
Disney, Roy, 146
Dizzy Dishes, 14, 100–101, 152
"Do-Do the Kid from Outer Space", 21
Donald Duck, 14, 15, 16, 17, 23, 38, 41–42, 105, 107, 122, 124–25, 162, 181
"Doonesbury Special, A", 20
Dot and the Line, The, 22
Dover Boys, The, 28, 182–83
Dr. Seuss, 65, 67
Droopy, 16, 18, 22, 127, 128
Duck Dodgers in the 24 ½th Century, 11, 44–47, 74
Duck Amuck, 29, 36–39
Duck! Rabbit! Duck!, 135
Dumbo, 16, 107, 130

Edison, Thomas, 10
Education for Death, 107, 186
Edwards, Cliff "Ukelele Ike", 91
Elmer Fudd, 16, 22, 24, 29, 31, 35, 38, 44, 74, 76, 133–36, 148, 178
Ersatz, 186
Eshbaugh, Ted, 186
Eugster, Al 125

"Famous Adventures of Mr. Magoo, The", 20
Fantasia, 23, 31, 35, 122, 130, 143, 178
Farmer Alfalfa, 13
Fast and Furryous, 17, 74, 186
Feed the Kitty, 29, 150–51
Feline Follies, 13
Felix in Hollywood, 22–23, 184–85
Felix the Cat, 13, 16, 37, 55, 92, 185
Ferdinand the Bull, 186
Ferguson, Norm, 73
Ferguson, Otto, 43
Figaro, Tony, 166
Fischinger, Oskar 176, 186
Flebus, 187
Fleischer, Dave, 97, 143
Fleischer, Max, 12–13, 22, 89, 91, 97, 143, 186
Fleischer Bros. Studios, 15–16, 23, 29, 88, 97, 99–101, 140, 142–3, 152, 162
Flip the Frog, 14, 101
"The Flintstones", 18–20, 22, 164
Flowers and Trees, 13, 15, 186
Foghorn Leghorn, 17
For Scentimental Reasons, 22, 74
Ford, Greg, 76, 125, 136
Foster, Alan, 170
Foster, Warren, 18, 22, 170
Fox and the Crow, The, 16
Foxy, 14
Frank Film, 187
Fred Flintstone 25
Freleng, Friz 20, 22–23, 25, 17–18, 38, 47, 77, 145–48, 187
Friedwald, Will, 165
Fritz the Cat, 20
Furies, The, 187

Gallopin' Goucho, The, 14, 122
Gerald McBoing Boing, 18–19, 28, 17, 64–67, 130
Geronimi, Clyde, 21, 186
Gertie the Dinosaur, 22, 28, 12, 15, 52, 55
"Gigantor", 20
Gillett, Bert, 186
"Goliath II", 18
Goofy Gophers, 22
Goofy, 122, 124–5
Gordon, George, 129
Gorilla My Dreams, 187
Gould, Chester, 84, 86–87
Gracie Films, 25
Graham, Graham, 34, 43
Gray, Milt, 182
Grant, Joe, 107
Great Piggy Bank Robbery, The, 84–87, 173
Green, Gene, 91
Griffin, George, 176
Groening, Matt, 25
Gulliver's Travels, 12, 97, 101

Hair-Raising Hare, 186
Hand, David, 186
Hanna, William, 16, 18, 19–20, 24–25, 129, 162, 164
Happy Harmonies, 15
Hardaway, Ben "Bugs", 24, 77
Hare Meets Hare, 77
Harman, Hugh, 14, 18, 47, 59, 46, 158, 162, 164, 173,
Harris, Ken, 135
Heckle and Jeckle, 17
Hilberman, Dave, 114
Hoberman, J., 173
Holmes, Sherlock, 84, 86–87
Honeymoon Hotel, 15
"How the Grinch Stole Christmas", 19, 21
Hubley, Faith, 176
Hubley, John, 18–20, 24, 67, 176, 114, 161
Hubley Studios, 187
"Huckleberry Hound", 20, 22, 164
Huemer, Dick, 107
Hurd, Earl, 12, 13
Hurtz, William, 114, 181

I Haven't Got a Hat, 15, 23, 46, 145–46
I Love to Singa, 187
Inge, M. Thomas, 73, 143
Ising, Rudolph, 14, 18, 47, 59, 146, 162, 164, 173
Iwerks, Ub, 13–14, 23, 78, 92, 101, 186

Jackson, Wilfred, 78, 186
"Jetsons, The", 19–20, 22, 164
Jiminy Cricket, 91
Johnston, Ollie, 80
Jones, Charles M. "Chuck", 16–18, 21, 22, 24–25, 28–29, 31, 33–35, 37–38, 44, 47, 49, 51, 74, 76, 134–36, 148, 151, 182, 187
"Jonny Quest", 19–20, 22, 164

Kane, Helen, 23, 100
Katzenjammer Kids, The, 13, 15
Kaufman, J. B., 79
Kieffer, Mike, 91
Kimball, Ward, 130, 182
King-Size Canary, 68–71
Kinney, Jack, 107
Kitty Kornered, 186
Knight, Arthur, 65
Knighty Knight Bugs, 18, 22, 77, 146
Koko the Clown, 13, 22, 23, 37, 94, 97, 152, 185

Koko's Earth Control, 186
Krazy Kat, 13, 15, 101, 85
Kricfalusi, John, 25, 87, 89

LaCava, Gregory, 15, 101
Lady Play Your Mandolin, 14, 173
Lady and the Tramp, 14
Langer, Mark, 152
Lantz, Walter, 14, 16, 20, 22, 24, 101, 111, 166–67. 186
Lantz, Grace, 24
Laurel and Hardy, 135, 148
Leaf, Carolyn, 176, 187
Lend a Paw, 122
Levitow, Abe, 18
Little Red Riding Rabbit, 156–57
Little Rural Riding Hood, 29, 57, 108–111
Little Nemo, 12–13, 22, 52, 186
Lloyd, Harold, 125
Lois Lane, 140
Lonesome Ghosts, 186
Long-Haired Hare, 84
Looney Tunes, 14, 23, 38, 46–47, 146, 170, 172
Lord of the Rings, 12
Love, Ed, 59
Lucas, George, 44
Lundy, Dick, 73
Lunick, Olga, 161
Lupo the Butcher, 187

Magoo's Puddle Jumper, 24
Maltese, Michael, 18, 20, 31, 51, 62, 74, 135–36, 145, 148
Maltin, Leonard, 12, 40, 46, 181
Man Who Planted Trees, The, 29, 168–69
Marvin Martian, 22, 34, 44
Mason, James, 113
Maxell-Petok-Petrovich Productions, 187
May, Billy, 170
Mayer, Louis B., 57
McCay, Winsor, 10, 12, 13, 15, 22. 28, 52, 55, 70, 187
McKimson, Robert, 17, 38, 47, 187
McLaren, Norman, 119, 176
Mechanical Monsters, 186
Melendez, Bill, 21, 100
Melody, 130
Mercer, Jack, 29, 89, 91
Merrie Melodies, 14, 15, 17, 23, 38, 46, 146, 173, 178
Merritt, Russell, 79
Messmer, Otto, 18, 20, 22, 19, 22–23, 92, 185
MGM, 14–17, 57, 59, 68, 70, 83, 108, 127, 129, 146, 159, 162, 164, 187
Michigan J. Frog, 22, 50–51
Mickey Mouse, 22–23, 29, 41–43, 55, 78–79, 89, 92, 100, 121–23, 124–25, 173 185
Mickey's Service Station, 186
Mickey's Trailer, 186
Miller, Jack 145
Miller, Jeff, 83
Minnie Mouse, 78–79, 121
Minnie the Moocher, 29, 98–101, 105
Moonbird, 187
Moore, Fred, 73, 121
Moore, Phil, 161
Mother Goose Goes Hollywood, 186
Mouris, Frank, 187
Mouse of Tomorrow, 16
Mouse Cleaning, 187
Moving Day, 186
Mr. Magoo, 18, 20, 24. 114, 181
Murakami-Wolf Films, 187
Music Land, 186
Mutt and Jeff, 12, 15, 185
Muybridge, Edward, 10

Nash, Clarence, 23
National Film Board of Canada, The, 19, 116, 139
Natwick, Myron "Grim", 23, 100, 101
"New Casper Cartoon Show, The", 20
Newgarden, Mark, 70
Newland, Marv, 155
"Newlyweds, The", 12
Night Watchman, The, 16
Noble, Maurice, 135
Northwest Hounded Police, 11, 126, 129

Old Grey Hare, The, 187
Old Man of the Mountain, The, 99, 186
Old Mill, The, 15, 28, 80–81
Olive Oyl, 89
One Froggy Evening, 29, 48–51, 74
Oswald the Lucky Rabbit, 14, 22, 122
Out of the Inkwell, 13

Paramount, 16, 19, 94, 97, 99–100, 140, 142–43, 152
Parmalee, Ted, 114
Peace on Earth, 29, 158–59
Pepe LePew, 17, 18, 22, 34
Petty, Sarah, 187
Pink Panther, 18, 22, 25, 146
Pink Phink, The, 19, 22, 25
Pinocchio, 130
Pintoff, Ernest, 187
Plane Crazy, 14, 78–79, 122, 186
Pluto, 73
Plympton, Bill, 127, 176, 187
Poe, Edgar Allan, 113
Pointer, The, 186
Poor Cinderella, 100, 186
Popeye 14, 22–23, 29, 89, 91, 97, 162
Popeye the Sailor Meets Ali Baba's Forty Thieves, 89, 186
Popeye the Sailor Meets Sindbad the Sailor, 15, 88–91
Porky Pig, 18, 22–24, 38, 44, 46, 60, 62–63, 84, 136, 145–46, 162, 173, 178
Porky in Wackyland, 60–63, 173, 175
Porky's Duck Hunt, 15, 46
Porky's Hare Hunt, 16
Porky's Duck Hunt, 38, 46, 77
Porky's Badtime Story, 15
Price, Michael H., 80
Private Snafu, 16, 34, 47
Professor Owl, 130
Pudgy, 23, 100
Pudovkin, V. I., 166

Quasi at the Quackadero, 28, 174–77
Questal, Mae, 23, 99
Quick Draw McGraw, 20, 164
Quimby, Fred, 129, 164

Rabbit Fire, 135, 148
Rabbit Hood, 187
Rabbit Seasoning, 29, 74, 132–35, 148
Rabbit of Seville, 74–77
Raggedy Ann and Andy, 20, 14, 101
Red Hot Riding Hood, 18, 22, 29, 16, 56–59
Reiniger, Lotte, 14, 176
Reitherman, Wolfgang, 43, 125
"Ren and Stimpy Show, The", 21, 25
Republic Pictures, 97
Rescuers Down Under, 21
Rhapsody Rabbit, 186
Rhapsody in Rivets, 186
Rickard , Dick, 186
Rikard, Dick, 80
Road Runner, 17, 18, 22, 25, 31, 34, 47
Rocky and Bullwinkle, 20, 25
"Rocky and His Friends", 18
"Roger Ramjet", 20
Rooty Toot Toot, 29, 101, 114, 160–161
Ross, Virgil, 18, 22, 103
"Ruff and Ready", 18. 20, 164
Ryan, Will, 91

Salkin, Leo, 114
Scaredy Cat, 186
Scarlet Pumpernickel, The, 136–37
Schleh, Jack, 20
Schlesinger, Leon, 24, 38, 47, 62, 145, 146, 147
Schmidt, Louis, 83
Schneider, Steve, 35, 86, 148, 151, 172
Schwartz, Zack, 114
Scott, Bill, 161
Scrappy, 14
Screwball Squirrel, 187
Screwy Squirrel, 16, 18, 22, 111
Scribner, Rod, 18
Sears, Ted, 73
Secret of Nimh, The, 20
Segar, E. C., 23
Seldes, Gilbert, 42
Señor Droopy, 187
Seven Dwarfs, 55, 94, 122
Sharpstein, Ben, 186
Show Biz Bugs, 38, 148
Shuster, Joe, 140
Siegel, Jerry, 140
Silly Symphonies, 14, 43, 92, 186
Simensky, Linda, 139, 157
"Simpsons, the", 21, 25
Singer Sam, 20
Sinkin' in the Bathtub, 14
Sinking of the Lusitania, 13
Skeleton Dance, The, 14, 29, 92–93
Snow White and the Seven Dwarfs, 43
Snow White, 94–97, 99, 101, 123, 155
Snyder Ken, 20
So Much for So Little, 22
Societe Radio-Canada, 169
Solomon, Charles, 92, 121, 169
Song of the South, 105
"Space Angel", 20
Speedy Gonzales, 22, 146
Spielberg, Steven, 21, 145
Stalling, Carl, 15, 18, 47, 92, 103, 135
Stanford, Leland, 10
Steamboat Wille, 13, 14, 28, 78–79, 122
Story of a Mosquito, The, 12, 52
Street, The, 187
Sullivan, Pat, 15–16, 23, 185
Superman, 16, 19, 21, 28. 97, 140–43
Sunshine Makers, The, 186
Swing Shift Cinderella, 57, 108, 111, 186
Sylvester, 17, 22, 24, 38, 47, 136, 146
Tale of Two Kitties, A, 186
Tashlin, Frank, 16, 18, 23, 62
Tasmanian Devil, 18
Tell-Tale Heart, The, 19, 28, 112–115
Tempo Productions, 114
Terry, Paul, 13, 16, 18
Terrytoons, 17–18, 19, 20, 164, 186
Thomas, Frank, 80, 121
Thompson, Bill, 128
Three Little Pigs, 15, 65, 72–73
Thru the Mirror, 186
Thurber, James, 181
Tin-Tin, 21
"Tiny Toon Adventures" 47
"Tom Terrific", 20
Tom and Jerry, 14, 16, 18, 20, 22, 24, 70, 162, 164, 165
Toot, Whistle, Plunk and Boom, 14, 17, 130–31
"Top Cat", 20
Tweetie Pie, 17, 22, 47, 146, 187
Tweety, 16, 18, 22, 24, 48, 146, 173
Tytla, Bill, 121

Unicorn in the Garden, A, 19, 29, 180–81
Universal Studios, 97
UPA (United Production Artists), 14–15, 17, 18–20, 24, 29, 65, 67, 101, 113, 130, 161, 181–2, 187

Van Beuren Studios, 13, 186
Vaughan, Lloyd, 135

Wallace, Ollie, 107
Walrus, 99
Ward, Jay, 19–20, 25
Warner Bros., 16–25, 30, 34, 36, 37, 47, 49, 50, 60, 74, 128, 133, 136, 145, 146, 148, 151, 157, 162, 170, 172, 173, 182, 186, 187
Warner, Jack, 18, 136
Washam, Ben, 135
What's Opera, Doc?, 29, 30–36, 74
When Magoo Flew, 24, 186
Who Framed Roger Rabbit?, 21, 100, 128, 145
Who Killed Cock Robin, 186
Wicked Queen, 94, 103
Wild Hare, A, 16, 187
Wile E. Coyote, 20–21, 34
Wilkerson, W. R., 161
Williams, Richard, 101
Willie Whopper, 101
Willie the Giant, 121
Wimpy, 89
Winkler, M. J., 185
Wise Little Hen, The, 23
"Wizards,", 20
Wolf, The, 57, 59, 108, 127, 157, 170
"Woody Woodpecker Show, The", 20
Woody Woodpecker, 14, 16, 17, 22, 24, 101, 166, 186
Woolery, Adrian, 114

Yellow Submarine, 20
Yogi Bear, 20, 22, 25, 164
Yosemite Sam, 17, 146
You Ought to Be in Pictures, 38, 144–147
Your Face, 187

Zagreb Studios, 18–19, 186

Acknowledgments

Putting this book together has been a ball, thanks to the efforts of project editor Lori Stein and all of my personal friends who contributed artwork, text, time, and their specialized knowledge: Chuck Jones, Mike and Jeanne Glad, Steve Schneider, Paul Mular, Jere Guldin, Will Ryan, Linda Simensky, Andrew J. Lederer, Cheryl Chase, Mike Barrier, Mark Kausler, Leonard Maltin, John Kricfalusi, Steve Segal, Will Friedwald, Mike Kiefer, Wendy Horowitz, Raymond Spum, Howard Lowery, Linda Jones, Dean Diaz, Darryl Van Citters, Leslie Cabarga, Doug Ranney of *The Whole Toon Catalog*, Ruth Clampett, Lorri O'Grady, Nancy Beiman, Karl Cohen, Antran Manoogian, and Nancy Johnson . . . this book is dedicated to you all. I'd like to especially thank the contributors who shared comments, insights, and wisdom with us and the collectors who lent us artwork (both groups are listed below).

Additional thanks are due to Dick May of Turner Entertainment/MGM; Lorri Bond, Kathie Helppie, and Charles Gaitz of Warner Bros. Animation; Rob Clampett, Margaret Adamic, Howard Green and David Smith of The Walt Disney Company; Ita Golzman of King Features; Lucie Bourgoinoin of Canadian Broadcasting System; John Sirabella at The National Film Board of Canada; Steve Worth and Lew Stude of Vintage Animation cel restoration; John Sammis; Chani Yammer; Etti Yammer; Susan Lurie; Deena Stein; Michelle Stein; Jared and Alyssa Miskoff; Dylan, Trevor, and Cory Kazaks; Jacob and Rebecca Cherry; Eric Marshall; Jay Hyams; and Alan Kellock. The staff at Turner Publishing, including Michael Reagan, art directors Michael Walsh and Karen Smith, editors Kathy Buttler and Walton Rawls, Zodie Spain, Lauren Emerson, Marty Moore, and Bee Edmunds Espy made special efforts, above and beyond the call of duty, to improve the book. —*Jerry Beck*

CONTRIBUTORS

Joe Adamson: Author of *Tex Avery: King of Comedy* and *Bugs Bunny: Fifty Years and Only One Grey Hare;* award-winng director/writer/editor of television documentaries.

Michael Barrier: Creator of *Funnyworld;* author of several volumes on comic books, and of a much-awaited history of animation.

Jami Bernard: Film critic for the *New York Post;* author of *First Films.*

Leslie Cabarga: Author of *The Fleischer Story;* commerical artist.

John Canemaker: Author of four books on animation history; producer, director, and designer of animation; head of animation program at New York University

Bob Clampett, Jr.: Director of Bob Clampett Productions.

Karl Cohen: President of ASIFA San Francisco; animation historian specializing in early TV animation and censorship

John Culhane: Writer for *Newsweek*, *The New York Times*, and other periodicals; author of several books on Disney including *Walt Disney's Fantasia* and *Aladdin: The Making of an Animated Film.*

Greg Ford: Animation historian; coproducer of *The Carl Stalling Project;* cowriter and director of Warner Bros. shorts, including *The Duxorcist* and *Blooper Bunny.*

Will Friedwald: Coauthor of *Looney Tunes and Merrie Melodies;* producer of compilations of vintage music.

Milt Gray: Producer/director/writer of animation; author of *Cartoon Animation: Introduction to a Career.*

M. Thomas Inge: Blackwell Professor of Humanities at Randolph-Macon College, editor of the University of Mississippi's *Studies in Popular Culture;* author of *Comics as Culture.*

John Kricfalusi: Creator of Ren and Stimpy.

Leonard Maltin: Film correspondent for "Entertainment Tonight"; author of *Of Mice and Magic.*

Jeff Miller: Film critic for *The Houston Chronicle.*

Mark Newgarden: Illustrator, designer, animation historian; cocreator of The Garbage Pail Kids.

Bill Plympton: Acclaimed animation director (*Your Face*).

Michael H. Price: Film critic and cartoonist for *The Fort Worth Star-Telegram;* film director; coauthor of several books.

Will Ryan: Voice artist and songwriter for Disney and Don Bluth; archivist for Elmo Aardvark.

Steve Schneider: Journalist; playwright; author of *That's All Folks* and guest curator of the Museum of Modern Art's Warner Bros. show.

Linda Simensky: Director of animation development for Nickelodeon; President of ASIFA, New York.

Charles Solomon: Book critic for the *Los Angeles Times;* animation historian; author of *Enchanted Drawings.*

ILLUSTRATION CREDITS

John and Dawn Altyn: pp. 21, 56.

Pat Ballew: pp. 43, 78, 79.

Mike Barrier: pp. 48, 144.

C & A Animation: pp. 19 center, 81, 156 bottom.

Leslie Cabarga: pp. 5 left, 13 top and center, 87, 100, 143 left.

Canadian Broadcasting System: pp. 168, 169.

John Canemaker: p. 53.

Bob Casino, Pixcelation: The Animation Source: pp. 124, 162, 163 top, 164 bottom.

Bob Clampett Productions: pp. 5 second from left; 60, 61, 62, 63; 85, 87; 102, 103, 104, 105; 170–73, 178–79.

Joel Cohen, House of Collectibles: p. 42.

Sally Cruickshank: pp. 174, 177.

Greg Dundis: pp. 167, 178 top right.

Steve Ferzoco: p. 77

Mike and Jeanne Glad: pp. 32, 33, 52 top, 54, 55, 64, 66, 67, 73 bottom, 80 bottom, 90, 91, 112, 114, 115, 160, 161, 180.

Harvey Entertainment; p. 17 left.

Mark Heller: p. 59 right.

Chuck Jones Enterprises: pp. 74, 75, 149.

George Kurz: pp. 49 top and center, 50 top and center, 51 top, bottom left, right.

Aaron Laken, Filmart: pp. 72, 73 top, 120 bottom, 121, 122, 163 bottom.

Heidi Leigh, Animazing Gallery: p. 30.

Howard Lowery Galleries: pp. 5 second from right; 11 top, 109 top, 110, 11, 126, 131.

Greg Martin/MacPhee Group: pp. 2–3 title page spread.

Pam Martin, Cel-ebration: pp. 125, 148 bottom.

Peter Merolo: pp. 40, 41, 96, 7.

Museum of Modern Art Film Stills Collection: pp. 10 top, 12, 13 bottom, 14 top left, 16 top.

National Film Board of Canada: pp. 116, 119; 138, 139.

Mark Newgarden: pp. 4 left, 31, 67, 92 bottom.

Marv Newland, International Rocketship: pp. 5 right, 154, 155.

Greg Nunnally: p. 80 top.

Cheryl Schatz Petrozelli: pp. 19 right top and bottom, 132, 165 top; photography by Carl Petrozelli.

Steve Schneider: pp. 4 second from left, right, 34, 35 top, 38 center, 69, 76, 84 bottom, 150, 157 bottom.

Silverstone Galleries: pp. 52 bottom, 140 bottom, 142 top, 143 top/bottom right.

Richie Singer: pp. 44 left, 47, 157 top.

Andrew Weinstein: pp. 11 bottom, 35 bottom, 44 right, 45, 46 bottom, 132; photography by Evan Austin.

World's Greatest Posters: pp. 72 bottom, 88 right, 120 top, 130 top; photography by Aden Keith.

Steve Worth, Vintage Animation: pp. 65, 130.